"Searing.... Harrowing.... Flook narrates painful events with remarkable poise ... a voice that is lyrical ... authoritative.... A powerful and disturbing book."

—Michiko Kakutani, *New York Times*

"Maria Flook has taken home the brass ring with her searing family biography.... A fierce, riveting tale."

—*Vanity Fair*

"A box of dark treasures.... A beautifully wrought story of the way things go wrong and the way people survive and exploit their detours of fate. Maria Flook writes with breathtaking artistry and precision. This book holds you in troubling and unpredictable ways. It is a mesmerizing work of nonfiction."

—James Ellroy

"Flook's fiction has always galvanized me with its irrepressible lyricism and high voltage. *My Sister Life* brings the same qualities to the nonfiction form with arresting results. Read this book."

—Rick Moody, author of *Purple America*

"This disturbing book by one of the most powerful American writers at work today takes us through the richocheting doppelganger-ing lives of two sisters and their eerie shipwreck shadows. I wished very much this book were fiction, but it is not."

—Annie Proulx, author of *The Shipping News*

"Striking authenticity ... crackles with emotional insight and with astonishing powers of recall and compassion ... burning with harsh truths about the irreparable wounds marking all families. *My Sister*

Life testifies with raw eloquence to Flook's unwavering commitment to her lost sister."

—Elle

"Flook, one of our best writers of fiction, gives us a starkly beautiful book, full of redemption . . . utterly memorable."

—Howard Norman, author of The Bird Artist

"A compelling story . . . the book takes flight. An unpredictable tale of wayward parallel lives."

—Boston Globe

MY SISTER LIFE

MARIA FLOOK

MY
SISTER LIFE

The Story of My Sister's Disappearance

BROADWAY BOOKS   *New York*

This is a true story.
Names have been changed in respect
to individuals and institutions who do not wish
their identity revealed.

BROADWAY

A hardcover edition of this book was originally published in 1998 by Pantheon Books. It is here reprinted by arrangement with Pantheon Books, a division of Random House, Inc.

MY SISTER LIFE. Copyright © 1998 by Maria Flook. All rights reserved. Printed in the United States of America. No part of this book may be reproduced or transmitted in any form or by any means, electronic or mechanical, including photocopying, recording, or by any information storage and retrieval system, without written permission from the publisher. For information, address Pantheon Books, a division of Random House, Inc., 201 East 50th Street, New York, NY 10022.

Broadway Books titles may be purchased for business or promotional use or for special sales. For information, please write to: Special Markets Department, Random House, Inc., 1540 Broadway, New York, NY 10036.

BROADWAY BOOKS and its logo, a letter B bisected on the diagonal, are trademarks of Broadway Books, a division of Random House, Inc.

First Broadway Books trade paperback edition published 1999.

Designed by M. Kristen Bearse

Library of Congress Cataloging-in-Publication Data
Flook, Maria.
My sister life : the story of my sister's disappearance / Maria Flook.
p.   cm.
ISBN 0-7679-0315-3
1. Flook, Maria—Family. 2. Women novelists, American—20th century—Biography.
3. Teenage girls—United States—Family relationships. 4. Sisters—United States—
Biography. 5. Missing persons—United States. I. Title.
PS3556.L583Z47 1999
813'.54—dc21

{b}

98-30823 CIP

99 00 01 02 03 10 9 8 7 6 5 4 3 2 1

ACKNOWLEDGMENTS

Several people have helped me in the writing of this book, and to collect shipwreck documents, hospital files and court records. My thanks to Claudine O'Hearn, Kim Witherspoon, Susan Norton, Emilia Dubicki, Jim Peters, Nancy Rosenblum, Tim Barry, Michael Stein, Renee Bowles and George Michelson. Special thanks to John Skoyles.

My deathless gratitude to Daniel Frank, my editor.

For A.D.

"We have collided with another ship.
Please. Ship in collision."

THE
MIRACLE GIRL

1964

WILMINGTON, DEL.

———

MY SISTER KAREN disappeared when she was fourteen years old. The *Wilmington Journal* ran a photograph of Karen with the word RUNAWAY? beneath her face. The next day they ran the same picture. The caption asked, DEAD OR ALIVE?

I was twelve years old. Karen told me, "I'm going to the corner, want anything? You want your Teaberry gum? Do you want a Hearn's cake?"

I sat at the kitchen table, writing five sheets of detention homework. My sister was dressed up, wearing smoky nylons and low heels that shifted her posture forward. Her lipstick was frosted salmon-pink. Her matte powder erased her features.

"I don't have money for sweets," I told her, fishing.

Karen said, "I've only got a dollar. That's not enough for both of us."

"Forget it," I said.

"I'm going to the store," Karen said again. She pinched the doorknob for a long time, I thought, before turning it. I saw the kitchen clock above her head; its second hand had become bent. As it circled the numbers, the needle scratched a silver gouge in the clock's white face. Then my sister went out.

WHEN KAREN HADN'T RETURNED after forty-eight hours, the Penny Hill police recognized that it wasn't a typical pout session or simple teen whimsy. Federal investigators were directed to our street. My father, Ray, laid out some of Karen's report cards with the teachers' comments. The FBI agent picked up one yellow booklet and read the teacher's remarks, "Karen is an agreeable student but too retiring. She should be encouraged to participate in class discussions."

"This says your daughter is the shy type?"

"She's quiet," Ray said.

"These shy kids don't usually take off. But sometimes a wallflower turns into a wild seed," the agent said.

Ray didn't like what the agent was suggesting, and he asked me to leave the room. I wasn't reluctant to leave because I could hear everything the agent said by standing inside the dining room chimney. Inside the mortared shaft, their conversation was amplified. I heard my mother sniffling. She ripped a tissue from its hollow box, and another. Veronica was giving a performance. The agent asked about our two older stepsiblings, each of them married and living on their own. Had Karen ever confided in one of them and run off to one of their homes?

"It wouldn't be an option," Veronica said.

Veronica was painting an icy picture of our family's splintered relations; she was implying that when people jump ship, it's every man for himself.

The FBI agent asked, "Does Karen have a nickname she goes by?"

" 'Peaches,' " Ray said.

"Oh, please," Veronica said. "Only Ray called her that."

"That's right, I call her 'Peaches,' " Ray told the agent.

The FBI man asked, "Was your daughter a virgin?"

Veronica asked Ray, "What's your guess?" Her voice had an edge.

"These days, I don't know," my father said, and the FBI agent chimed in with his similar beliefs. "These days," he echoed Ray. The agent was careful to indict the age and not the girl herself. He wanted a list of Karen's boyfriends.

"Karen didn't have any boyfriends," Veronica said flatly.

"None? Are we sure?" Ray said.

"If she had had any boyfriends, do you think she'd have been so gloomy all the time?"

"Love is strange," the FBI man said.

There was a tight silence.

"In fact, if your daughter acted gloomy, that's a good sign she was in over her head," the agent told my parents.

I was asked to return to the room to relate the details of Karen's departure. "What did Karen tell you?" the agent asked.

I told the agent what my sister had said, " 'Do you want a Hearn's cake?' "

"What's that?" he said.

I described the tiny sponge cakes that were sold at a nearby grocery store. The cakes were the size of scented guest soaps and iced with a satin glaze, a buffed pearl patina in hues of shell pink and Wedgwood blue. These tea cakes triggered my greediest impulses. Each compact confection was not meant to be shared, but should be centered on the tongue in one languorous and prolonged absorption of its delicate extracts—vanilla and *rose water*. Hearn's cakes had an almost sinister power over the senses and sometimes seemed to—especially right then—affect my moral decisions and issues of conscience. Perhaps, if I had asked Karen to bring me one little cake, she might have returned home. She might never have disappeared.

The agent was impressed by my description of the sweets. He smiled at me. He asked, "What did Karen take with her when she left the house?"

I told the government official that Karen did not take a single thing. I looked down at my white sneakers, which were smeared with soot from the hearth.

"We have all the suitcases," Ray told the man.

The agent said, "She could have hidden a grip in the bushes."

"She didn't take anything," I said.

"We have all the suitcases," Ray said another time, as if he had lost sight of exactly what was missing.

The agent wanted to look around outside. We walked him full circle around our huge house, a fieldstone ranch. It was one hundred feet long, with blazing picture windows, massive squares of glass you could drive a tank through. These windows framed my youth; interior and exterior worlds merged or collided along these ten-foot transparent skins. Neighborhood families exhibited mirrored balls on pedestals, sport trophies, heirloom lamps, even a huge orchestral harp. Across the street our neighbors watched the FBI agent from *their* picture windows. I recognized Mr. Ossi peering at us, dressed only in his bathrobe and holding a baked apple in a dish.

"Where did you last see your sister?" the agent asked me.

"Right here on these kitchen steps."

I sat down on the fieldstone risers and squashed tiny red spiders with my thumb. The agent looked inside our sunken garbage cans, four sheet metal canisters recessed below the flagstone sidewalk. Karen and I had stood in these tin wells, daring one another to squat inside and close the lids. But their stench was too strong and the compartments too eerie, like drawers in a morgue. Once, maggots had infested an odd sliver of garbage until it twitched and curled like a living finger.

The agent stepped on the pedals until each heavy lid pried open. "She could have hid a suitcase in one of these cans," he said.

Ray was losing his patience. He insisted that he could account for every odd tote bag, duffel and valise. Ray told the agent that Karen had started a job after school at the Holiday Lanes. They might know something. The agent took down the address of the bowling alley. He looked grim, but he assured my father that some girls ran away with just the clothes on their backs.

KAREN AND I SHARED A ROOM. Once, I had drawn an imaginary line down the middle of our bedroom, and if Karen put anything of her own on my side, I claimed it. When Karen was missing, all of her possessions were arranged in their proper places; there was no chance of them moving over the boundary and becoming my rightful property. I collected china horses and arranged them in formal rows across my dresser according to each one's temperament and conformation. These prancing mounts no longer allured me, and from my bed I studied the treasures on Karen's bureau glass. In the Nite Lite's dull arc, I saw her ceramic Siamese cat, slope-shouldered, with almond eyes and an emerald collar, a novelty shampoo bottle Karen had saved. I saw my sister's comb and brush, her blond hair coiled around the bristles. I saw her golden paperweight, a fossilized chunk of amber sap in which tiny bubbles of air were trapped.

The hours with my sister were too short. Our entire brief union could fit into the tiny oval of Karen's hand mirror: One school night, I ask Karen to brush my hair. I hold the hand mirror extended and watch my reflection as Karen pulls the bristles over the crest of my scalp, scouring my accentuated widow's peak. She angles the untame strands until my mane is plowed and parted. If I turn the mirror slightly, I can see Karen's face, a pink barrette between her teeth. She wrinkles her nose when our eyes meet. She fastens the clasp around a tight hunk of hair until the roots at my temples are stinging.

This hand mirror often comes back to haunt me. It is like a silver garden pond in memory, a bright oval of light splashed upon the ceiling of the psyche.

I WENT TO THE CELLAR to retrieve a doll I had punished and tossed into the laundry chute. One of its eyes was jammed shut and I shook the doll until its eyes rolled open. Standing on a pile of soiled shirts, I looked up the chute and found my sister's face floating one floor above me. She leaned deep into its sheet-metal duct; I saw her profile repeated, mirrored on all four sides of the shiny burrow. Her blond hair fell in silky kinks, like curled ribbon.

Karen scolded me for standing on Ray's white Van Heusens. Her voice trailed off when she noticed our mother's hose wound in a tight, erotic knob, like a nautilus perched on the pile of laundry. Finding Veronica's female items in the subterranean washing room made her jittery. Karen and I had often watched Veronica dress for cocktail parties. Together, we lolled on our parents' king bed, sharing a bowl of bridge mix as Veronica trekked back and forth from her bureau to the closet dressed only in her strapless bra and panties. Karen became hypnotized, her eyes pinned on our mother during every stage. I sat beside Karen and sucked the chocolate satin from the peanuts and spit the messy nuts into the palm of my hand. Without taking her eyes off our mother, Karen unfurled a Kleenex and I centered my discarded candy in its gauzy tarpaulin.

Veronica stood back to inspect two cocktail dresses swirled across the bed. Her face was both dreamy and overly alert as she examined the gowns and imagined her party night. She picked the blue Chanel and became all business as she assembled her shoes and matching accessories for her outfit. Before stepping into her dress, we watched her shiver loose powder and spritz her French Jean Patou perfume, pinching the rubber bulb of a cut-crystal atomizer. Next, she stooped before the full-length mirror to adjust her seamed stockings.

To protect against runs when she tugged on her hose, Veronica put on the short white cotton gloves that she wore to church each Sunday. With insulated palms, she caressed each ankle and smoothed the fine mesh, following her natural curves, urging the nude silk over her knees and higher. She pinched and patted her stockings until each seam was straight. She secured her ribbon garters. The metal tabs snapped open and shut like the tight jaws of tiny, unnameable reptiles. I was fascinated by Veronica's exotic apparatus, but Karen's face suddenly blanched, as if she recognized the scene from a deeper level. She collected the Kleenex tote of smeary chocolate drops and left the room.

Veronica's lace undergarments were hints and markers suggesting that *sex was a highway*. Soon my sister and I would enter that busy esplanade and merge with the traffic.

Families take pride in their piety or in their prosperity, rejoicing in a father-and-son business venture, in a gifted child's scholarship or in a prized commission in the military. But in our household, Veronica's enterprising sexuality overwhelmed our individual goals and spilled into family matters. Her erotic aspect emerged in her every routine and came more naturally to her than maternal duty.

I reached for Veronica's balled-up hose, a silk mollusk.

"Don't touch that," Karen said. I looked up the silver chute and saw my sister's face. She smiled. Our childhood was safe in that tight mirrored flume, safer than it would ever be.

I TRIED TO PICTURE my sister dead. I invented a scene: I saw an angel, its ragged wings flapping without forward propulsion, the way a rock dove stalls when it's struck by buckshot. If I pictured my sister's motionless body in a grassy trench along the Delaware River, I felt like I'd murdered her myself. It disturbed me more to believe she still survived, survived without thinking of me.

If she drove off in a detailed Chrysler pimp ride and set up housekeeping with moody grifters and addicted vets, outlawing with some oddball foster family, I knew she was going to come back to collect me. She didn't forget about me.

In our anonymity to one another we grew codependent, we grew closer. Now, in my early forties, if I were to reactivate a search, where would I start? Which one of us will surface first?

THE DELAWARE MEMORIAL BRIDGE is two identical spans, one flowing east and one flowing west across the marbled, toxin-scalded Delaware River. The dual structures were tagged the "Twin Bridges" or they were called the "Two Sisters." Ray used these twin bridges as a logo for his company. Complimentary Sheaffer pens, Zippo lighters and decks of playing cards were printed with the company name, MITCHELL INDUSTRIAL SUPPLY, above a graphic of the sweeping double span. All his company trucks and Econoline vans were stenciled with the twin arches.

When my sister disappeared, I believed that she had crossed the Twin Bridges and was swept away on that fluid artery, the highway of sex. It was natural for me to think that my sister and I would utilize these bridges to escape our home town and evacuate our childhood. On the other side was New Jersey, its famous turnpike, a wide highway edged by truck farms, indifferent scenery and undistinguished landmarks until the New York skyline lifted on the horizon, a granite cloudscape of riches and devils. Veronica alluded to it too; she seemed to know Karen was in that stream of traffic.

MY SISTER AND I WERE LED to believe that the route out of childhood was marriage. Our older stepsiblings had veered off, into stinging unions made slapdash because of the nearing due dates of unplanned babies. These celebrations were hushed and awkward, as if the tradition of marriage was merely a method for sweeping errors under the rug. I began to notice the phenomena of "sudden fate." In Veronica's *Woman's Day* magazine, I read about wedding tragedies, bride-and-groom head-ons and such. In one example, an entire wedding party—husband, wife, bridesmaids and ushers—had drowned in a cistern at a wedding dance. The reception was held in a decrepit hall. The floorboards were rotted and couldn't support the shifting crowd when they danced in a conga line. The joists sagged and broke away from the bearing walls, immediately creating a lurching funnel.

The hall was built over an *open cistern* with thirty feet of standing water.

Just before the dance, the wedding guests had been photographed on the steps of the building where they would be killed. The magazine had circled the faces of the victims, specifying their relationships to the bride and groom. I recognized the bride's timid countenance, a wary cameo, and the groom's handsome face, serious, ready to father his children. Bachelor ushers, grinning with another year's freedom. Nineteen were drowned in their formal attire, cummerbunds, corsages and garters. The flower girl—a five-year-old in daisy chains—was spared. I can see these circled faces even now, as if it were a reliable graph from which to gauge my own risk, my own fortune. Certainly, this couple was not meant to be; so evil was their union that a score of innocents were sacrificed to ensure its termination.

WHEN ONE CHILD goes missing, the remaining child is left untethered. I have seen a dog pull free from its collar and in its sudden freedom shudder, as if any connection it had had to the world remained in the coil of leather.

When my sister disappeared, the physical world was immediately altered. The morning after she left, the refineries at Marcus Hook spewed microscopic droplets of oil across the leeward neighborhoods. Our picture windows filmed; my hair sagged with petroleum mist as I stood at the bus stop. The sun itself was masked, as if behind a vinyl shower curtain.

At night, Karen's closet door wouldn't latch and drifted loose. I saw her dresses hanging on the closet pole; their shoulders slumping off the hangers seemed animate and shrugging. I got out of bed to shut the door and again it fell open as if the room itself were turning and the wall was rotating to become the ceiling. I propped a pair of shoes against the doorframe—Karen's cordovan Weejuns with spidery tassels, as if she had just stepped out of them.

That same week, a neighbor drove his car through a plate-glass slider. I went directly to the scene with my father, who penned measurements for a replacement door. The car had to sit on the plush carpet until the insurance inspectors arrived. I felt the cold air rushing through the interior rooms of our neighbor's house, a chilly spectacle of freedom.

A missing child and a car in someone's living room have immediate shock value. When Karen disappeared, I was jostled and freed by a *charmed* destructive force, from every tether of childhood.

Absence is a fat seed.

When a loss occurs, it occurs in perpetuity; it keeps regenerating like a flowering vine. What vanished once keeps vanishing, in perennial mutations. For years I have been cloaked in the glutinous caul of our childhood, that steeping, unleavened bread that should have been long ago consumed, used up, the way a chick devours its yolk and emerges individual and clean, with no memory of its confinement. Our childhood never came to a valid completion; days never accrued in a natural progression. Our childhood just stopped.

I want Karen to retell it.

With only an eighth-grade education, events have never been inked. I hurry to transcribe it before it all evaporates.

Karen walks ahead of me through these pages. She's holding a shoe box of scraps, notes with her half of the story. I am writing this down as it happens.

THE

MIRACLE GIRL

W HEN THE OCEAN liner SS *Andrea Doria* collided with the
Stockholm on July 25, 1956, my sister and I were at home in
the suburbs of Wilmington, asleep in our horsehair beds. I was four
years old, my sister was six. Less than two weeks earlier, we had
crossed the Atlantic, returning from Turin, where Ray had worked as
an engineer at Fiat. The Italian auto manufacturer prized Ray and had
treated him like a king. They assigned to him two personal translators,
one at either elbow, but Ray longed for America and after two years in
Italy he decided to bring us home. Ray had booked passage on the
Doria, but he used his Fiat office to wedge us on an earlier crossing
aboard the *Giulio Cesare*, another ship from the Italian Line. Veronica
kept our original ticket vouchers for the doomed ship, complete with
the historic dates and cabin numbers, the adjoining staterooms 52 and
54, on the starboard side, right under the Promenade Deck. In fog, the
Stockholm had steamed straight into the *Doria*, ramming these exact
sleeping compartments. The *Doria* sank, killing fifty-one people.

In stateroom 52, two *other* sisters were sleeping when the blind
ship punctured the *Doria*'s hull. The youngest girl was killed, but her
fourteen-year-old sister was scooped from her bunk and trapped in the
crumpled prow of the Swedish liner, which carried her off. Two days
later, when the disabled *Stockholm* berthed in New York, they discovered the surviving sister, Linda Morgan, in the bow wreckage, like a
battered figurehead swaddled in sheet metal.

Rescue workers administered morphine sulfate, writing on a piece
of tape across the girl's forehead the dosage amount, M. S. GR. ¼, a

lugubrious strip she wore to the hospital. Newspapers called her the "Miracle Girl." Having seen her picture with the adhesive marker, I can't get it out of my mind.

Karen and I had the ticket with the exact date and cabin number, the same accommodations as Linda Morgan and her doomed sister—stateroom 52. We were not aboard ship that night, but I have always felt as if we were its dreaming passengers, "dreaming passengers" until that mix-up.

When the *Doria* sank without us, that's when our wakeful journey begins.

During our childhood, Veronica often extended an end-table drawer and fanned open the tickets. "You girls would have died," she told us, as if a plan, greater than her own making, had been foiled. "We couldn't have saved you. Ray and I would have been dancing in the Belvedere Lounge. There's always a big party on the last night of the crossing. Little girls would have been in bed. The steward kept your names on a card."

The fact that Karen and I should have been broadside of a Swedish liner but two other sisters doubled for us has been a perplexing burden. Veronica told us, "The fog was like soup." She said, "Scientists blamed sunspots for the radar failure." I couldn't imagine these "sunspots," but I pictured the *Doria*'s running lights and golden portholes winking out, disappearing, until she was invisible in the fog. I pictured the compartment I would have shared with my sister, and our one unspoken desire for shore and safety—for our parents to finish their indulgent night in the Belvedere Lounge and to come to check on us.

THE STEAMSHIP COLLISION was suggestive of our dangerous journey through youth with parents who were under the spell of an intense erotic sorcery. This was the challenge of our household—how to maintain family life against a backdrop of carnal spectacles. Veronica flirted and vamped for our father, but her antics extended to everyday merchants, her bachelor bridge partners, even the handsome breadman who came to the door in his brilliant white jacket with a basket of sweets on his arm. The scent of iced cinnamon rolls and spice cake filtered through every room of the house before Veronica finished flirting and she allowed him to continue his route. The new principal at the elementary school, Mr. Forcetti, was her target for a year. Veronica liked his Latin looks and went into his office with a box of pencils that said MITCHELL INDUSTRIAL SUPPLY or to donate our old encyclopedia set. She was insatiable and could never get enough attention; Veronica was not like Cinderella who lost a slipper—she *was* the empty glass slipper.

Veronica looked remarkably like Vivien Leigh, but our mother was more sultry. I once heard Veronica say that Vivien Leigh was too wan and she'd benefit from a cure at Vichy. But Veronica's looks were both a blessing and a curse to her, just as she had always said her name was a curse. She was named after the saint who had stopped Jesus on his way to Calvary to offer him a cloth to wipe his face. The stains of Christ's sweat and tears left a permanent image upon the swatch.

I have watched Veronica avert her eyes from mirrors in lobbies or restaurants. Perhaps it was in simple modesty, but she seemed well aware of the fact that when people saw her they were startled, devoured by longing. She recognized their famished expressions and avoided sighting her own image, the source of it all.

Veronica was small-waisted, with the full hips of Italian starlets. Her heart-shaped face was framed by rich brunet hair pulled back from her temples in deep ropes. She had a habit of removing her hairpins and shaking her hair loose, perhaps while standing in line at the bank, or waiting for her number to be called at the butcher. The mannerism suggested that she wasn't at all pleased to be kept waiting. She created a minispectacle and the waves usually parted. But when her number was called, she took her time rewinding her braids and spearing the knots, her elbows lifted over her head.

Veronica understood that her beauty was at once an asset and a liability. She was careful to never flatter me for my looks, whether I deserved the praise or not. If someone said to her, "Maria looks pretty in her smocked dress," Veronica would say, "Shush, she'll get a big head." As a youngster, I imagined my head expanding like a balloon until it exploded. Later, if I buried my nose in a book, she warned me again. "Don't be an *egg*head. Men don't like egghead women."

Veronica never complimented Karen but often told her to smile. She told Karen, "You're pretty when you smile." Veronica tried to cajole the right facial wince that would trigger Karen's flat, expressionless mouth for an instant.

"*Gory*-orgeous," Veronica scolded.

Veronica used her beauty as a shield as people might employ their lameness or retreat behind a strawberry birthmark to hide worse traits and unforgivable character flaws. She excused herself from social obligations. She couldn't be a chaperone at the school dance or supervise a table at the church bazaar. Her ankles were too delicate and she couldn't be expected to stand behind a punch bowl for hours at a time.

When I was small, I heard people call Veronica "statuesque" and I imagined that Veronica must have walked off her pedestal in a state of dreamy amnesia. An odd thing happened once that exaggerated my childish perception. In France, Veronica took Karen and me to visit a family plot in an ancient cemetery. There were rows and rows of aboveground crypts, each sunbaked coffin marked by marble angels, and statues of the Virgin. To our astonishment, Veronica climbed on top of a cemetery monument to imitate the pose of its voluptuous ornament, a life-sized nymph. In the glaring Mediterranean heat, Veronica crooked her arm around the nymph's waist and leaned back and forth, swinging her bare leg. She held onto her stone partner, arched her back and kicked, as if practicing the cancan. The dance seemed choreographed; their likeness was so remarkable, the stone nymph seemed in compliance. Veronica played on that perch, beside the marble goddess for several minutes. She didn't invite me or Karen to jump up beside her.

She was shooed off the statue by two crones dressed in mourning frocks and heavy black cotton stockings, who had arrived at a neighboring mausoleum. They scolded Veronica, but she brushed them off in her haughty, perfect French. All that afternoon Veronica seemed refreshed, transformed by her romp with the nymph.

That instant in the arid, baked-clay cemetery was one of the singular times Veronica seemed happy. She tossed her straw hat into the weeds and threw her head back. She pranced on the pedestal beside the nymph, as if relishing her status. "I'm flesh and blood. I'm alive. The rest of you can rot," she chided those who rested beneath the sunbleached stones and also chided us, her living offspring.

Veronica told us that good looks attracted the wrong kind of people. This was how she claimed her innocence after she was jilted by her first husband. At nineteen, Veronica married an Arrow Collar model, Curtis Pettibone. He was the son of a prominent Chicago obstetrician, worthless at everything until he tried posing for pictures. He was one of the last models toward the end of the collar era when Arrow made separate collars before making shirts with attached collars. His looks were so remarkable an asset that he was kept stateside during the war where his only duty was to sit in a kissing booth in Times Square to recruit WACS. Women lined up around the corner to earn a kiss from the model after signing their enlistment papers.

The model wasn't faithful and humiliated Veronica at every turn. After fathering her first two children, he left her. She was forced to live with her parents, puritanical French immigrants. When her parents came to America, they opened a successful restaurant and bought several apartment buildings, but Veronica had first been raised in rural France, in a house built directly over a livestock barn. The stench from the cows and chickens lifted into the kitchen and parlors. If a piglet or a lamb took sick, it was brought upstairs and corralled by the stove, taking precedence over Veronica's needs. When Veronica wanted to level a complaint against me or Karen, after we had done something coarse or stupid, she had said "Don't be an *immigrant*" instead of "Don't be an idiot."

Veronica saved tear sheets of her first husband's Arrow Collar ads from the *New York Times*, the *Saturday Evening Post* and *Collier's*. Periodically, Veronica received air-mail envelopes from her ex-husband, gaudy postcards from Rio or Buenos Aires. These notes from the model were bald-faced announcements of a progression of betrothals and matrimonial tie-ups. The model was married seven times in all. Veronica wondered why he bothered to tell her that he was still at it. Veronica suffered for hours at her desk writing a response, trying to make it *look* dashed-off, something to snub him. Karen and I found these notes and clippings left scattered on the foldout leaf of the antique secretary where Veronica wrote letters. We examined Veronica's scribblings beside the ancient clippings, some of them torn up and taped together again. Karen said, "These look like love letters to me. But how would I know?"

The model's chiseled face, his stupid erotic gaze from the advertisement columns, became a vivid part of my childhood. His disappearance was a strange erotic stimulus, as if his *absence*, itself, was the seduction. Perhaps Karen had watched Veronica's obsession and thought that to earn her mother's adoration she too would have to remove herself from the scene.

When the Arrow Collar model disappeared for good, Veronica sued for divorce, claiming "mindful neglect, desertion." It wasn't long until she got to know my father, Ray Mitchell, who had married an old classmate of hers from the Sisters of Loretto Academy. Before the model left Veronica, the two couples had often double-dated and went dancing at the Palmer House. With Curtis Pettibone out of the picture, Ray took Veronica under his wing and they went as a threesome. They didn't see it happen overnight, but, just as when mice chew through the insulation around a lamp cord, a live current started to crackle. Ray courted Veronica. She didn't have second thoughts about her girlfriend, but she thought she'd be "slumming" if she dated an open-hearth foreman. Yet Ray was handsome. He was lean and muscular, with a slight stoop from an injury he had incurred shoveling coke into a blast furnace, but he had all the masculine vigor you might expect of a foreman at a steel mill.

Ray's first wife was consumptive, with worsening lung symptoms. Before she became sick, she had actually been quite pretty and held an uncanny resemblance to the sixties' orange juice spokesperson Anita Bryant. In my youth, watching TV in our den in Wilmington, Veronica would rise from her chair in a fury to flip the channel whenever Anita Bryant flashed on the screen. The tall brunette stood in a Florida orange grove, praising the golden juice as if it were a potion she might have used to snare Ray.

Veronica encouraged Ray to take her to the Chicago dance halls while his wife was an invalid. Ray left his wife in her sickbed and Veronica brought her babies to her parents' busy French restaurant where the kids were put to bed in empty kitchen drawers lined with feather pillows. Ray took Veronica to the Palmer House, to the Aragon Ballroom in North Chicago, or to the Trianon on the South Side where they heard Frankie Laine and Wayne King. These were postwar glittering nights, full of new hope and second chances. Under Veronica's

spell, Ray placed his wife in a TB sanatorium. He submerged himself in
Veronica's element and remained there, helplessly, the way a fish lives
in a mesh bucket in the river, zigzagging against the current in the
confines of its trap.

Ray himself had been a victim of a dramatic betrayal. When Ray's
father died of blood poisoning in 1917, his mother turned him over to
Girard School, an orphanage for "white boys" in Philadelphia. Every
day his mother walked to work and callously passed the front gate of
the institution where she had abandoned her son. Ray stood at the
wrought-iron fence and reached through the tines to clutch the hem of
her coat. She tugged it out of his hands and she didn't turn around
when he called "Mama!"

Abandoned by his own mother at the age of seven, Ray recognized
Veronica's maternal flatness, and he thought he could step in to claim
Veronica's two babies. Then again, wasn't it just plain lust for their
mother which made him undertake the responsibility of those children? Lust creates a cyclone effect; it swirls all the commonsense facts
when a man is organizing his "pros and cons."

"Physical attraction," Ray once warned me, "is the opposite of
clear thought."

When his wife wouldn't sign divorce papers, Ray fled to Arkansas
for a six-week quickie. He told himself that he might be leaving one
woman, but he was rescuing another. Assuming responsibility for
Veronica and her two children after the philandering model had abandoned them was a charitable and decent act.

In order to get his divorce, Ray had to leave his job at Carnegie Illinois South Works, Open Hearth No. 4, where he was ascending into
top management. He had to abandon his post and assume residence in
Arkansas to get his divorce paperwork. He had loved his work at the
open hearth, monitoring its stacks, flues and checkers, and managing
its heavy schedule of steel production while meeting the escalating
standards of the railroads and special wartime industries. How could
he walk away?

In my possession, I have Ray's huge tome "Open Hearth Melting
Practice," a five-hundred-page text he authored in 1945, from which he
gave weekly lectures to workers at Carnegie Illinois South Works. Ray

offered me the text when Veronica wasn't looking. Veronica didn't want him to prize his "other life" or hand down evidence to his children.

"You'll want this," he told me when he gave me the book. "Remember, the pen is lighter than the coal scuttle."

I thumbed through its frail tissue pages, which had been painstakingly cut from stencils long before there was Xerox. Mysterious graphs depicted technical procedures like the timing of "skins" on different ingot molds. Despite its technical diction, the book is a love poem to the steelworks, a paean to steel as if it were his own flesh.

For a new life with Veronica, Ray left his calling.

He took a job selling floor tiles and siding in Little Rock, then moved Veronica and my two stepsiblings across the border into Hamilton, Ontario, where his first wife couldn't serve support papers on him. Veronica said, "The model forgot me, so why should we send *her* a check every month? Just because you were hitched?" Veronica was insulted by the double standard.

In Canada, Ray took a pedestrian job in the industry, far below his previous position at South Works. He often joked to cover up his homesickness for South Works. He pinned his old South Works ID medallion to his barbecue apron, unable to part with the precious badge.

KAREN'S BIRTH WAS unexpected. Ray had been childless with his first wife, and he had accepted the blame for their infertility, considering his exposure to heavy metals, extreme temperatures and asbestos at the steelworks. Veronica thought marriage, especially a second time around, should be preserved for man and wife alone. She was distressed when her pregnancy interrupted her honeymoon. Children were intrusions. The Arrow Collar model had wandered when Veronica became a mother, and she worried Ray might do the same. In those early years, when all four children lived together in one house, our schemes toward family unity were immediately quelled by Veronica's rigid program of romance with Ray. It started with cocktails. Then she made dinner for two at a late hour when he might have ordinarily worked on a jigsaw puzzle or played cribbage with my older siblings; he had bought them a beautiful board shaped like the Cape Cod peninsula. Ray enjoyed walking the cocker spaniel, Star, and pushing the baby carriage with Karen and I tucked beneath tasseled blankets. But Veronica whipped the leash from Ray's hands and gave the chore to Alex. She awarded Christine the honor of steering the baby pram. "Come back before dark," she told them.

Ray was disappointed that the family outing was vetoed, but Veronica told him, "We can't *all* walk the dog. It's only got one neck."

SOON AFTER KAREN and I were born, our older siblings were ingeniously dispersed first to boarding schools, then boot camp, early college admission, sudden nuptials or mental institutions. Like the bizarre habit of arctic geese who shove their fledglings off high cliffs only to watch the goslings bounce from boulder to boulder until each downy neck is broken, Veronica hinted to us that it would be Karen's turn to go next, then mine.

Veronica never explained where she expected us to go, but when Karen and I were not more than twelve and ten, Veronica began to assemble a "trousseau" for each of us. She collected housewares, linens; she bought sets of Oneida flatware, tumblers, wine goblets, Willowware place settings, cast-iron frying pans and two sets of the *Woman's Day Encyclopedia of Cookery*, thirteen volumes in all. These items, Veronica told us, would be ours when we eventually left home.

Veronica kept our trousseau boxes in a storeroom in the basement beside the oil furnace. The same way other little girls played with miniature tea sets, Karen and I often sorted and arranged the full-sized items we would be using when we were adults and living on our own. Veronica had spared no expense in her organization of kitchen gizmos, household helpers and Emily Post accessories. In one of our surveys, Karen and I discovered identical white boxes. Each box held a set of ceramic place markers. The small china cards stood independently and were meant to be displayed above place settings at a formal dinner. The blank china plaques came with a wax pencil. A hostess was supposed to write the names of her dinner guests on the face of each marker and arrange her seating according to gender or for "maximum conversation clusters."

At ten, I tried to imagine the people who would attend my dinner parties—what indeed was expected at these events? The future seemed a dizzying way off, and yet Veronica seemed willing to let it fall into our laps.

Karen took one of the wax pencils and wrote my name on one blank marker.

"Dinner at seven?" she said. "Is that a good time for you?"

"Seven is okay," I told her.

I wrote *her* name on one of my markers and returned it with the rest of the set to my cache of domestic treasures. Our bond was made. She would come to my house for dinner, I would go to hers. It was written.

Our mysterious trousseaux might have seemed like sensible gifts from a mother with generous foresight. She had seen Christine and Alex marry prematurely due to unplanned pregnancies. Christine was wed to a Ph.D. candidate in Chinese philosophy and moved with him from Cambridge to Ann Arbor. Alex knocked up a blond teen and married her in a swift ceremony at St. Helena's Church, but not before her belly had begun to protrude. His bride held her bouquet against her waist to hide her little bulge, but its trembling cloud of baby's breath only called attention to her predicament. Karen and I had watched our family deconstructed in a systematic progression. Unlike migrating butterflies or even the African termite, we would never reorganize in flight, we could make no migratory formations, no collective flock. We scattered.

KAREN WONDERED WHEN Ray had changed horses. She knew that Ray's first wife had been abandoned in a sanatorium in Downers Grove, but she took an exceptional interest in the dates. She calculated the math and insisted that she must be the child of Ray's *first* wife, the one who looked like Anita Bryant. She wasn't Veronica's daughter. "I think I should look into that," Karen told me.

Indeed, Karen didn't really resemble Veronica in any way. But if it were true that Veronica wasn't Karen's real mother, I didn't see how such a revelation would deliver Karen from her rejected station in our household. I told Karen I was willing to go along if she ever decided to search for Ray's first wife. Even Alex had said he might one day try to track down the model. If Karen and Alex had secret progenitors, other bonds they could research and renew, perhaps they'd have their second chances. This idea tinted my childhood. Who belonged to whom? I wondered if the broken tether was love or if it was blood.

VERONICA STRUGGLED to find harmony between romance and pro-creative duty; it's so easy to fail at one or both. Because she had once been an abandoned wife, Veronica spent a great deal of time sitting in Ray's lap, her arms around his neck. She seemed to be trying to forget her first husband and his unpredictable nights. One time, Curtis Petti-bone returned home wearing two different shoes. The right shoe was his own wing tip, but the left one was a polished oxford belonging to another woman's husband. The unknown woman possessed a similar pair of mismatched shoes and had boldly telephoned Veronica to sort it out.

Sitting in Ray's lap every night, she usurped our rights. Karen and I often stole up to Ray and Veronica to swipe the orange slices and maraschino cherries from their Old-Fashioned glasses. Did I gain my predisposition to alcohol addiction and substance abuse from devour-ing, nightly, the fully marinated compote after they drained their glasses? Veronica didn't want us at Ray's feet and she shooed us away, bribing us with these embalmed twists of whiskey-soaked citrus.

Karen and I were allotted only one good-night kiss, which Veronica performed hurriedly, gracelessly, with her hands knotted behind her back. Veronica was so erect and uncomfortable, she might have been administering inoculations. Karen was two and half years older than me. I was "littlest" but very canny, and I suffered these small rations better than she. My "tomboy" shell was thick. Karen sensed Veronica was halfhearted and she spurned her mother's feeble advances.

When Veronica hovered, perfunctorily, over Karen's pillow to de-liver an arid peck on her cheek, Karen tugged the sheet over her head and *refused* her kiss.

"Just one kiss?" Veronica said.

Karen shook her head beneath the taut Wamsutta.

"One kiss. We won't turn to stone," Veronica told her.

"No," Karen said, her voice muted behind the impromptu curtain.

Our mother gave up and left the room. In the dark, I watched Karen's wraith-white profile under the Wamsutta until at last she jerked the hem away from her face.

When I witnessed these nightly contests, my sympathies were divided. I felt unhappy for Veronica when Karen refused to accept her kiss. Certainly, no act of affection should be slighted. Yet, I understood that my sister didn't want a cursory handout.

Veronica brought Karen to a dermatologist the first time Karen suffered a mild case of acne. The physician prescribed an acrid lotion, its sulfur odor a noxious blend of rotten eggs and astringent calamine. Veronica pestered Karen to apply the solution every night at bedtime, and I protested.

"I have to sleep in this room," I told Veronica. My preadolescent complexion was silky and even. I had not studied a mirror or examined my pores as I would later on in my teens, when a silty pollen of oil and dirt collected across my forehead. Safely tucked in my smooth, dormant skin, I felt guilty. I watched Veronica shun Karen because of her imperfections and keep her at bay. Then, at her menarche, Karen suddenly became a different threat. Karen's sexuality erased her gawky characteristics. Karen's hormones increased, leveled off and adjusted to the monthly tasks of womanhood; her curves filled out her clothing. Her dress seams were tested at the hips and bosom. Karen adjusted her posture and hunched her shoulders so her bust wouldn't thrust out. Veronica began to monitor Karen's food intake, categorizing Karen's transformation as "weight," and not the natural bloom of adolescence. Veronica purchased boxes of Metrecal cookies and cans of Metrecal milk shakes. When Karen came home from school, she was permitted to have one Diet-Rite soda and three dry-as-dust Metrecal cookies, or she could detour the cookies and have instead one Metrecal shake.

I could eat anything, and I often removed a half gallon of Sealtest "Neapolitan" ice cream from the freezer and ate it directly from the dripping carton. I was lithe, athletic, and my physical dexterity gave people the impression I was self-confident. In truth, I was self-assured about only one thing: I was a sprinter. I could run short distances at a high rate of speed. I could shoot ahead and keep out of harm's way, at least for the time being.

One final Halloween, Karen and I dressed up as winos, our faces smudged with burned cork. On our return, I watched in numb bliss and confusion when Veronica went through Karen's treats and gave most of them to me. Veronica awarded me all the chocolate bars, peanut butter cups, foil kisses and whatever else she presumed might be high-caloric or might aggravate Karen's acne.

I sat across from Karen on the oriental carpet in the living room. Veronica sorted through our cache of treats. Each time Veronica tossed a candy bar in front of me, I shoved it across the rug to my sister. Veronica intercepted it again and handed it back to me. Again, I tried to inch a Hershey bar across the floor to Karen, who sat with her arms around her knees. I couldn't bear being the recipient of these riches which didn't belong to me. "I don't want *hers*," I told Veronica.

"Karen can't have it. You might as well take it. It's yours."

Karen was left with a mound of bland sweets: Necco wafers, broken candy corns and squares of branny Bit-O-Honey that I would have forfeited gladly under any circumstances. But being allotted Karen's rightful share of the premium candy loot added to my comet trail of guilt that had been accruing throughout our childhood.

I had always been awarded the position of the "cute one," the "favorite," "littlest." I was given priority. Perhaps I earned more attention because, born at only four pounds, I had been a "preemie" and deserved the extra fawning. I gained their notice because I "bounced back" from every neglect and didn't retreat like Karen. Veronica had often rubbed my back when we watched *Bonanza*. She explained to Karen, "Your little sister needs her back rubbed because she stayed in an incubator for weeks." Yes, nurses had massaged me every hour, like clockwork, reaching into the incubator through rubber hands attached to the glass box. I was never removed from the glass box.

When Veronica made popcorn, she always gave me the larger portion. She salted the dome of white kernels for me before handing the shaker to Karen.

I tried to believe that Veronica was teaching Karen the eating habits, dieting regimens and skin-care techniques that would allow Karen to prosper in the highly competitive theater of femme fatales in which our mother reigned supreme. Perhaps by confiscating her Halloween rewards, Veronica was giving Karen a leg up. Yes, perhaps Veronica was ready to hand the baton to Karen—beauty, with all its rewards and burdens, was Veronica's domain, and she herself would bestow it on Karen.

Karen faced Veronica. In direct body language, shoulders slumping and head bowed, she seemed to be saying she didn't wish to compete. She surrendered. Veronica was perfection. Karen could never imitate her beauty tricks and cosmetic routines because she didn't have the small bones, olive complexion and hot green eyes to begin with. She could never live up to it.

IN HIS EARLY TWENTIES, my stepbrother Alex began to accrue money and status in real estate development and speculation. His industry was sparked by his obsession to impress his mother, and he often left a building site in the middle of the day to visit Veronica. He brought her a little gift, an antique bottle or a rare Canton dish he had seen in a shopwindow and purchased on a whim to please her. He pulled into the driveway in his ruby Jaguar XK-E, which had his initials stenciled on the driver's side door in one-inch-high Gothic letters, a tiny gold period after each one. A.P.—Alex Pettibone. Alex refused to take Ray's surname, Mitchell. He visited Veronica in the afternoon so he wouldn't have to see Ray. His sole competition was the ghost of his own father, the handsome model, whose presence was always felt. Alex looked so much like his philandering father that he might as well throw himself against that breastplate and shoulder its burden.

Yet Alex had never even met his own father, who had left Veronica before he was born. Veronica had returned to her parents' house with her first baby when the model came back to "borrow" cash. During this impromptu visit, Curtis Pettibone made love to Veronica one last time. While still in her arms, he reached over to her bureau and took her change purse. He started counting out the tens and singles. He picked up a pen to write an IOU. He was writing! Then he stole her sterling hand mirror and matching silver hairbrush to unload them at a pawnshop. After that last session in bed, Veronica was pregnant with Alex.

Alex was attached to *me*. He often brought me trinkets, and when he was on tour in Korea after the war, he sent me peculiar packages from overseas. A glossy jewelry box with a row of Chinese ponies galloping over the landscape of black enamel, their nostrils flared open like pink lotus petals. I don't remember him shipping things to Karen.

I watched my stepbrother shift in his chair as Veronica unwrapped the surprise he had brought her. "How nice," she said. "It's different." She balled the paper in her fist, admired the gleaming china bowl and placed it on the mantel beside other recent offerings. I could tell she didn't really like it. She usually said a gift was "different" or "interesting" when it flopped. The exchange was quite tight-lipped, perhaps because I was present. Alex lit Veronica's Kent cigarette. Then he drove off to his building site to supervise a delivery of ReadyMix cement.

Following Alex's example, I showered Veronica with gifts. Blue jay feathers, a swallowtail chrysalis with its golden spots and a Vargas pinup I had ripped out of a men's magazine that had been left out on a neighbor's porch glider. The cool, creamy skin of the reclining coed, her buttocks clearly outlined in a pair of gauzy culottes, surprisingly evoked Veronica. The similarity planted in me a seed of chaos and confusion, and I wanted to know what Veronica would think of her twin. I left the pinup on the kitchen table. My punishment for tearing a page from a men's magazine:

No riding lessons for two weeks.

No contact with horses.

No horse flesh, no leather *fix*.

I writhed on the floor before my mother, braiding my arms in a beggar's contortion, an anguished prayer made authentic by a colossal boots and saddle jones no one could quibble with. Veronica didn't budge. She looked down at my twisted shape on the Persian carpet, a long runner with peculiar geometric symbols and "cartouche."

"Get up off the *prayer rug*," she said. I just assumed that the rug was named for my begging sessions, those times when I was down on my hands and knees. Years later, I learned that "prayer rug" was the correct term for the antique carpet. Its name had nothing to do with me. Had Veronica seen the oddball irony and allowed it to escalate between us?

OUR BEAUTIFUL MOTHER was the mysterious kernel, the blister, the contagion seed in our family's doomed whole. It extends to each of us, it feeds us, and in turn we nourish and invigorate its taproot.

Being youngest, I have often posed questions to my older siblings, each at their different levels and stations of estrangement: "Was Veronica always this removed? Had she once been sweet and loving? What made her drift away?"

When electricity is interrupted, a lineman can follow the cables to the source of trouble, finding the exploded transformer or the severed wires. Children often imagine that they are to blame when a family breaks up. Of course, it couldn't have been us, in our diminutive ranks. In our innocence. Yet, tiny wrens or swallows, little puffballs that weigh next to nothing, when perched en masse can rupture support rigging and black out an isolated grid of electrical service.

PARIS

In the summer of 1964, Ray took Veronica, Karen and me to Europe for an extended business trip. At the end of August, we were scheduled to take the boat train from Paris to the transatlantic port at Le Havre. We might have returned to the states on TWA, but Ray had purchased a luxury Citroën for Veronica's birthday and we had to bring it back on the SS *France*. An automobile could not be shipped to the states on the ocean liner unless accompanied by valid ticket holders.

During those weeks in Europe, a novel silence overtook my sister. For weeks, she was typically mute, riding beside me in the back seat of the Citroën, staring out the window at the sweeping fields of lavender in the south of France and averting her eyes from pedestrians as Ray idled the car at crosswalks in Paris. Her new blankness seemed expert and engineered. She no longer suffered her condition, she *employed* it. She no longer accepted the chocolate wafers from which I had licked off all the frosting, nor the pretzels, the denuded knots, after I had licked off the salt. These snacking rituals between us had ended with her adolescence. Our bedtime routines playing Old Maid and War or sharing our comics had come to an end. Karen's tolerance and deference to me had been stripped off with a torch. In its place, a new connection had formed between us. I was no less important to my sister, but *she* took the reins. She instructed me, bossed me. She explained briskly what role I was to play. Karen was on the brink of womanhood with all its trompe l'oeil, false doors and dangers; I was one step behind her and for the time being acted as her valet or assistant. She told me when to polish her shoes with Ray's kit. She instructed me to arrange her hairpins on a dish while she rolled and set her hair. She gave me her drip-dry shifts and sweaters to wash in the hotel sink, but she washed her panties herself with the bathroom door locked.

Veronica didn't care to show us ruins or paintings. We were pulled along to get what we could from it while our father sold contracts for industrial supplies. My favorite pastime that summer was swiping my mother's unfiltered Gitanes and smoking them in the bathrooms of the small hotels we stayed in. Mornings, I went into my parents' bedroom to dunk my brioche in their pot of coffee. Ray was in the *salle de bain* shaving. I saw another empty Maalox bottle in the trash basket when I looted the carton of cigarettes. My father's stomach condition wasn't getting any better, but Veronica played it down. She said that everyone has a "physical weakness." I wondered what my physical weakness might be. Veronica said, "Girls have bladder 'complaints.'" This was news to me. I had never heard the term 'complaints' for physical aches and pains, and I pictured an internal organ on stilt legs, a cartoon bladder making acid remarks and grumpy asides, bitching and moaning.

As Veronica sat on the edge of her bed to paint her toenails, I sunk the pack of cigarettes in the waistband of my underpants. I watched my mother's back, her small waist and the flare of her hips highlighted by her worn satin peignoir robe. Just as Karen had learned from her, Veronica started her day with some sort of cosmetic ritual. I always dressed hurriedly and went to play on the old-fashioned cage elevator—reaching through the accordion gate to finger the thick green lubrication on the cable. I smeared the grease from my fingers on the inside hem of my shorts.

Seeing my mother performing her morning toilette always unnerved me. Her sexuality was brimming, no dressing gown or bathrobe could disguise it. She had often embarrassed me when she strolled into Silverside Elementary School to deliver my raincoat or my forgotten homework. Veronica would arrive dressed in Capri pants or pastel stretch tights that highlighted her smooth hips, the flex of her calves, and worst of all, the distinct little hill of her pubis. Other "home room mothers" were plump, wore floral shirtwaist dresses and carried cookie sheets of marshmallow krispies. Veronica caused a ripple in the teachers' lounge each time she poked her head in to ask questions or to find the poor soul assigned to teach me. No one could ignore the tenacious clicking sound of her cleated ballet flats when she came into the school to retrieve me for a dentist appointment or for whatever reason she had to enter my world of broken pencils and composition-book dishevelments. She found me at my desk erasing multiplication errors until my math test was wrinkled and blank. I left the ravaged paper on the desk and followed Veronica outside the building. I'd rather get a tooth drilled than stay in school.

Veronica's eyes are true glass-green, with a band of smoky topaz around the pupils. In his early courtship, Ray invented a nickname to tame his immediate lust and he tagged Veronica for her most ethereal feature: "Green Eyes." But when she peered at me or Karen point-blank, it was a chilly scrutiny and her eyes turned cold green like a medicine bottle.

Somewhere in her French ancestry there was Basque influence, and her deep, black hair was rich and wavy. Despite her green eyes, with such dark hair she could never be Iseult or Rapunzel, but Veronica likes to tell the story about the time she was approached by two distinguished men on a city street in Chicago, in front of the huge glass doors of the Continental Illinois Bank. The men asked her if she would *sell* her hair, right there and then. Of course, these fellows were cons. One of the men removed a shears from his breast pocket while the other man opened a roomy muslin sack. They could have clipped her tresses and run off. With cropped hair, Veronica might have walked away from the icy rime and niveous zone of the beauty goddess. But Veronica refused to sell it. How could she? Her beauty was her primary, perhaps her sole, resource.

THE LAST WEEK IN PARIS, waiting to take the boat train, Karen left the hotel every night. She climbed out the third-floor window and went backward down the fire escape, which dropped her in full view of the front office. The evening manager chose to ignore her. Karen had met an Algerian boy, Imran Mamdouh, and they "dated" like this. She brought me along, perhaps fearing I might squawk if I stayed behind, but I think she wanted me there for company. She was embarking on the perilous activity of fighting off loneliness with lust. Whether she cleaved to my tomboy image or flaunted herself before it, I couldn't tell. I was her tolerant kin; she wanted my intact purity nearby as she endeavored otherwise. I waited on the sidewalk as she and the boy crumpled to their knees in an alley behind a pharmacy and he pumped her head above his crotch. Once, she lifted her face and I saw the glistening phallus, wet from Karen's saliva. I looked away and watched the traffic going by in the street. I practiced my inhalation technique with the remaining cigarettes in the pack. After the young man had finished, he led us in circles around the same block like a hot walker at a racetrack. Then, Imran stopped us in front of our hotel and my sister slipped back into her girlhood, as if the boy had snapped his fingers. She climbed the wrought-iron ladder into our hotel bedroom, pulling me up behind her. My sister brushed her teeth for longer than necessary. She told me she didn't want to use the bidet. It was a disgusting invention, why should she try it? After all, she was still a virgin.

I thought, how could she still be a virgin when she took his thing in her mouth? I was sure she was mistaken. "How can you suck it?" I said.

"Nothing to it," she said. She fanned herself with her hand mirror as she talked; its oval of light flickered across her face, across the ceiling.

I wanted to ask her, "What did it taste like?" Karen and I were always comparing brands of chewing gum according to how quickly the minty taste diminished. I had my doubts that I would ever submit myself to a one-on-one with a man or participate in such a peculiar oral exercise as that. I read in Dr. Spock that *babies* explore the world with their mouths. They suck rattles and plastic blocks, examining their physical environment. Was it the same in the theater of sex?

Karen and I played cards for an hour, then we turned out the light and discussed the girls we knew stateside, classmates at the junior high school, listing their weaknesses and then their endearing traits.

FOR THE LAST SEVERAL NIGHTS in Paris, I trailed behind the couple. I was impressed by my older sister—how had she attracted this stranger, handsome and lithe, with deep saffron-toned skin? He handed me cigarettes and occasionally would light them for me. I started to inhale without the immediate cough. I was learning the style of it, then the nicotine assumed its importance.

One morning in our hotel room, Karen was taking a bath in the giant porcelain tub, deep as a sea. She washed her hair and reclined beneath the surface to rinse out the suds. She held her breath and went under. Her wavy hair floated like golden kelp. When she surfaced for air, she was annoyed to find me watching her and she shooed me away.

When we were younger, Karen and I had often bathed together. I missed those days when I was small and Karen had assumed our mother's duties when our parents' routine cocktail hour dragged on too long and I was still dressed in my muddied breeches from my riding lesson. The ramshackle riding stable was often cited by the Board of Health for its abundance of rat pellets and dried rat urine. The pellets were swept up, but inspectors could view the rat urine with ultraviolet goggles.

My sister saw I needed to be washed, and without a cue from Veronica, Karen initiated the evening ritual. She ran the hot water and sifted the Calgon bubble bath under the churning faucet. She put my plastic bath cap on my head, adjusting it correctly at my hairline, tucking the elastic behind my ears so I was sure to wash them. Karen undressed and we sat in the bath, facing one another. I cupped bubbles in the palm of my hand, watching shiny windows slide across them. I looked up and saw that Karen wasn't busy washing. She was watching me.

"What?" I said.

"Nothing," she told me.

I instinctively turned around to look at the ceramic tile behind me, expecting to find a silverfish or a centipede zooming at a diagonal. There wasn't anything.

I turned back to look at Karen, who was still eyeing me. "It's in your plastic cap," she said. "It's big."

She couldn't stand it anymore and Karen pulled her own cap off and tossed her hair. I reached up for mine, but she grabbed my wrist. She said, "Wait, let me think."

The spider was trapped inside the elastic hem; I felt it tickle my temple, thumping against the thin polyethylene.

I felt my eyelids flutter in a peculiar silent spasm. Karen pinched the shower cap between her thumb and forefinger, but the spider wriggled through the crown of my hair trying to escape. Again, she pinched it. We heard its carcass snap. She smeared it between her fingertips to finish it off. She carefully removed the shower cap from my head. I studied its dismembered legs, black as boar bristles from a hairbrush. By now the water was lukewarm and she ran more hot. She wet my head with a plastic drinking glass and lathered my hair with Prell.

I STOOD FULLY CLOTHED in the big, high-windowed Parisian bathroom while my sister still bathed. "Do you mind?" Karen said as she poured Breck's pearl-pink creme rinse directly on her hair and massaged it in. Her nudity was a compelling vision each time I intruded upon it. She seemed years ahead of me. When I wouldn't leave, she said more forcefully, "Get out of here, Stick!"

I had already had my bath, at which time I unlooped the silver shower hose, aiming its pulsing ivory spout between my legs until the tight spray triggered the sensation that still surprised me each time it happened. Finally, I left Karen in the bath and walked into the other room. That morning, I smoked a half pack of Gitanes, lighting a new one each time the cigarette was only halfway consumed. I threw the lighted butts out the balcony window. I soon learned that the hotel's doorman, really not much older than a boy, was standing on the sidewalk right below our room. My cigarettes fell onto his hair and shoulders, bounced to the pavement, and rolled off the curb. He picked up the smoldering butts and looked up at our window. I had ducked inside to light up another and had no idea I was showering sparks upon the epaulets of the uniformed victim. His supervisor saw him holding cigarettes in his hand and came outside to scold him. He was not permitted to smoke on the job. The boy explained what had happened, but his boss didn't believe him.

The young doorman and the concierge appeared at our room. Karen was wrapped in a bath sheet, tucking her hair around giant foam rollers. Ray said that the French had shown unusual sympathy toward Americans that summer, only months after our president had been shot. The hotel office might have attributed Karen's erratic behavior to that and looked the other way when she climbed out the window at night, but the barrage of burning cigarettes was a different matter. They stared at my sister; the moist sheet loosened around her curves as she lifted her arms to insert a bobby pin across the pink foam rubber. In pantomime, the boy explained to his employer how the cigarettes originated from our balcony, in an endless strafing, he was sure of it. He pretended to smoke an invisible cigarette, then he walked to the window and tossed it off. He struck an imaginary match, inhaled again. His performance was comical, and since I had consumed the last real cigarette and had discarded the cellophane packet, it seemed ridiculous. There wasn't a dirtied ashtray to confirm the doorman's accusation.

The manager left us, called to the telephone, but the boy remained. He was looking at my sister. She was smiling at his foolishness.

She stood up and walked across the room, her hips pulled left and right just a little, enough to suggest that she had the floor if she wanted it. She told him, "I don't smoke. It was *her*." She pointed to me and smiled the way a dog lover smiles at a puppy who has chewed a slipper. "It's on her breath. Go see. She shouldn't be smoking those things, should she?"

The doorman didn't bother to come over to me and investigate my smoky tonsils. He had approached Karen and was already moving just the heels of his hands over her breasts, keeping his fingertips carefully lifted off her flesh, as if to touch her with his actual fingertips would be more excitement than he could possibly bear. Her breasts were released from their dewey sarong and the sheet fell to the carpet. He spoke in French, some words I thought I understood only from their heat. I went out to the balcony and looked at the foreign cars going past. I searched for American models and saw a Ford Fairlane parked below the hotel, its tires rolled onto the sidewalk to afford room to the narrow street.

After a few moments, Karen pushed the doorman away and he went out of the room, his face still flushed with his greed. Karen said, "Mare, try not to get us in another jam like that." I promised my sister I would flush my butts. Once, when our mother came in unexpectedly, I crammed the lighted stub in the toe of my shoe and later suffered for it. The tips of my toes were mildly seared; two pale blisters swelled until they burst, revealing the raw tips underneath.

ALL THAT SUMMER, I was witness to my sister's carnal exchanges with members of the service industries in Italy and France. Busboys, cabdrivers, vending machine operators. She pulled me along on bizarre hikes into stockrooms and kitchens, or out to the streets and into the Métro. Once, a man drove us in his Renault to the Bois de Vincennes, where he made me wait on a bench stained with bird milk while he took Karen into the dark arbor for an hour.

"What happened?" I asked her.

"He couldn't."

"Couldn't what?"

She looked at me. She was gauging her responsibility. What should or shouldn't she explain to me? "What have you had to eat?" she asked me. She always tried to consider whether my stomach was empty or not. Would I gag at what she might tell me? Other nights we walked or took the train and prowled after hours in the formal gardens of the Tuileries and the Champ de Mars. Karen scolded me for having such dirty hair. "I'm ashamed to be seen with you! How can you go around like that, you oil rag!"

Despite her criticism, I continued to practice hygiene habits unacceptable to my sister. She tried to teach me the White Rain doctrine, "wash, rinse, repeat," but I wanted my hair dirty. I was twelve and already I was finding rosy stains on the crotch of my panties. I was worried that menstruation would change everything. I might lose my hard, angular figure. I would lose my swiftness, my agility when I walked a post and rail fence like a balance beam. I started hunching my shoulders a little to hide my own bustline, which manifested in two ridiculous conical lumps. Karen's breasts were full and heavy. I refused to plunge into the transformation and I rejected feminine ritual. My hair was greasy and hung in several limp hunks. I grew up on the TV shows Have Gun Will Travel, and Rawhide, identifying with the gunslingers and cowhands and not the prairie maidens. I was "horse crazy," Ray said. I thought that fathers called it "horse crazy" out of jealousy. My relationships with horses were entirely sane. Horses are just huge, dumb animals with acute muscle definition; men deride them because they must see in horses something of themselves—a physical nature that calls for the same pampering.

I spent hours mucking stalls, grooming ponies and oiling saddles at Highland Stables to earn my riding privileges. It was my home away from home, and my obsession was not deterred by a huge sign across the barn roof that said RIDE AT YOUR OWN RISK.

From western heroes, I graduated to secret agents—James Bond and Napoleon Solo. I was not "in love" with Bond; I wanted to *be* Bond. The summer of '64 was my last stand. And yet, I couldn't deny my fascination for what was happening to my sister. I listened to the cooing notes coming from the Algerian boy, his breathing brisk and humid, startled at his release. I was excited by the structure of his authority with Karen until that one wild, uncontrolled moment when it shifted to her, and she was superior to him.

Back in our hotel room, we traded French edition *Archie*s until we turned out the light. If I had trouble falling asleep, Karen told me, "Think of a field of daisies. Think of a field of daisies and count each one."

Think of a field of daisies. I wondered if that's what Karen saw when she shut her eyes. If it wasn't what Karen was seeing, wasn't it generous of her to think it up just for me?

Even if she counted daisies at night, during the day Karen was moody and sad-eyed, and I couldn't cheer her. On a car trip to Lyon, she sat in the back seat and fingered the velveteen hand rest or plucked the lid of the ashtray open and shut. She was "depressed."

Veronica asked her, "What have you got to be depressed about? What in the world ever happened to you?"

I was easily bribed by ice cream and laughed readily, enough to amuse my parents and make them think I was happy. I wasn't really certain I wasn't happy, although I was beginning to see the outlines of a personal despair I had yet to greet head-on. Ray and Veronica understood Karen's silence as a surly disregard for the privileges they showered upon her. Nothing, of course, but her room and meals were paid for, a few little trinkets here and there, but Veronica announced she could no longer buffer Karen from her emerging "destiny." Veronica often referred to the biblical image of the "the right path," and "the wrong path." Karen and I were free to choose for ourselves, yet Veronica assumed we would err.

ONE NIGHT IN ITALY, when Ray's old friend and translator from Fiat met us for dinner, Ray started reminiscing about the steel industry. Ray still missed that line of work, and his step-by-step narrations of open-hearth melting practices sometimes overtook the table talk.

Throughout our childhood, Karen and I had learned the matter-of-fact and the Gothic thrill of metallurgy. We knew about semikilled steel and dead-killed steel, slag viscosities and how to condition an ingot mold with an aluminum wash, in a tar tank or with graphite. I was the only kid at the grade school who understood that steel wasn't mined. It was man-made.

"It's dangerous work," Ray said. "I might not be here today—"

Veronica groaned. "Oh, please, don't start. Not the old one about rescuing Mr. Trojanowski."

"I like that story," Karen said, pouring some salt on.

"Trojanowski was injured, caught on a scaffold just as a ladle was ready to pour," Ray said. "I have to figure I can get to him by going up to the second tier and coming down the other side, but the shortest route to get to Trojanowski is to run beneath the ladle. I can run right over there, see, but the nozzle is ready to tip. It's twenty feet as the crow flies. What am I deciding? In a second, it's going to tip." Ray was grinning at the translator and looking back and forth at his two girls.

Veronica said, "It's stupid to run beneath molten steel."

"Trojanowski was in trouble. I was the supervisor."

"So, you saved one Polish guy. There's always someone next in line. Tell everyone how that fellow ended up."

"Yes, Trojanowski had another accident the same year."

"All for naught," Veronica said, as if she was summing up his whole career.

Ray was already irritated and then he saw Karen's silent smirk. He hit her. I saw he was going to strike her when his face turned garnet and his fork quivered as if all his self-control were balanced on its tines. Yet, it was Veronica who had incited his outburst. She had glared at Ray as he told his story, shifting her posture, adjusting her weight imperceptibly upon her seat bones. His anger wasn't even caused by Karen, it was a combination of Veronica's dismissal of his passion and Karen's remote unhappiness. He couldn't find middle ground and finally he turned against Karen. He lost control abruptly, like when a teeter-totter loses its counterweight and crashes. He smacked her.

That wasn't the only time. Earlier that summer, in Venice, Ray knocked Karen off a canvas director's chair in the Piazza San Marco.

The fragile chair collapsed around Karen like wild, spindly stork legs. It happened after a grueling day. We had spent a long, blistering afternoon at Lido Beach during which Karen had run off with a man, riding away on the back of his motor scooter while my mother and I sunbathed. Karen just disappeared off the crowded beach. Perhaps she had drowned. Our mother said, "I bet she's out there with all those cabin cruisers. She swam over there for a party—" We scanned the anchored pleasure boats, searching the gaudy clusters of swimmers and tourists but couldn't find Karen anywhere.

At dusk, the beach was closed and we waited at the Lido police office as Ray filled out forms and gave my sister's description. "Missing Persons" was not the forte of this particular police barracks. The uniformed officers shrugged and opened their hands, gesturing their empty palms in a familiar Italian caricature.

I went outside and bounced pebbles on the slate sidewalk. I wondered if my sister had really drowned in the sea, but I was certain she had not.

After several hours, word came that an American girl had been stopped for riding a motorcycle wearing only a two-piece bathing outfit. Riding mopeds dressed in indecent attire was an offense that carried a stiff fine. Karen had a serious pipe burn on her inner ankle where she had touched the exhaust. The next day, we were both grounded in our hotel room four floors above the dirty canal. There was a nest of ants in the window box and I passed the time plucking them off the geranium leaves and throwing the tiny victims into the water. Karen was in pain from the pipe burn and she whimpered now and then from the dark interior of our bedroom. She wasn't complaining. She seemed to expect these war wounds. She expected to suffer more injuries until either she or her field of enemies surrendered.

TWO DAYS BEFORE we were scheduled to take the boat train, Ray discovered our nightly sojourns with Imran. When we came back to the fire escape and looked up, our windows were blazing and molten voices showered down on us. I heard Veronica's livid accusations and Ray's lowered voice as he made steady reprisals against himself. Karen looked into my eyes. "Shit. He's taking the blame," she said. "He's making it worse for me." Karen decided to use the lift like a civilized person and face the music head-on.

Veronica said Karen was "uncontrollable" and needed a psychiatric evaluation. Ray decided to take her home to Philadelphia where a medical sleuth could figure out what was causing her to act this way.

Of course, there was the matter of the Citroën.

My mother and I would have to cross on the SS *France* in order to ship the car home. My parents wouldn't have their second honeymoon onboard the luxury liner, all because of Karen. I went with Ray to get the car ready for the boat train. To my surprise, body-shop mechanics removed its glossy fenders and placed them inside the car on the velveteen passenger seats. The dismembered car with its exposed wheel wells added to my general feeling of insecurity.

Ray made several transatlantic telephone calls to the Cheltenham Institute in Philadelphia, arranging for my sister to be seen.

The next day, Karen left with Ray.

I watched the two of them get into a taxi, Ray in his familiar striped suit, my sister in her rayon travel dress, a drip-dry shift that came in its own plastic envelope. When Ray kissed me, I could taste the chalky residue of his antacid on his lips; it left a minty dust at the corners of his mouth. His stomach trouble had worsened all summer. He often tapped his fist against his diaphragm as if his inflamed ulcer was a trapped bird fluttering behind his rib cage and he wished to free it. I started to see how his stomach trouble probably wasn't caused by too much wine or too much pepper but by a flock of anxieties.

When the cab took them off to Orly Airport, both Karen and Ray looked relieved to be rid of us. Even at twelve, I understood that my father deserved a little respite from his wife's scrutiny. He might take a high road with Karen, if left to himself.

Karen had been monosyllabic all summer, but I had depended on her company. I felt lost without her. Those nights together, I fell asleep listening to the hollow rustle of her hairbrush as she pulled it through her tamed hair one hundred times. I grew accustomed to the smell of her acne lotion, a vinegar odor that remained all day on the rolled pillows. When Karen was gone, I was left by myself at the hotel for a whole day while my mother went alone to visit her cousins on the

Right Bank. I prowled the hotel gardens by myself. I certainly wasn't going to solicit men's attentions like Karen had done. I went into the park, wandering in and out of the prams and bicycles. I tried to buy an ice-cream cone, but I had only the old currency, which wasn't enough. France had just changed the franc, and the large piece I held in my palm was defunct. Karen knew the currency and would have avoided these embarrassments with vendors. When I returned to the hotel, I called room service and ordered three deep ramekins of crème caramel and ate each one. The first dish was for me. The second for Karen. In honor of Imran, I dipped my glazed spoon into the last custard on the tray.

THE MORNING BEFORE we were to take the boat train, my mother made an appointment at Galeries Lafayette to buy a few high-fashion cocktail dresses. We arrived at the store at nine o'clock. A manager told us where to report for Veronica's private showing and fittings. The lavish, sequestered salon was upstairs. Veronica started up the escalator and suddenly turned around. She pushed me off the escalator and jumped down after me. Her face was white as a sheet and her eyes looked swimmy.

She couldn't bring herself to ride the flowing stairway.

"What's the matter?" I said, but I knew she was frightened. This had happened before at department stores in the States. At Lord & Taylor, where the mechanical stairs had white tread that looked remarkably like giant teeth in an opened jaw, Veronica wouldn't step on. Veronica could ride the DOWN escalator, but she refused to ascend on the motorized runway. She was disturbed when the stairway crested and the silver risers disappeared under the floor again. Veronica feared its "forward propulsion." She was even frightened to drive her car onto access ramps and to merge with the expressway traffic. "Retreat" didn't seem to disturb her, it was always "getting to" somewhere that panicked her. An escalator makes its slow and eerie ascension and delivers its passengers at the threshold of the unknown, the blank plateau.

A clerk showed us to a stairwell, and we hiked up the marble landings until we reached the third floor, where we were greeted by two gorgeous saleswomen, like Chanel models. Veronica was perspiring, and she dabbed at her face with one of my father's handkerchiefs. She passed the crumpled linen beneath her nose once and again, as if she wanted the smell of him; his smell would snap her out of it.

In the fancy salon, I sat on a plush chair and watched the two women dress my mother in a fiery lamé jersey gown, then in a gauzy dress of metallic net. Veronica was looking only at gold dresses. I watched the saleswomen dressing and undressing my mother in these provocative golden frocks, tucking waistbands, fastening the tiny hook-and-eye closures, peeling necklines away from her shoulders. Again, I understood that *sex is a highway*; it was its own destination. God forbid there should ever be an UP escalator along the way.

Veronica revolved before a three-paneled mirror as if standing before identical sisters. But she had been an only child and I knew few details of her youth.

Her father died before I was born. My French grandmother lived in Chicago but rarely visited Wilmington. I knew my grandmother only from the boxes of *Domino* sugar cubes she sent in the mail, whole cartons of sugar dots which I fed to the horses at Highland Stables. When my grandmother sent pounds and pounds of cubed sugar to our household did she think it would compensate for Veronica's acridity? I filled the sugar bowls on the silver tea service and hoarded the remaining boxes for the next time I went to the stables.

When I was nine years old, Veronica took Karen and me to Chicago. Her mother was dying and Veronica pushed me into the sickroom and left me standing at the old woman's footboard. Veronica and Karen watched from the doorway when my grandmother asked me to sing the whimsical French love song "Dites-moi Pourquoi"—"Tell Me Why."

> Dites-moi pourquoi
> La vie est belle,
> Dites-moi pourquoi
> La vie est gaie,
> Dites-moi pourquoi,
> Chère mademoiselle?
> Est-ce que, parce-que
> Vous m'aimez?

I sang it without a glitch. My singing French was perfect. The old woman, skinny and weak from heart disease and diabetes, peered at me, her quilt up to her chin. She appeared so sweet and contrite, how could my mother hate her?

Hate her own mother?

I looked at my grandmother, who looked at my mother, who looked at my sister Karen. I did not yet recognize my station on that shriveling vine. The fruit of that vine was indeed as fragile and easily blemished as squash blossoms that emerge and wither in a period of hours.

I asked my grandmother, "When will you be in heaven?"

"I'll send you a sign."

"What will it be?"

"A white pigeon will fly down and peck your head," my grandmother said in dead seriousness. I believed she was telling me the truth. When a white pigeon lands on my head, I'll know that God is real. It didn't seem impossible as my grandmother described it.

Hearing her mother's crazy half-English, Veronica grabbed the hem of my skirt and pulled me out of the room. "Don't believe her. A bird won't land on your head," she warned me.

After her mother's death, Veronica told me stories about her unhappy childhood. Her parents had been industrious French immigrants and had worked long hours at their restaurant, preparing continental cuisine for business clients who had tired of the bland Irish and Polish entrees routinely offered on local Chicago menus. Afternoons, Veronica did her homework at the restaurant, her books spread across one of the empty tables. She was given her dinner there and at 7 P.M. she was sent home.

After she had had her bath, her parents had routinely locked her up in their Chicago apartment with a padlock. Each night Veronica was shut away alone while her parents returned to their busy restaurant until late in the evening. She heard the hasp secured and the lock clicked shut, and she ran to the window to watch her parents walk down the sidewalk, arm in arm, cross the street and turn the corner. Then she banged the wall to rouse the neighbor who tried to soothe her through the door although he didn't have a key to free her. Her parents owned the building and none of the tenants spoke up in her behalf. Her parents believed she was safe; what could happen to her in her own home? Veronica told me that being locked inside those small, familiar rooms in a monotony of domestic landmarks was more tortuous than being left abandoned on an open plain.

Summers, her parents sent Veronica away on the overnight train from Chicago to Massachusetts, a piece of paper with an uncle's name and address pinned to her collar. Male passengers tried to fondle her and she called for the conductor, but it was usually too late. Veronica expected to see my alarmed reaction each time she told me these stories. She seemed to be saying, "You think *you* kids have it bad, well, when I was a child—"

Once, she went to a desk drawer and searched for a tiny antique lock similar to the one her father had used to jail her. She held it in the palm of her hand for my inspection. It was a common heart-shaped padlock with a crooked slit where the key must be inserted and yanked to release the hook. I was uncomfortable looking at the unhappy heirloom. It had an uncanny likeness to a tiny iron vulva. Did my mother see its sexual suggestion? Was it just my imagination?

More than once she told me about her father's fit of violent anger when he heaved her bicycle down the basement stairwell. The bicycle was destroyed; its frame was hideously bent, its wheels skewed.

Then he forced her to ride it.

If she ever complained or caused trouble, he took out the misshapen bicycle and insisted that she try to balance it.

Each night, her parents locked the apartment door and she was trapped inside. Perhaps this was the seed of Veronica's strange habit of always checking the doors of our ranch house. Routinely, after Ray locked up at night, Veronica followed behind him to twist the dead bolt open again to make sure it wasn't stuck. In a moment of panic, she tugged the door ajar to make sure she wasn't locked *in*. This obsessive-compulsive tic must have been triggered in her childhood when she was imprisoned.

At eighteen, Veronica was a popular coed at DePaul, and she was often the subject of romantic sonnets and villanelles written by handsome English majors. She kept some of these faded pages in her desk drawer in the house in Wilmington. The fountain-pen ink had bleached away, leaving pale violet couplets impossible to decode. Veronica had dropped out of college after her first year. Events turned when she met the Arrow Collar model.

One night, in the dead of winter, he walked into her parents' restaurant.

THE TRAIN TO LE HAVRE was crowded, but somber. The wheels rolled over the track in a remote, clattering dirge. I imagined five days at sea with my mother. Veronica announced that there were two swimming pools on board, one fresh water, one seawater. How could she think I would have fun in the pool without Karen, who always spread her legs apart so I could swim through the underwater bridge?

Onboard the SS *France*, we followed a steward to our cabin but found it already occupied by newlyweds. The young wife opened the door in her slip, cupping a flute of champagne in her tiny, upturned hand. "But we're already unpacked!" she shrieked.

Veronica told the steward that, of course, the couple should stay in the room. Veronica was showing her business savvy; she understood that the ship was completely booked except for its larger staterooms.

"This will do just fine," she said, when the steward showed us to the Sun Deck, the ship's topmost tier of accommodations. According to the tradition of the "Compagnie Transatlantique" each luxury suite bears the name of a French province, and its armorial shield was displayed at the entrance. An original painting, inset in the decoration, conjured up the landscape typical of each region. The steward told us that international statesmen and movie stars, perhaps even Yves Montand himself, had booked the exact room. I imagined Yves Montand sitting on the bidet and, of course, the toilet.

"Look at these windows," Veronica said. But I didn't like seeing the breadth of the ocean without Karen. I watched the receding shoreline, an evaporating green line. If I should fret about sinking, Karen would have said, "Think of a field of daisies." Veronica pointed out the glistening lifeboats that were just outside the window, almost within our reach.

I pictured Karen at the psychiatrist. How was she surviving her interrogation? I heard Ray mention an inkblot test my sister might be asked to complete during her doctor's examination. I didn't know exactly what kind of procedure it was and confused it with "Chinese water torture," which was described in an Ian Fleming paperback. I pictured my sister strapped to a bed and balls of indelible ink dripping onto her forehead until her golden hair was saturated, her oat-straw eyebrows permanently stained.

That night, in the First Class card room, a man in a silk evening jacket pestered Veronica, trying to win her attention. He claimed to be an expert on the *Titanic* disaster and other shipping mishaps. He explained to us how all radio messages from the *Titanic* were ignored until it was too late.

The playboy went on to describe what had happened aboard the *Lusitania*. He stared at me hotly as he explained to Veronica that when the *Lusitania* was sinking, her captain thought it most humane to put the babies and children in the first two lifeboats. The crew placed the tiny infants right in the arms of the children and the boats were quickly lowered into the rough surf with their thoughtfully assembled innocents. But in their panic, the crew released the winches too abruptly. Both lifeboats of tots flipped over, spilling infants and children into the sea, long ahead of their rightful parents.

The man finished his story and smiled furiously at me. He hoped I'd run off and leave Veronica by his side. That night I dreamed I stood on deck beside another girl, but it wasn't my sister Karen. It was the Miracle Girl, Linda Morgan, from stateroom 52, wearing her adhesive strip with the abbreviation for one dose of morphine sulfate.

The stern was bucking; everything on deck was sliding—lounge chairs, pedestal ice buckets still chilling their green wine bottles, fringed carpets curled over like mock waves, flower urns toppled—that's when I saw her. Veronica was far out in the water, already disembarked in a lifeboat. Veronica had gone off without me. I was slipping into the salty vortex as the liner stirred in a slow circle like a soup ladle.

And beside me was the familiar girl—my peer, my equal.

SHARING THE OPULENT CABIN with Veronica was the first time I had ever slept in the same room with my mother. From my bed, I could

hear the huge ocean liner's engines, a steady thrumming from somewhere belowdecks. It was a soothing, reliable rumble, not loud enough
on the topmost deck to be disturbing, but it was there if I listened for
it. I associated its warm chugging drone with my mother's presence. I
adopted the idea that it was our *connection*, our kinship underscored
by the peril of an ocean crossing, that engendered its steady tonal resonance. Why not attribute the machine-made lullaby to my nearby maternal source.

I was forever trying to reinvent new routes and manifestations of
true mothering that Veronica might assume to meet me halfway.

On our third day in open water, Veronica suffered a severe attack of
"gout." The ship's physician came to our suite at midnight. Veronica
asked the doctor to knead her thigh, which she claimed was knotted in
spasm, but it looked smooth as silk. She suffered from night sweats
and palpitations. Her pulse was racing. The doctor listened to her heart
and gave Veronica three little pills of nitroglycerin. He told her, "If you
have discomfort, dissolve one of these pills under your tongue." He
told Veronica that her symptoms hinted at a dangerous predisposition
to a massive coronary. Veronica made light of it and asked him to mas-
sage the gout spasm in her leg.

The next night, she again called the ship's doctor to her bedside.

"And tonight, what are your symptoms?" he said in a slow exact
English.

"Oh, I don't know," she told him. "I just feel punk."

The doctor asked her, "Will your husband meet you in New York?"

"Yes. He's reserved a suite at the Hotel Volney. He's been shooting
a full page for Brooks Brothers—"

To my surprise Veronica told the doctor about the Arrow Collar
model; she didn't tell him about Ray. Veronica described her handsome
first husband as if she had seen him yesterday.

"I'm sure you've seen the Arrow Collar ads?"

"The man with the patch over his eye?" the doctor asked.

"No, no, that's the 'Hathaway Man,' a minor competitor," she told
him.

"You'll feel better when we arrive in port," the doctor told her. He
patted her knee and dropped his hand.

"Oh, sure, I'll be fine. My husband will drive us home in our new Citroën as soon as its fenders are welded back on."

I listened carefully, trying to keep my alarm off my face, but I kept shifting under the covers. Could she still be in love with the model? When Veronica saw I was awake, she began to speak French to the doctor, so I couldn't understand half of what she said.

I wondered if Veronica's physical complaints might have been invented just as she was fibbing to the doctor about which husband she would be meeting in New York. She was betraying Ray in her charades, in her compulsion to describe to the handsome doctor a different romance from her past. But even at the age of twelve, I understood that sometimes a lie, in itself, was telling the truth, the *real* truth.

GRIER SCHOOL

Veronica told Ray that she wanted expert documentation proving Karen's behavior was not in sync with other girls her age. If Karen's actions were gauged at the far end of the spectrum, it wasn't behavior Veronica would have to adjust to or absorb in her household the way other parents accepted their children's turbulent "teen years." Karen was interviewed by a fashionable psychiatrist who asked her to describe her nights in Paris with Imran. He decided that Karen might be better off in boarding school and told her, one-to-one, that he just might be delivering her from "the icy environment which nurtured her symptoms of promiscuity."

When Karen was enrolled in boarding school, Veronica seemed renewed by a peculiar domestic energy—the same "nesting reflex" some women feel prior to the *birth*, not the departure, of a child. She helped Karen collect her possessions and put what she didn't want into boxes for Goodwill. Nothing was left in Karen's bureau drawers. The morning Karen was to depart for Grier School, Veronica didn't wait to strip Karen's bed and fold the blankets. The blankets were stored on the top shelf in the closet, too close to the lightbulb. Within an hour the wool was scorched and emitted an acrid odor. Veronica discarded the charred covers. I was alarmed by a distinct perception—that due to a strange progression of events both Karen and even Karen's bedding were removed from the room where she had once slept.

"Boarding school is a privilege," Veronica told Karen. "It's a springboard."

I tried to imagine this "springboard," and all I could see was an empty swimming pool.

Karen had said, "Why can't I just go to the Friends School?" Karen and I had met girls who attended the Quaker academy. A collective aura of inner bliss radiated from their tier on the bleachers whenever they attended sporting events at the public school. One of these Quaker girls lived in our neighborhood. Every spring, her family cared for different orphaned lambs rescued from a relative's farm. We watched the lamb flick its long, unbobbed tail and romp across their two-acre suburban property, adding to the gentle mystique of that closed Quaker society. If they could adopt a lamb, why not Karen?

The Friends School was out of the question, Veronica said. She said that the point was to get Karen in a different "setting," some place far enough from home to spark a new academic commitment. Grier School was over a hundred miles away.

Karen received a mimeographed list from Grier School explaining what was acceptable prep school attire: "Six pairs kneesocks, forest green. Dickies acceptable. Forest-green or nut-brown."

"Nut-brown?" I asked Karen. "What's that?"

"Squirrel-shit color, I guess," Karen told me. Karen didn't necessarily want to stay at home any longer, but she didn't much like the idea of the school our parents had found for her, which emphasized "Equestrian Arts." Together, Karen and I had attended Boots and Saddles day camp, but Karen wasn't a good rider. Karen was a little hippy and didn't have the sexless flexibility of an athlete. But I had a good seat on a horse, and I won the cash pot every time I entered "Dollar Bareback" at the horse shows. Most of the money flutters to the turf. But I rode in only my swimsuit and used the horse's sweat to glue the dollar between its frothy hide and my white skin.

Once a du Pont funded the gymkhana and handed out *twenties* to the contestants. Each bill was brand new and repelled moisture, but I urged the money higher up my thigh until I was almost sitting on it and I won the whole kitty. The bareback competition hinted at sexual commerce and perhaps Karen recognized it years before I did.

I continued my lessons at the rat-infested riding academy, where I spent much of my time mucking out stalls. When the exterminators came every month, they let me look through their ultraviolet lenses, which illuminated rats' urine trails. I held the contraption in front of my eyes. The barn was crisscrossed with a thousand electric paths from the hay loft to every feed bin, along every rail and gate and across the very benches where we sat. Even the telephone receiver was scrawled with violet streaks of dried urine. I was curious about these invisible rat trails, and I imagined our "invisible" human thoughts, our deepest spiritual desires and worse, our unhappy prayers for the deaths of our enemies. Perhaps our secrets excreted unreadable stains, a magic waste on everything we touched.

THE NEW CITROËN was packed with my sister's possessions: six pairs of forest-green socks. New pajamas with a matching robe. Karen swore she would never wear these matching items at the same time. Grier School was located in the mountainous wasteland of western Pennsylvania. The campus buildings looked Gothic and cold. Although I teased my sister about her new surroundings, my heart was in my throat. How could we drive off and leave her there like that? Our parents went inside an office to sign forms and write further deposit checks for schoolbooks and gym clothes. Karen and I walked through the stables. A horse, with one blinded eye like a big smoky marble, nosed over its canvas stall guard and Karen stroked its muzzle, sorry for it.

"Well, this is good-bye," Karen said to me.

Did she mean, "This is good-bye *for now,*" or "good-bye *forever?*" I tested the finality in her voice and said, "You'll be back in a couple months. You could get yourself expelled."

Karen shrugged. "I don't really want to go home."

I tried not to feel stung.

She smiled at me. It was a strange, enlightened expression. She looked as if she had a baby aspirin dissolving on her tongue, its sweetness overpowered by the bitter ingredient. All of her childhood seemed condensed in this little pill. Soon it would be only a pink stain on the roof of her mouth.

KAREN'S MONTHS AT GRIER SCHOOL were not successful. She couldn't manage her classroom duties and wasn't adopted by any of the cliques of girls in the dormitory. She often had headaches and was sent to the infirmary, where she had to lie on a green leather couch with a cold pack on her forehead. If she lifted the ice off her brow to regulate its cold, the nurse scolded her and she had to replace the rubber bag although it made her headache worse.

One afternoon in late fall, Karen walked away from the Grier campus. She followed the gravel shoulder on the county road for three miles wearing her Weejun loafers, which chafed. Her heels had swollen red knots, and pink stripes crept up her achilles tendons. She got as far as a VFW lodge, a small cement-block structure, where she entered the kitchen door and told the woman who cooked that she'd like to find work. The cook took one look at her and knew Karen had come from the boarding school. But Karen looked serious about working; Karen's desperation gave her an older appearance, an earned maturity, as if she had suffered her share of hard breaks. The cook gave Karen a colander of potatoes to peel for the "Hunters' Banquet" scheduled for later that evening. The potatoes were to be added to the venison stew. The cook stepped back from a big tiled tabletop. Karen saw the deer meat already coarsely chopped. The meat looked strange, a deep purple heap of cubes with whorls of gristle. Karen knew she was going to be sick, and she stepped outside the kitchen door before she retched. Nothing came up. She went back into the VFW kitchen and started to scrape the potatoes.

By dusk, Karen had performed many tasks for the cook and started to understand that she had been manipulated by the older woman, who sat at the table reading magazines while Karen worked. She left the building, heading out the front door where men had already assembled for their party. She caused quite a ripple, and a man followed Karen outside. He put her in his car, a sedan with an altered cab, half car, half pickup, complete with a gun rack and coils of bungee cord to tie on slaughtered whitetail bucks.

"Where to?" he said.

"You tell me," she told him.

RAY RECEIVED A TELEPHONE CALL from the headmistress at Grier School. Karen was missing. A week later, Karen turned up at her dormitory, but she was sent to the hospital with "bladder spasms." Somehow, Karen's urinary meatus had been traumatized and she needed a catheter. Karen was discharged from the hospital and sent home.

When she returned to Wilmington, Veronica told her that on the very next business day Karen would have to go alone to the office at Mt. Pleasant and get reenrolled in the high school. "I'm not doing it for you. You had your opportunity at Grier," Veronica said. "Now you have to return to your homeroom and face the teacher." Veronica looked truly disturbed, as if she herself would be forced to stand at the front of the classroom and explain why Karen had been banished from prep school.

In our bedroom that night, Karen said, "I can't stand another day with Veronica."

"Can't you just ignore her," I said.

"How?"

"You could say, 'I'm rubber, you're glue. Whatever you say bounces off me and sticks to you.'"

Karen looked at me, again, as if I was a kitten fighting in a paper bag. "Do those rhymes work for you?"

I had never stopped to ask myself how I survived our mother's belittling remarks. I suppose I stayed outdoors and kept late hours at the riding stables, shoveling manure in exchange for time in the saddle.

KAREN GAVE ME three pairs of her forest-green kneesocks, but the elastic was stretched and they didn't stay up. Karen was a little heavier than me, and our figures were in sharp contrast. Veronica told Karen, "You know what I've been thinking? You might need some diet pills." The next Thursday, I went with Karen to the family doctor. I waited in the room outside where they had the big Norman Rockwell. When my sister came out, I could smell the syrups and alcohol from the open bottles the doctor kept on his desk. Karen was holding a prescription that had the words "Marbles, three times a day" scrolled across it. The doctor didn't prescribe diet pills after all. Veronica paid the doctor. He took a roll of bills out of his pocket, removed a rubber band, added Veronica's cash and again snapped the elastic around the scroll of money. He put it back in his pocket.

"You don't think a prescription could help?" Veronica asked Dr. Kerrigan.

"Help who?" he said.

Karen had been crying. I could see it right off because Karen had the kind of eyelashes that kept the tears in place long after there was any cause.

Driving home, we stopped at Hoy's Five & Ten, but Karen wouldn't get out of the car. I went in the store with Veronica because I liked the aisle with the white mice; the hairless babies suckling their mothers looked like rows of worn-down pink erasers. We came outside with a fifty-cent bag of marbles. In the car, I said, "Three times a day isn't too bad." I was just prying.

Veronica said, "If you have to know, your sister has flat feet. She has to pick up the marbles with her toes."

"Shit," Karen said.

I said, "I think it's good we bring it all out in the open."

"It's none of your business," Karen said.

We bickered until Veronica said, "Your father." She often said these words—*Your father*—when Karen and I argued. It meant that we should stop what we were doing and think of Ray. I pictured his big chair in the corner of the living room, a new recliner. With Veronica settled in his lap and his legs extended, I could never approach my father. This had me feeling sorry for myself and I forgot about Karen's condition.

KAREN PRACTICED WITH THE MARBLES in the privacy of our bedroom. She had a tin wastebasket, and as she picked up the marbles with her toes, she dropped them in the can. We could hear it throughout the house. We could hear it out on the sidewalk, a sad plink, plink, plink.

One day, Karen took an ink pad and she made some footprints on a paper bag. They were flat as ever. I couldn't keep out of it, and my own high arch left only a thin crescent on the paper. My slender footprint made me feel guilty, and I tried to remind Karen of my own imperfections.

I told her, "I was a preemie, remember? I spent weeks in an incubator. No one held me."

Nurses inserted their arms in huge rubber sleeves, like Playtex living gloves attached to the heated cubicle. "That must be why I'm skinny. I have to drink that fish oil to increase my appetite—it's awful stuff." But this was the wrong example to make because Karen, along with her flat feet, had a low center of gravity and it made her feel clumsy.

"Oh, never mind," she told me, and she crumpled our footprints and threw them in the waste can.

During those weeks after Karen came home, our domestic rituals became increasingly tense. Dinners, dishwashing, television. All our tasks were preceded by, endured and finalized by silences. Karen moved through the house like a ghost wearing a stranger's skirts and sweaters, a stranger's curves and flesh. Karen stopped playing the piano. After six years at the Wilmington Music School, she declined to return to her lessons on Thursday afternoons. She told Veronica that her music instructor had said something suggestive, but Veronica didn't go down to the music school to confront the maestro.

Karen never again sat down at the piano bench. Her silences permeated the house, room to room. In the dead plateau after dinner when Karen had usually practiced, I yanked open the desk drawers to look through family photograph albums. My obsession was to rearrange snapshots and put out-of-place items in a particular order to create a historical narrative of my own making. I had an allegiance to the facts coupled with the "gift of imagination."

"Imagination," that magical guesswork that sometimes reaches a feverish fugue state—is it a gift or is it a burden?

I sorted out photographs and arranged my face next to Karen's, but the snapshots were difficult to align without calling attention to our differences. Her mouth was flat, my smile too cherubic or conniving, and these cameos didn't jibe with one another.

I told stories and was a natural liar, a deadpan perjurer, a rubber-healed high jumper, but Karen's expertise was a practiced silence. So I tried to find a photo from our annual Cape Cod vacations, a sun-drenched fan of sea spray, or perhaps a Christmas goose on a platter, encircled by a wreath of golden roast potatoes—something that might spark a conversation. Instead, I discovered a childhood photograph of Veronica that had been lost beneath the pastel shelf paper in the bottom of a desk drawer.

In the picture, Veronica stands centered in a tier of classmates, a prize student, favored by all the nuns at the Sisters of Loretto Academy. Around her neck, Veronica wears an odd necklace—a new *pencil* dangles on a long piece of thread—a gift from the nuns. The dark thread is tied off until the pencil point skims just below her waist; its glisten-ing lead tip aims at the knob of her uterus, where I would grow.

KAREN BEGAN TO HOARD MONEY from Ray's desk. She gave cash away to win momentary friendships, just as she would soon square re-ceipts with a pimp. I stood beside her as she looted Ray's drawer and stuffed the bills in her pockets. Her allegiance to our family had been so severely thwarted, she didn't feel remorse for the pilfering she did. "Here, this is for you," she said, handing me two dollars. I followed her outside and saw her get into a car with someone. He was driving her to buy liquor and Karen wouldn't have a penny left. I watched her seek shelter in outsiders, punks in pegged jeans who hung around the Holi-day Lanes or an occasional older straggler who had long ago dropped out of high school. She had no vision of herself without a circle of cheap admirers. In our room at night, Karen stared at herself in the closet mirror. She stood stock-still for stretches of twenty minutes, studying her face, as if she waited for her image to evaporate like steam. She read to me from a book in which the experts agreed, in a unanimous statement: "There have been diverse eyewitness accounts of apparitions materialized in mirrors, but no one has ever successfully developed an actual snapshot of a ghost."

ONE DAY AFTER SCHOOL, Karen sat across from me at the kitchen table. She swirled a glass of Tab but didn't lift the cola to sip it.

She went away to change her clothes. She returned in ten minutes and told me, "I'm going to the corner, want anything? You want your Teaberry gum? Do you want a Hearn's cake?"

I said, "I don't have any money." Karen could have loaned me a dol-lar. She had started working a part-time job behind the soda counter at Holiday Lanes, but I didn't ask for charity. I might have pulled my jacket from its hook and trailed her, the same way I followed her and Imran those nights in Paris. But I didn't go with her. She didn't ask me. I watched her hand on the kitchen door, the way she pinched the knob and released it and pinched the knob again. Karen walked down the sidewalk. It was only three blocks to the Philadelphia Pike, where she waited on the corner of Silverside Road, in front of Ed Honey's Liquor Mart. Then, she sat down in a Glo-waxed Chrysler.

JUST AS WE RODE the boat train to Le Havre, again Veronica and I were thrown together. We sat facing front without talking. We watched television. The screen showed the chalk outline of a body. It was a detective series and it usually started out this way. Two months had passed with no word about my sister. I was still waiting for Karen to call me. I saw the chalk outline and told my mother, "Look, it's Karen." I was sometimes mean-spirited in my new adolescence, feeling jaded and wearied by it already. I didn't flinch when my mother stood up in a tide of anger, flicked the television off and turned to face me.

I went down the hall to the bedroom I had shared with my sister.

Karen's closet door won't latch and sweeps open. I see her dresses hanging on the closet pole. I borrow my sister's comb and brush, then return them in order to her dresser. I pick up her hand mirror. Karen walks ahead of me through these pages. She's holding a shoe box of scraps, notes with her half of the story. I am writing this down as it happens.

THE
PARIS THEATER

———

1965–67

VIRGINIA BEACH

(KAREN)

I COUNT NINE LIGHTED WINDOWS outside in Bailey's Trailer Village. People stay up pretty late. Each of these units seems to have its own clock. People work all hours, but you wouldn't know it from what they have to show for it. Every trailer looks junked. Cheap plywood skirts hide the hitch and undercarriage, but the plywood warps from the humidity or heaves with the frost. Roll-out canopies flap from metal poles. Scraps of linoleum and carpet remnants stretch out before each stoop. These runways are weighted down with bricks where the edges are curling up. There's one trailer in back with some pretty white lattice and a row of shrubs.

James Robinson says its stupid to put down roots in a trailer park.

These tin cans have all sorts of goings on—who can tell who's here and for how long? There's a row of mailboxes out on the road, most of them blank. One guy has put up signs around his trailer, burned with an electric tool: NEVER LET YOUR HITCH GET RUSTY, or IF THIS TRAILER'S ROCKIN', AIN'T NO USE KNOCKIN'. IF IT'S ROLLIN', KEEP STROLLIN'.

Today, I watched two men on a scaffold brushing fresh tar on our old friend Goldwater. They smoothed wet sheets across the senator's picture until they had a new Marlboro ad big as a sunset. Tonight the billboard is lit up. It's the same cowboy I've seen on signs at home in Wilmington.

Poor Goldwater—I guess it's all over for him.

The space heater is almost useless; the heat can't work its way to this end. It's a 1956 ten-wide Ventoura "Land Yacht." Its walls are thin and dented. Cold air sips through the rivet holes, like a colander. Each room opens up into the next down a narrow corridor, through three tiny archways. The walls and ceiling are smooth, lacquered birch veneer. It's like being inside a seashell.

The trailer is perfect for any couple, except Ruth Snow is still living here with James and me. Ruth owns the pink slip for the Ventoura, but she's letting James stay on a little while longer. She and James share the fold-out Castro and I get the window bunk in the "kids' room." Sometimes it's the other way around and I sleep with James in the Castro.

Ruth raised both her boys in this park, and the first thing Ruth said to me when I arrived was her *one rule* about living in a house trailer. The rule is this: "You don't take anything out unless you put something away."

She showed me around the kitchenette, the size of a closet. It has four hooks to hang cooking pots and utensils. She keeps one fry-pan on the stovetop and four saucepans on the hooks. If she takes one pan down, she replaces the one she isn't using back on an empty hook. No counter space. The drawers are jammed. She sewed magnets on her kitchen towels so they'll stick to the icebox. Library books have to go back on time whether she reads them or not. She can't keep more than a few books on that one shelf. I was surprised to see that familiar picture *Head of Christ* laminated to the refrigerator. James has a wallet-size *Head of Christ* that he's saved ever since he was in the service.

James tells me, "They used to hand out *Head of Christ* to everyone going over. This GI wallet-size *Head of Christ* is a collector's item. Today, recruits are leaving NoFuck for Nam without the blessing of the Lord. Not even a wallet-size blessing."

I still jump when James says "NoFuck."

"NoFuck, Virginia." Recruits learn to say "NoFuck" on their first Cinderella liberty when they have to be back on base by midnight without getting "any."

The room where I sleep is crowded floor-to-ceiling with sizable cardboard cartons. The boxes are stenciled with the words SPERRY & HUTCHINSON, INC. There's a pillar in here and at least a hundred more cartons of S&H Green Stamps outside in the Alum-a-room shack. James has even more cartons stacked beneath a plastic tarpaulin under the Expando awning. He acquired a half a truckload at a box trailer lockup. Thousands and thousands of Green Stamps worth less than a penny a piece, but glued into books they get him silver-plate items and small appliances. Ruth calls that Alum-a-room "Fort Knox." She likes to insult James, but he gives it right back. She tells me that when her kids were bad, James locked them in that Alum-a-room, so I better watch out. James expects me to glue all these stamps until they're finished. He says it will keep me busy.

He calls me a Minor in Need of Supervision. "Miss MINS," he says. That's what girls are called in those juvie joints, he tells me. Well, it's going to take weeks to glue all these stamps. James says he's done all right with this particular game, collecting television sets from redemption centers in Maryland and Virginia. I worked four hours at it today until I ran out of the booklets that James has to pick up at the supermarket. I start licking the stamps, but James says, "Don't waste that talent on stamps." He puts a wet sponge on a saucer and pulls a sheet of stamps across it. He presses the moistened sheet on the page all in one motion. I copy his method until I can do ten pages a minute, that's six seconds a page. Every book was full, their leaves stiff and bulky, like a paperback novel after it falls in the bathtub. I did seventy-six books kneeling on the floor until my ankles went numb and I couldn't feel my feet.

We have to go to the A&P and Winn Dixie and collect the booklets from the stands outside the customer service counter. We can't take all the booklets without looking suspicious. We leave some in the rack and drive over to another market to get more. Gulf and Esso has them. On these trips outside of Bailey's Trailer Village, James takes me to the Seventh Wonder Diner at the foot of the Chesapeake Bay Bridge-Tunnel. The bridge-tunnel is supposed to be one of the "seven engineering wonders of the world." He orders a grilled cheese. I'd like to eat both halves myself, but he wants to share it. I say, "Do you think we could order another one of these?"

He says, "We have had an excellent sufficiency."

"Excuse me?"

"We've had an *excellent sufficiency*." He drops his napkin on the plate.

I see he's too cheap to buy me another grilled cheese.

When I ask him again, he orders it for me. He waits until the waitress brings me a second sandwich. I reach for it, but James picks up the whole plate and turns it over on the countertop. The potato chips scatter, but my sandwich is under the china plate. He waits to see what I do.

"I guess I lost my appetite," I tell him.

We leave the Seventh Wonder and James stops at the Elbow Room for "fortification." He says he has to "wet the baby's head" after being straight for the last ten hours. The cocktail waitress, Penny, tells him most of those hours he was sleeping, which doesn't deserve credit. I see the waitress is wearing copper earrings made from coins squashed flat on a railroad track. "I like your earrings," I tell her.

She says, "Yeah, my boyfriend makes these at the switching yard."

James says, "They turn your ears green after a while."

The Elbow Room tavern is packed. There's not an empty seat, with just five booths and a row of high chair-stools at the bar. Ruth says these regulars are washed-up bookies and grifters. Barflies with nothing to talk about but ancient history. That's why James feels at home there. Ruth says: "It's a perfect place for a true booze artist like James. There's nothing worse than hearing the same old stories from a washed-up con."

Penny knows I'm underage, but she's spiking my ginger ale with whatever James is having. The gin creeps up on me. I watch the busy sign in the window. Two neon-pink martini glasses tip back and forth in a little dance until I'm hypnotized.

JAMES IS MAKING a production about getting rid of my old clothes. I've got goose pimples while he tears my skirt into little strips, shredding its acetate lining. He's pulling the seams apart the way Ray used to tear old shirts for the car wash. James is almost fifty years old, but he's still blond as a lion. He wears his hair to his collar like that swashbuckler actor Errol Flynn. James keeps his hair wild because he had to wear it short for nine years in the navy. He doesn't have much body hair. Ruth says that's because he's Finnish. I thought she said he was *finished*, like washed up. His lips are hot and his breath is tarry from Pall Malls—that much I learned in the first five minutes.

I just can't stop laughing.

He's snipping my blouse with a meat scissors and feeding the scraps to the blazing ring on the compact gas range.

"You're crazy," Ruth tells him. She looks at me: "James is a hundred percent paranoid. He smokes dope and thinks there are eyes in the wallpaper."

James doesn't listen to Ruth. He burns ribbons of my clothes and wipes the ash from the enamel stovetop with a wet rag. The greasy Nu-Tone sucks away the smoke. He sees my winter coat is too much to incinerate and he crams it in the trash can. There is nothing left of my belongings.

"It's a good feeling, isn't it?" he tells me.

"I guess. But shoot, I'm freezing."

James hands me a large bag from Sears. I've been waiting all afternoon to take a peek, but he wouldn't let me open it. I pull the sweaters and slacks from the tissue paper. Silky triangles fall to the floor, new panties with tiny hearts and polka dots. A pink jersey nightgown with eyelet lace at the collar. I tell James that he picked out some really nice things for me. I'm shivering, so I start to put on my new clothes, but James won't let me.

Ruth says, "She's naked as a cashew. Let her get dressed."

James wraps me up in an electric blanket instead. He puts the big dial into my hands. He walks me to the other end of the trailer. He plugs the blanket cord into a socket. I stand before him as the wire mesh in the automatic blanket starts to heat up.

"You'll need more things," he tells me. "We'll get it."

I nod.

"You're here now, we're clear on that?"

"Sure," I tell him. "Where am I going to go?"

"Shit, honey, if you left your own home, you can break away anytime."

"I'm here."

"That's what we're saying."

We curl up on the Castro, and James and I are alone for a while. I can smell Ruth's hair spray on the pillows. Helene Curtis. Ruth comes in and tells James she wants the bed. She tugs his shoulder and whispers his nickname.

His name is James Robinson, but Ruth calls him "Crusoe," like the shipwrecked victim.

I get up from the sleep sofa and go into the other room. It was Ruth's kids' room until they went to Greensboro to live with their grandmother. Ruth's husband is in jail for operating under the influence and crashing a speedboat into a finger pier, killing two people. Ruth says, "He went from land to water like a reptile."

The bunk is cold next to the icy birch veneer. I'd rather be with James where it's warm. The whole room smells like glue from the stamps. It's a smell I know pretty well.

JAMES TELLS ME we're doing the right thing. He's saving my life. He tells Ruth, "She's lucky I found her."

"You mean *you* got lucky. Just like when you got lucky and found Vanessa."

I say, "Who's this Vanessa?"

Ruth says, "James found her last year. He likes finding girls, but they don't stick around. Now Vanessa works for me at the Paris." Ruth laughs at James as if she doesn't think much of him, but she's nice to me. Sometimes I think she's still in love with James. She reminds me of Phyllis Diller, that comic with the husband named Fang. Even when Phyllis Diller is saying something mean about Fang, like when Ruth calls James "Crusoe," it comes out like love talk.

I met James Robinson in Wilmington at the Holiday Lanes. I was working behind the soda fountain filling Cokes, Tuesday and Thursday my first week back at school. At 7 P.M., another girl of legal age came in to draw beers. James ordered a drink from his intercom at lane 8, and I brought him a big glass of Royal Crown with a straw standing erect in the chipped ice. The fry cook taught me to peel only half of the straw and leave a paper cuff on it. James picked up the straw and blew the paper cuff in my direction. Now that was a flirt, wasn't it?

I went back to the soda fountain. I leaned on the counter and watched him bowl. He was better than average. He had a nice fluid release and the ball didn't make that loud crack that signals an amateur. He buzzed me on the intercom. He said, "I've got a bone to pick with you."

I said, "What is it? The wishbone?"

He was surprised I could hand it back. He laughed. It sounded tinny coming through the speaker, like a doll's laugh when you pull a string on its back. "This cola is all ice," he said. "Forty-five cents for ice? I need a refill already."

I brought him another cola with just one scoop of ice chips. There wasn't anyone waiting at the soda counter, so I stayed in his horseshoe booth and sat at the little table. I turned on the tiny overhead light and scored his game for two sets. I noticed James's street shoes. Shiny black ankle boots with zippers, his nylon socks rolled up in each one. I picked up the stubby pencil. When the machine raked the pins, I wrote down the right numbers, but I was telling him my life story. If he had a spare and we waited for the single pin to ride up and come back down in its proper place, I realized I had spilled my guts. In the other lanes, pins were crashing and I had to raise my voice. James never stopped bowling, but I could see he was interested in helping me out. He rubbed his Brunswick with his handkerchief, white-on-white just like my father's, and I believed he was feeling something for me.

"You're my problem now," he told me in the back seat of his car. "Don't worry about a thing. You're my problem."

He said he was in Wilmington visiting his sister. She had lung trouble after working as a spinner operator at Burlington Textiles and her emphysema put her back in the hospital. We went over to Wilmington General once or twice to see her. The second time I met him, he took me out on a little date. We rode into Chester, where he took me inside a bar called Dave's Kozy-In. The barman didn't size me up. He didn't care who was paired up with who. I don't exactly look twenty-one, but I can act it. We drank beer from mugs with the Ballantine logo. Three intersecting circles. James said these were the number of wedding bands he'd thrown away already.

"Is that right?" I said, but I had never hinted I wanted to get married. He was setting his limits down for nothing. James listened to my troubles. That's when he first said, "You're my problem now." Soon he started saying, "You're my girl now." I took it as a compliment—who wouldn't?

When his sister was discharged from Wilmington General, we

drove her home. Her apartment was in a project near the river. Some women were burning garbage outside in a big steel sink. Trash and kitchen scraps, including the whole rib cage of a turkey or a big capon, I don't know. The smoke shifted and the odor was getting on me. His sister had a new oxygen tank on casters, and James helped carry it into her apartment. He set up the slim tank in her bedroom. I could hear a slight hissing sound when the oxygen started to roll out. When his sister was sitting in front of the TV, we left her. James told me he was ready to go back to Virginia Beach. He invited me to come along. He said, "It's a different world south of the Mason-Dixon. Really nice folks."

I didn't try to think about it more than one minute. I said, "Okay. When are we going?" I was sniffing my fingertips—that burnt carcass smell was still on me.

James told me he wanted to go the next night.

The next day, I was at the curb in front of Ed Honey's Liquor Mart, watching my Bazooka wrapper twist over and over with the autumn leaves. He pulled up beside me. I got into his car. A nice old Chrysler Newport with graceful fins, although the chrome was flaking off, leaving tiny Dalmation spots. He just came from the Claymont Car Wash where he got it Glo-waxed for an extra dollar. A big Coleman jug filled with Hi-C was resting right there in the middle of the front seat. We could tip it and fill our cups at any time we felt thirsty, all the way to Virginia. Its orangeade scent smelled familiar as we drove along into farm country. We passed a sign that said WELCOME TO MARYLAND, and James said, "We cross this state line and Mr. Mann's toe is throbbing."

"Mr. Man? Who's that? Like Mr. Green Jeans?"

"*Mann*—that's with a double *n*. Ever hear of the Mann Act?"

I took a cookie from the package on the seat. James had brought macaroons, but macaroons make my throat close up. I started choking on the flecks of coconut.

FOUR DAYS AFTER we arrived in Virginia Beach, he burns my clothes. He tells me not to answer the telephone. A man named Piers, a skinny guy dressed in coveralls, arrives every day at about three o'clock, and he and James go into the Alum-a-room shed and rearrange some cases of bootleg cigarettes. They look at the appliances. I guess these TVs and clock radios are booty from the stamps, and the fellow doesn't want me watching what he puts in his truck. I tell Ruth I never heard of someone named Piers. Ruth says, "You know the saying: A pier is a disappointed bridge."

"Oh, I guess so," I tell her. I see she doesn't like James's friend and I'm not getting in the middle.

James tells me to wait on the stoop. In a minute he comes back out, but it's just to give me an old windbreaker with the Clemson tiger's paw.

The stoop is just a wobbly cement block put here for a step-up, but it's an accident waiting to happen. I see that some of these trailers have retractable aluminum stairs, like the kind attached to airplanes. Either way, when people have to move, they just put the cement block inside the trailer and take their doorstep with them. I sit down on the concrete block. I can feel the cold right through these nylon underpants, so I sit on my hands.

The trailers are parked so tight I can look right inside our neighbor's window. The blinds are pulled down halfway, but I can see their kitchen table and on it two nine-inch cakes. A woman is frosting the first layer. I can only see her hands. She turns the plate a quarter turn and smoothes the butter cream on the sides of the cake, then over the flat center. I watch her fit the other nine-inch cake on top. She's doing real good, turning the plate and wetting the knife in a cup of water. I watch her hands. She swirls the knife over the icing, then wipes the extra frosting off the remaining inch of plate, all the way around, until it's clean.

I spy on the pair of hands until they're gone.

Yesterday, James took me and Piers to look at the Norfolk Mace, a huge ornamental weapon made of silver. "Solid silver would bring a solid return," James tells Piers. The mace is like the official symbol of the city, and it's on permanent exhibition in the Sovran National Bank building. James was thinking about pinching it right from its display case in the bank, but Piers says the job is a large-scale operation, too big for just the two of them. "I'm not fucking around in a bank just for an ornament," Piers said.

James says: "This thing would bring in a few grand, at least. It weighs in at thirty-five pounds. What's sterling going for an ounce? See what I'm saying?"

"You won't get that much," Piers says. "You can't get the top price like you would get in a bank, asshole."

They forget I'm standing there looking at the mace until Piers says, "Shit. She's got big eyes."

I guess my eyes are wide as dollars because right then I understand I'm hooked up with a thief. I feel my lips twisted in a smirk. I can't help it. Like the time I lifted Veronica's cigarette from the ashtray when her back was turned, and I put it down the opposite way so when she reached for it again, she picked up its burning tip. This smirk just runs across my face without my trying.

THE ELECTRIC BLANKET is old and threadbare and some of the wires get too hot. I shift it off my shoulders and let James take a big drink of me. The bed is already pulled out.

James and I do it so much it doesn't hurt anymore. I guess I'm getting stretched, but that Ortho foam still burns. I just want to soak in a bath, but in this trailer you can't sit down in a tub. The water heater doesn't have a very big tank and James tells me to take a "navy shower."

Turn on the water. Turn it off. Soap up. Rinse.

He says if we go to a hotel sometime I can take a "Hollywood shower" and stay in there all I want.

My slit is still stinging, and Ruth showed me how to make a hot compress. She took a Tampax from the cardboard applicator and ran it under the hot-water tap until the cotton swelled up like a fat sponge. Ruth said, "Tuck this in your continental divide where it's sore." I pressed the warm compress high between my legs. It helps, but I still can't sleep.

One time when I was small, I was playing in the grass and I got some chiggers in my underpants. They bit me right in between the legs. In the middle of the night my bites were itching. I went to Veronica, but she didn't get out of bed. She told me to go into the bathroom and get the Vaseline. I went to the medicine cabinet. I took down a jar. I rubbed the ointment on my chigger bites. I could smell that awful menthol, then I felt it stinging. It was Vicks VapoRub, not Vaseline. I screamed.

When I wouldn't stop screaming, Veronica got up and told me, "You'll wake the dead."

This scared me. I didn't want the dead to come after me. "Are they coming?" I said.

RUTH HEARS ME SHIFTING in bed. She comes out and tells me, "Still sore? I think you're allergic to that Ortho gel."

"Do you think so?"

"It burns some girls."

"That's what's happening to me," I tell her.

She goes into the kitchenette and comes back with a plastic bag of "Petite Frozen Peas."

Ruth holds out the frosted bag. "Put this between your legs," she tells me.

"These petite peas?"

"Frozen peas are good for a bee sting, so maybe it'll work on your privates."

I take the bag of peas and press it between my legs. The icy sensation fights with the burning sensation. I don't know which is worse, but I don't tell Ruth. She's just trying to help out.

JAMES THINKS HE CAN teach me, but I'm pretending I already know. The worst part is when he asks me, "You like this? Or this?"

I just say, "Sure, that's fine—"

One time he asked me, "Do you like a cherry turnover?" He wasn't talking about Danish pastries. He moved me around so I was looking at the floor. I didn't tell him to stop.

If I fall asleep in the Castro, Ruth comes in and taps my arm. She leads me to my bunk as if I was her little sister who got groggy watching a double *Perry Mason*. She makes sure I find the blanket and tug it up to my chin. She goes back in there to be with James.

WHEN I CAN'T SLEEP, I press my nose to the window and try to see into that trailer next door where I saw the pair of hands frosting the cake. Or I can wipe my mind clean by thinking of a field of daisies, a field of daisies with a thousand black eyes, rolling across like waves on the ocean. I might dream about my little sister. She has a notch between her front teeth that fills up with frosting, or maybe it's toothpaste. To tease me, she tucks a whiskey-soaked orange rind behind her lips and smiles like that Cheshire cat in *Alice in Wonderland*. There's that big wolf spider trapped in her shower cap. She has no idea it's waiting there.

There's nothing I can do about it.

RUTH CAN'T HELP ME with the stamps. She's going in to work. Ruth manages a Norgetown franchise attached to a small auditorium called the Paris Theater right near the Little Creek Naval Amphibious Base, just west of the Chesapeake Bay Bridge-Tunnel. Ruth's Norgetown laundry is more or less a wire room for placing bets. James doesn't want me to go there with Ruth, but she's been taking me sometimes. James says, "There's too many baby cigar butts trying to operate."

Ruth says the washers are there for the public if they want to come in and use them. But navy housewives don't like what's going on, so the coin-op is always empty. A bum might come in once in a while to wash the one set of clothes he owns. He peels off his stinking layers and stands around in his dirty shorts while the washer completes the cycle. The gambling operation is run by Ruth's younger brother, Russell Stover. *Russell Stover*—just like the boxed candy. Ruth calls him "Turtle," and I think of those chocolate-covered caramels. Turtle and some of his cousins hang around with their dope sheets and betting slips, jamming the pay telephones.

The theater runs films days and evenings, and there's a different schedule for girls working the peep windows. James calls Ruth's place a "Flesh Showroom," as if he wouldn't step foot in there himself. He says he doesn't go in there because the whole place stinks from the solvent recycled in those big dry-cleaning machines. The smell seeps into the auditorium seats.

Behind the auditorium there are some paneled rooms just like a Motel 6, each with a bedside stand, a clock radio, and lamps with bonbon fringe. Ruth's girls can take a date in these rooms day or night. Daytime hours, Ruth arranges "coffee breaks" and "hot lunches" for some regular customers. She calls them Mr. Tuesday, Mr. Wednesday, and like that. "Maybe you'll do hot lunches after you've licked all the stamps," Ruth teases.

James says to Ruth, "Get your eyes off her."

"Who says?" Ruth answers.

"She's off-limits," he tells her.

Ruth laughs. "You make the rules now? Since when?"

I look back and forth. In my whole life, I never saw two people try to claim dibs on me.

Ruth shifts her voice. "Why can't she sit in the laundry and clean the lint traps? She can wipe up the spilled soap and restock the Tide machine. Can't she do that?"

James says, "I don't want her standing there like sucker bait while your brother and his minimobsters take receipts. She just got here, for Christ sake, and you want to put her to work?"

"Shit. She's working for you licking these stamps. These pull in just about nothing. It's pitiful, Crusoe."

Ruth sits tailor-style on the carpet gluing stamps with me while the teakettle boils. Every night, she makes a thermos to take with her to the theater. I'm learning her routines, and seeing how sensible she is. She tells James, "These stamps are a stupid racket. It's a *Romper Room* con. It's too much time and trouble." A row of stamps is stuck to the heel of her hand and she nips it with her teeth. James doesn't make enough money from the stamps. Ruth writes his checks. Ruth says her children are my age or a little older, and it's just as well they aren't around to be influenced by James. I can't imagine Ruth has kids my age. I can't imagine they're anything like me.

Ruth has a tattoo "chain" that runs all the way around her wrist, a blue braid with inked charms that say the names of her two sons, RORY and NICK. The bracelet can't jangle with these silent blue charms.

"When did you get that tattoo?" I ask her.

"That's from a corporate retreat she took with some business associates," James says.

"Shut up," Ruth tells him.

"One of those getaway vacations compliments of Richmond County Jail."

I rub the book of stamps with the heel of my hand to get it to shut. Ruth's the kind of person Ray calls a "productive individual." When she fries hamburger patties for me and James, she drains the grease, wipes out the pan, rinses it and hangs it up before she sits down to eat. We haven't even unscrewed the ketchup bottle and she's already cleaned up the sink. Ruth seems to like me even though I don't have any of her skills.

RUTH SAYS HER BOYS like steak sauce on their burgers—did I get that at my house? I tell her my mother never tried it. I ask Ruth if she thinks Veronica is used to the fact I'm gone.

Ruth says, "Shit, honey, every family is a jigsaw puzzle with one or two missing pieces, lost for good."

I look through the S&H gift catalogue we picked up at the Winn Dixie. "Hey, maybe we can get one of these," I tell James. I point to the glossy Siamese cat, as big as an umbrella stand. "I got one of these china cats back home. I like to collect them."

James looks at the picture. "That's just a cheap figurine. It's only a few books. Sure I'll get you one of those."

"Now where is she going to put that cat?" Ruth says. "On the roof? We don't have any space for collectibles. We can't even have a live cat."

"Karen can have one of these," James tells her. He tosses the catalogue at Ruth.

"Shit, you knocked my earring off," Ruth says.

We comb the rug with our fingers to look for it. The carpet never gets vacuumed, and I see everything in it—sand and gravel, cookie crumbs, little gold flecks of stale pretzel, dimes standing on their sides. I think I see fingernail clippings. Ruth sees it too and doesn't say anything. I don't take my eyes off that filthy rug until I find that tiny gold hoop, lift it out and hand it to her.

I USED TO GLUE S&H stamps with my little sister. We sat in the dining room with newspaper spread out to protect the walnut table. We looked at the catalogue together. My sister wanted a three-foot doll called Patty Play Pal, I think just for its novelty value. Veronica used the stamps for a bouffant hair dryer.

For our Saturday chores, Veronica had us glue stamps or polish silver. I licked stamps and Maria took out the bottle of Twinkle polish and tipped it on a cloth. She wiped a sterling tray and the cloth turned black with tarnish. She squirted more polish on the rag and wrote something in script across the huge platter. She rinsed it off. She brought it over to me. She held it up like she was serving something fancy on the tray, but it was just my own name in bright silver letters. Just the one name, K-a-r-e-n, glittering there.

The day I left, my sister was in trouble again, sassing a teacher. She had to turn in five sheets of detention homework to the vice principal's office the next morning. I hated that vice principal. He interviewed me once, explaining how he was making a special file referring to the percentage of the student population who were "menstruating females." He was "acquiring data in order to *substantiate* the necessity for Kotex machines in the girls rest rooms." I don't think he was authorized to discuss that subject with me.

Last year, Maria was suspended for screwing up the Pledge of Allegiance. Instead of saying "and to the republic for which it stands," she said, "and to the Republic *of South Africa*." She didn't know what she was saying. She was just playing with the words. She's always shifting words around until they backfire.

She's always in trouble. I left her to finish those sheets and walked out the kitchen door. I waited for James at the corner. A neighbor was buying a whole case of Heaven Hill at Ed Honey's Liquor Mart, but I don't think he saw me.

Veronica saw I was giving her some competition. Like the time we walked down the sidewalk at the Merchandise Mart and we saw a man who looked just like that actor who plays 007. He carried a skinny metal suitcase like the one with Ray's electric drill, but Veronica told me, no, it was a special briefcase for transporting precious gems, maybe diamonds, back and forth to jewelry stores. Well, this man noticed me *first*. He saw me and winced, as if he'd suffered a shooting pain, a stitch in his ribs. Then he nodded to Veronica, like he was asking for her understanding. He *couldn't help* looking at me—but she wouldn't excuse him, or me.

After that, Veronica drove me to the seamstress in Claymont. The bungalow was tumbledown, but I noticed that all the curtains, even the pillows on the divan, were hand-stitched; the piping was perfect. The seamstress asked me to take off my dress and my shoes. I stood in her sunlit kitchen, right next to a chicken trussed on a sideboard. An open can of white lard rested on the counter with its lid beside it. Lard wasn't something Veronica kept around our house. I was standing almost naked in that strange kitchen. My pale skin was whiter than lard.

The seamstress shook out her tape and took my measurements. Veronica told me that the plain gray herringbone would minimize my hips. Why should they be minimized? I decided to choose a plaid, knowing I would never wear it. In this way I could victimize my mother, or at least my mother's pocketbook.

"I want this one," I said. I lifted the scratchy bolt of red and green cross weave.

"That's loud," Veronica said.

"Not really, I like it."

"A tartan is classic," the seamstress said. I could see she was hoping to unload it.

I told my mother, "That's the one I want."

The seamstress finished the skirt within the week. Its seams were correctly aligned and the rows of plaid corresponded. The skirt had a full lining like a sheet of ice against my bare thighs. I wore the skirt the day I walked out of the house. James ripped the plaid into strips and fed the gas range with it.

RUTH MAKES A PITCHER of pink lemonade from a frozen can, and she tips some Gilbey's in it. I can feel the gin begin to work. My tongue feels fuzzy. I forget to blink my eyes. I guess I'm getting faced.

They start laughing at my slurred words. James cradles my foot and rubs my toes through my socks; he rests the heel of my foot on his crotch. Then James leads me down the hall into the bedroom and puts me in the Castro. Ruth follows him and waits as he rolls down my kneesocks and tugs them off my feet.

"Why can't she keep her socks on?" Ruth asks.

"Look, who's going to fuck her? You or me?"

"I guess you are."

"Give us a couple minutes," he tells her. He wads my underpants in his hand and gives them to Ruth. She takes them and puts them on the doorknob. James slips the palms of his hands down the inside of my thighs and presses them apart.

Ruth folds her arms and waits.

James shoves his trousers down. James is already big as I've ever seen him. Ruth is watching him too, smiling. When his eyes pinch shut, she winks at me and leaves the room.

SOMETIMES AT NIGHT I have the dream about the white footprints. I see these white footprints in a line on the Persian carpet. I follow them straight into the front hall and right out the front door. I trace them up the flagstone sidewalk. They're getting thinner until they disappear at the curb.

I was in charge of my little sister as she polished her shoes with that chalky bottle that comes with a fur-tipped applicator. She was fixing her shoes for Sunday school, Veronica's orders. Before I know it, she's painted the soles of her Mary Janes. She's walking through the living room leaving a mess on the three-thousand-dollar carpet. Veronica starts screaming.

Maria disappears. I follow her footprints out to the street. She's run off somewhere. Veronica says, "Don't come home until you find your sister." I look everywhere in the neighborhood until I remember the apple tree up the street. Her hiding spot. I duck under the branches that fold down like a huge hoop skirt. I look up and see those white soles dangling from a branch high up. It's always the same dream, but sometimes I look up and can't find those white Mary Janes anywhere.

THIS WHOLE PART OF Virginia is swarming with the military. Anywhere you look, there's white hats off duty. New recruits go everywhere in packs. James was in the navy a few years back. He has a grudge. He spends his drinking time moaning about his Section Eight after nine years stationed at Bakersfield and then at Norfolk. He had problems with his senior officers. "It's a doomed system. Rubber rungs on the ladder," James said.

Ruth tells me if it weren't for the navy her adult entertainment business would be washed up.

I say, "Why is the navy so important? Men are men, aren't they?"

I'm thinking of that one thing they all have in common. I just can't stop thinking about it, now that I've seen it for myself.

Ruth looks at me. She says, "Honey, you're probably right. Uniforms don't help much." Ruth looks at James. "They all have the same number of beans in their jar." She's smiling. "But what we have here is a *concentration of manpower*."

"A concentration of manpower?"

"Everyone knows that these navy men are away from their wives and families. Most of 'em are boys. The local politicians protect us because we're doing a service for the government. These boys ship out for months. We can't help that, but when they're in port the population triples. They're starved for sex. They're at a low point. Their eyes are bigger than their stomachs. Even those Wally Cox types. They get an appetite. They don't want Tastee-Freez, do they?"

"Shit. Is there a Tastee-Freez around here? I haven't seen one." My voice sounds funny, tight in my throat. It's the alcohol, or maybe it's just some childish begging. I can't look at either of them. James stands up and gets his car keys. Ruth pulls her coat on. I can't believe how sweet these people are to me. I didn't even have to ask about going out for ice cream. We get into the front seat of the Newport and drive down to the strip.

I EAT MY BOAT of soft-serve vanilla. James has a dipped cone. He's lifting the chocolate coating off whole, like a dunce cap, and eating it with his fingers. I notice that the ice cream isn't melting at all. It doesn't even taste like *ice* cream. Ruth says it's corn starch whipped up with air. The night is cold and bleary and the ice cream doesn't make me feel much better. Ever since I came down here with James, meals have been organized around other things and I'm always feeling hungry. We're driving past some restaurants with SEAFOOD listed on marquees the way they list movies. It's a good selection even in the off season. "CRAB CAKES," I read the sign out loud. "SHRIMP BASKET—"

James doesn't seem to be interested in getting some real food. We're just a few miles from Bailey's when James is pulled over.

The police cruiser doesn't use a siren; it just spills its revolving light over our back windshield and James immediately turns onto the shoulder. He's trying too hard to look innocent. I would have waited a few more seconds to see if the cruiser just wanted to pass us.

The officer parks behind us and comes up beside the window. James has his wallet open and he tugs his license free. Ruth opens the glove box and gives James the registration card. The officer takes the license and registration back to his cruiser.

"Is that driver's license real?" I ask Ruth, expecting that it must be a forgery. I don't think James could have a real ID on him if he's selling TVs right and left.

"Sure it's real."

"It's got his name on it?" I ask.

Ruth pinches her two lips together with her thumb and index finger like I'm supposed to shut up.

"It's my own goddamn name. I didn't steal it," James says.

When the policeman returns to the window, he tells James, "Your bulb over the plate is loose. It flickers when you hit a bump."

"Excuse me? You're saying my plate is loose?"

"The light. It's shorting out or something. It flickers when you hit a dip. Get it checked out." He steps back from the car.

"Since when are they pulling you over for a thirty-cent bulb?" James whispers. He steers onto the road. The cop does a three-point and heads the other way. We drive on for a few minutes. James's profile looks hard and still. I'm holding my plastic ice cream dish in my lap. No one talks. James pulls the Chrysler off the road again. He tells me to get out.

"What?" I ask him.

"Get out of the car."

I push open the passenger door. I stand up on the gravel shoulder. When I'm out of the car, Ruth moves over on the seat and arranges her purse between herself and James. I'm out there by myself and Ruth slams the car door. The wind opens the collar of my windbreaker. I try to close the lapels and I drop the plastic ice cream boat. It flips over several times in the wind and disappears up the road.

Oh, I see. A little attention from the cops and that's it. I'm getting ditched.

James gets out of the car and walks around to the back. He twists the little bulb above the plate to make sure it's in tight. He walks back to the driver's side. "Now Karen, watch my rear end, see if the light blinks."

"Which light? That little one?"

"Over the plate," James says, and he sits down behind the steering wheel. He drives the car away.

I'm left alone in the dark. I watch the taillights of the Chrysler and the tiny glow above the license plate. It remains steady as James disappears around a curve. I am certain that this is something final. I had been ditched before. High school boys had left me at the Big Boy or at the Charcoal Pit without any formal good-byes. My father drove away from Grier School and left me standing in the turnaround. He didn't even look back. Maybe he didn't find his chance. Maria turned around in the back seat to face me as Ray drove down the hill. I watched her tiny face sink away.

Some traffic passes me. A tractor-trailer with tiers of hogs rolls down the highway, leaving a stink in the air behind it. I start walking back to Bailey's Trailer Village. I imagine I know the way. I follow Shore Road for a quarter mile. I can see the lights of the Chesapeake Bay Bridge-Tunnel. I hike along the shoulder for two minutes until James pulls up. I get back into the car. I report that the light didn't flicker, as far as I could tell.

"I knew it," James said. "These Virginia mounties are always fussing with me. They're pimples on my ass."

Ruth says, "We didn't hit a bump. Maybe she should get out and watch where the road is broke up." Ruth is teasing me, but James takes her seriously. He steers onto a side street and rides two miles across the declining neighborhood until he hits a railroad crossing. He drops me off fifty feet from the signal. The wind is icy with a hint of winter. I pull my nylon jacket shut, but it's just a thin shell. I watch James ride the car over the tracks a little too fast. The shocks jiggle and shiver. The Newport disappears around a corner. In a minute it comes back in my direction. James does a U-turn and rides across the tracks again. I don't see the plate light flicker once. When I sit down in the front seat next to Ruth, she says, "That little fucker blinked, am I right?"

"No, actually it—"

She elbows me.

I realize we would be at it all night unless I lied. "It flickered just for a second. The cop wasn't seeing things," I tell James.

"All right, then?" Ruth says to him. "Your cock's always caught in a zipper over nothing. You should get that bulb fixture replaced."

THE

PARIS THEATER

———

(KAREN)

JAMES WENT UP to D.C. for the day with Piers. I ask Ruth, "Just who is this Piers?"

"He drives for Great Neck Trucking. He's the one who boosted the stamps."

"No wonder I don't like him."

"Honey, you don't have to lick those stamps. Put your foot down."

"I guess I will."

Ruth says, "You can work for me at the Paris anytime. You decide." Because James is gone, she takes me into work. She says I can sit in the laundry and make change for customers, or I can sell tickets for the movies. I can have my choice. She'll get me an ID. "You look older than fourteen, but you never know who might want to see it in writing."

The lightbulbs in the big billboard marquee are shot out. It's a blank. Ruth says she's not exactly running the hits *Mary Poppins* or *My Fair Lady*. The city doesn't want her to advertise her vice den. But they don't mind it being there. Instead of the big marquee, Ruth puts up a tiny felt bulletin board with the names of the movies. This week it's Russ Meyers's *Eroticon, Europe in the Raw* and his new release, *Mudhoney*. Ruth tells me that before each full-length feature, they run a string of fifteen-minute stags. She's got a storeroom of 8mm cans and she keeps getting new ones. They're black market. Filmmakers invent porn pen names: "directed by Will B. Hard," or "photographed by A. Wise Guy." Sometimes it's pretty rough stuff, since they're made by amateurs in their own homes.

"God knows what they have in mind, but it doesn't matter as long as the actor aims for the camera," Ruth says. "I don't even screen them anymore. Let the audience be the critics. We don't hear any complaints."

The full-length features come from a distributor and have to go back after their two-week run. Ruth says the men don't care what's playing. They've seen everything at least once.

"They don't mind watching the same ones? Isn't the ending ruined that way?" I say.

Ruth looks at me. "Honey, endings are always the same. It ends with the money shot."

"The money shot?"

"The moment they wait for."

"Oh, that."

"Just watch any of these. Even the old ones, *Wonders of the Unseen World*, *A Free Ride* or that antique, *Grass Sandwich*. That's one of the first stags. He pulls out and shoots on her backside or shoots right into the camera like he's spraying the first row. If he's not ready yet, he has to pump it with his hand. It's a race against time. Rule is, we get to see him shoot. That's the one rule."

Ruth tells me that in these first films the men are wearing a disguise—a wig, a mask or a rubber hook nose to hide their identity, but women have to be whoever they are.

The Norgetown is to the left of the lobby. I can see the dryers twirling as I stand at the ticket booth. Seeing the machines calms me down as Ruth explains the ticket booth to me. Ruth introduces me to Rose Pearson, who sits on a stool behind the Plexiglas window. Rose is smoking a cigarette screwed into a long wand with a spearmint filter just like Gloria Swanson. When she's not at the ticket booth, Rose works the regular "lounge" and she also works the live window. Rose introduces me to a few of the other girls who are standing around the lobby. One girl named Sharon is pushing a Bissel carpet sweeper, but it's not picking up anything. I ask about Vanessa. "She's in back," Rose says. I'm thinking, Did Vanessa dump James or vice versa?

These girls look a little tired out. Maybe it's the way they're dressed, like it's a pajama party—satin loungewear and baby-doll pajamas over flesh-tone body stockings. These nightgowns don't look right in broad daylight. Rose is wearing stretch pants two sizes too small for her. I don't like to notice, but the seam cuts into her crotch like a knife divides a stick of butter.

Tired or not, these girls are knockouts and tall as a kick line. I straighten up to see if I'm the right height when a man comes up to the Plexiglas booth to buy a ticket for the movie. Rose shows me the routine. "I sit here and push tickets through this slot. See? I collect the two dollars in this silver tray. Like this." She pushes a lever and a little metal dish swings out. The man puts a twenty in the clip, then Rose pulls it back. The man waits, his hands in his pockets. His shoulders are slumped. He's looking sheepish, which I think is on my account. She changes the man's twenty and folds his cash change before she inserts it in a spring clip on the little dish. She pushes the dish toward the man. I'm thinking, even if she doesn't touch this guy's fingers, she's touching his money, which started out in his own hands.

Ruth brings me into the laundry, a narrow room with a string of Norge washers. The dryers are spinning and the air is too hot to breathe. Like James said, the dry-cleaning solvent hangs in the air. A girl, not much older than me, is doing her wash while her toddler is walking around without any pants. I guess the young mother stripped him down to wash all his clothes at once. Two men are sitting around waiting for their wash. I don't see these men doing squat. They don't have the usual wicker laundry baskets, no bottles of bluing or softening rinse, none of the usual. One of these men is on the pay telephone, just listening to the other end.

Ruth tells me, "Nights, it's harness or dog track. Sometimes there's a prize fight. Sundays, it's football and they're taking point spreads. Four years ago, we did a lot of business during the election, but Goldwater and Johnson weren't really a contest. Kennedy and Nixon, now that one was close. That race had people laying down their houses and automobiles. It was that tight in 1960."

"You mean he's taking bets?"

"Honey, it's numbers, all kinds."

She introduces me to her brother, Turtle. I put out my hand. He pinches just the pads of my fingertips like he's testing grapes, and lets go. He's not impressed to meet me. Ruth tells me to check a dryer. She smells something burning up. I walk over to the dryer and stick my hand in. It's a tattered flannel blanket. Ruth doesn't have to tell me that these dryers keep spinning the same old blankets just for looks. When they're dry, they go back in the washer. Something has to keep happening.

Ruth takes me back through the theater and into her office. There's a narrow stairway leading up to another level with a frayed panel curtain hanging to the floor. Ruth tells me the stairs lead up to the projectors. A man named Hendrick switches the reels and comes down the ladder to sit in a vinyl recliner in Ruth's office. There are film cans everywhere. Tiny silver wheels the size of tea plates. "This is Hendrick. He's our projectionist." Ruth pokes him with her fingertip. Hendrick is dressed in a bathrobe. His hair is wrapped in a silk turban like a rajah. I see his eyelashes are glued on. I can see the little seams stuck to his eyelids.

"Is that a real turban?" I ask him.

"Sweetheart, this ain't no turban, it's a cloche. There's a difference between."

I can't keep from staring at Hendrick. His breasts jiggle beneath the lapels of his kimono.

"He's had injections," Ruth tells me. "Same as Rose and Val. You won't need any injections."

Hendrick says, "Shit. This baby one can go au naturel." He nods at Ruth, not at me. I can hear the movie's sound effects through the wall, but I can't hear any dialogue.

"Is this a silent movie?" I ask Hendrick.

"There's not much talking in these. Sometimes they're in German. German films have the blonds. Then we have the ones from Japan. A lot of these are homemade."

"What about French?" I say.

Ruth looks up from her stack of receipts. Then she takes a scissors and cuts the "Word Jumble" from the newspaper. The "Word Jumble" is one of her hobbies. She eyes Hendrick and smiles. "She's right. They're all in *French.*"

I tell Ruth, "You know my mother is a hundred percent French extraction, so I'm half-French. Can you see any French in me?"

They look me up and down with a new curiosity, like I told them I have a glass eye.

"My mother plays Yves Montand records in the middle of the afternoon with the windows wide open so the whole neighborhood can hear it."

"She does what?" Ruth says. I see she's not listening to me as she arranges scraps of paper on a spindle.

I guess Ruth never even heard of Yves Montand. Not everyone has heard of the French singer.

Ruth takes me into the back to show me the layout of the place. Behind the wall with the movie screen, there's a narrow hallway with a vinyl accordion door. We go down this hallway and Ruth says, "This is the lounge. The girls call it the 'pillow room,' the 'velvet pocket,' the 'playpen,' whatever. It's just for icebreakers."

I'm surprised to see that the tiny room has got *fur* wallpaper. Gold fur like a puppy's coat. It's filled with all kinds of plush, overstuffed pillows. Satin hearts, huge puffy cushions, feather rolls. There's a love seat and an ottoman. I see it's even got one of those little canvas trampolines. Big enough for one person at a time.

"They do it on that trampoline?"

"No, there's no sex in this room, just introductions and negotiations. That trampoline sweetens the deal. The girls speed up the transaction if they jiggle their merchandise a little bit."

"Oh, I get it. But I've never learned trampoline. I guess you have to have good balance. I wasn't so great at tumbling—"

"Tumbling? Shit, you just tumble in bed and tumble out. You'll get the knack."

The lounge room has a saloon door leading to a hallway with walk-in "closets." Each of these booths has its own window that looks onto one central room. The room is like an empty stage, furnished with one of those old-fashioned fainting sofas. Across from the sofa is a single bed and an end table with a vase of silk flowers that never wilt. The arrangement has collected a layer of peculiar dust. The windows in each booth have vinyl shades with dirty circle pulls.

"The shade goes up and down as he wants. To prolong his climax," Ruth tells me.

That word rolls right off Ruth's tongue, but it still shocks me.

Ruth says the booths are rented by the quarter hour, but when it's busy, Ruth pounds on the doors. "Some men can do it a few times, if they're lucky. After their time is up, they have to pay extra or I chase them out."

The hallway is L-shaped, so when all the booths are occupied, a man might see another customer lifting a shade, catty-corner across the dim room. Ruth says this gives some men an extra jolt. Vanessa Shore and Sharon Martone work weekends, a busy time. During the week Peaches and Valerie, and of course, Rose Pearson, do the live show.

"Peaches?"

"That's right. Peaches isn't her real name—it's one of the oldest in the business."

I rub my lips to wipe away my surprise.

Ruth says, "Pepper. Candi. Kitty. Peaches. Sugar. It's usually something spicy or something sweet, you know?"

I wonder if Ray knows that "Peaches" is a business name.

Ruth is saying they have good days and bad days. Ruth says the girls change their routines now and then but these men don't really want to be surprised. She eyes me for my reaction. "The girls try to change their props on a regular basis, just to keep repeat customers wondering what another day will bring."

I say, "Yeah, I guess props have to keep changing." I try to keep up with what she's saying. I think of the prop closet backstage at Mt. Pleasant High school, the chipped Libbey glassware, old rotary telephones and fringed lampshades donated to the high school theater program.

Ruth is trying to prepare me for what I am going to see next. Sharon Martone has just started her routine for two customers on opposite sides. Ruth pulls me up to the glass. In the dim light, I see the fainting couch, its slipcover stained and frayed along the skirt. Across the room, there's the single bed with a lopsided dust ruffle almost like the kind Veronica has on the guest bed in the spare bedroom.

I look at the girl. She's naked except for some high-heel shoes and a fake ruby choker like a slit throat. The shoes are amazing three-inch spikes, blazing chili-pepper red, with shiny brass toe shields. These *toe shields* are amazing. I've never seen shoes with armored toes like that. I keep my eyes on her feet for a long time while the girl does her act.

She's sitting on the sofa with her knees drawn up, filling her cunt with a squeeze bottle of Jergens, the common pink hand lotion. Now I have to admit this is my first time seeing something like this. She inserts the nozzle inside her and when she's full, she tells her audience, "Okay, boys, are we ready? No, not yet?"

She fills up again.

"Ready, boys?"

She squirts the Jergens almost across the room.

Ruth says, "Point is, they want to shoot at the same time. That's the game. She uses Jergens or Johnson's baby powder. Powder makes 'smoke rings.'"

I understand that it's baby powder making the strange white dust on the artificial flowers.

Ruth sprays the glass with Windex so I can't see anymore. Ruth says, "They're pigs. They shoot right on the glass and don't wipe up. I have to do the housekeeping. I don't ask my girls to do it." Ruth scrubs the window with a paper towel. She swipes blue paper sheets from the Sinclair station across the street. A couple times a night, Ruth takes a bottle of Windex and a handful of towels into the booths. She jokes, "I'll be back in a few minutes, Hendrick, I've got to clean the windshields."

She didn't ask me to help, but I take the Windex from her and I spray the glass. She scrubs the dried juice off.

At the end of the hall, I see some men go into the "playpen" to wait for their dates. I guess Ruth's running a regular whorehouse, but the movie theater, peep windows and coin laundry make it seem like a weird kind of underground shopping mall, like one of those basement arcades where you can find anything—a fortune-teller or a place to get your boots reheeled or your alarm clock repaired—just about anything.

Ruth is saying I'm a "fully employable individual." Any girl is a "candidate for the workforce." She's not talking about working at a bowling alley or a drugstore.

The Paris Theater doesn't shock me. Sharon ejaculating Jergens or making smoke rings from her cunt almost seems comical. Ruth says, "We laugh it off and put the cash right in our passbook accounts."

If I start to feel queasy, I remember my home life that delivered me here. What I like about Ruth is the way she helps me to see into the distance. I can make progress working here at the Paris. Or I can lick stamps and make love with James. Love isn't the same as progress. If I come down to the Paris to take tickets, or work in the laundry room, it's a professional arrangement. I prefer something professional.

Ruth says I can collect as a baby-pro. Ruth tells me, "I'll arrange things and take you along gradually. I have a talker who won't even touch you. That would be to start. He'll want to talk hot with you. You just have to sit there and keep a straight face. Keeping a straight face is harder than you think while he's talking silly smut. Anyway, that's one opportunity. Myself, I hate talkers and sightseers, they're a pain, but if someone wants fresh talent, he'll pay for it. Think about it."

"Sure," I tell her.

"James isn't ready to let you go yet, but he knows sooner or later you'll get tired of doing his housework. If it's not Green Stamps, it will be something else."

"How much business can I get?"

"Karen, that's not the question. The question is, how many hours are in a day?"

"You mean all twenty-four?"

"Norfolk is swarming with kids leaving for tours in Viet Nam. That Gulf of Tonkin thing. It's a boost to us. They're going over in droves. They get weekend liberty before shipping out, and you'd think it was their last supper. It's the first time for some of them, but they think it's their *last* time. They're out there looking for something just like you."

"Shit. Maybe they are."

Ruth says, "It's cash and carry. But, you're too sweet. You're a candy-butt, too premium for white hats. We'll get you an older customer. Meet him for coffee breaks, honey, that's just fifteen minutes. Mondays, Wednesdays and Fridays. Then you can lay out the rest of the week. Something like that. At your age, you can be fully financed by an oldster and work on your back as little as possible. Girls like you attract champagne tricks. As soon as you get broke in, it's harder to pull off. Whores are like this—you know that dyed money the bank gives a crook? Once you get in the Game, Karen, it's like that dye gets on your skin. You're marked."

Ruth slaps my hands. I'm biting my cuticles and can't break the habit.

"That's why you're a specialty right now, but that doesn't last for a minute. You hear what I'm saying? There's no reward for seniority. You break out of the gate, then, in a couple years time, you've run every race. That's that. But you're still wrapped in cellophane."

"Yeah, I guess I am," I tell her. I can feel my cheeks get hot. I'm embarrassed to have these feelings. I guess it's false pride, or I don't know, maybe it's butterflies. Ruth likes to flatter me for her own reasons. But I like to hear when she spells out my potential. I say, "You're right. Why not get some money."

Ruth says, "Nobody's forcing you. You're not in the street like some girls and they don't have a choice. But Karen, how long you going to feel sorry for James?"

"I don't know."

"This year coming up is your best year. When new is new."

When new is new.

"I might try it out," I tell her.

Ruth doesn't even blink. She starts explaining some precautions. "This is an established spot," she tells me, "we've been here ten years. We don't get too much crap off uniforms, but once in a while some dick walks in here because he needs to fill his sheet. He'll want to bring a girl downtown just for his paperwork. You don't have to worry about this. I'm starting you out front. Selling tickets, you'll get to know some faces. If somebody comes back to the lounge and we don't know him, we're careful what we say. First rule, we don't ever talk about cash. We don't talk about the sex. Police want to nail you for putting up a figure. You'll learn the regular code. Every trick knows the back-and-forth. Just act dumb. A trick will play along. Let him talk, like he's selling life insurance. He's going to put out the figure, not you. He'll say, 'Honey, I just got paid,' or 'I got my Christmas bonus,' or 'My mom just gave me my allowance and I'm sharing it with you.' They're comedians, and he'll dish out some figure. Whatever he throws out, you just let *him* keep going until he hits it right.

"When he gets specific and says what he's interested in—half and half, flatback, ass fuck, just nod your head, don't say a word. Don't hustle. Let *him* tell you. And don't ever sell your hair. Locks sell for twenty-five, that sounds irresistible, but before you know it, you won't have any hair left. And I don't want you cutting up my wigs and selling locks from them."

What Ruth seemed to be saying was this: I can do it, get paid for it and do it again. But I should never say out loud what it is I'm doing. In a court of law, it's words alone can put us in the tank.

I SOMETIMES THINK OF RAY. I didn't leave home because of him. On the other hand, I didn't stay.

Ray falls asleep every night in his recliner. This recliner has a bad history. Ray made a deal with one of his clients who owed him money. The client told Ray he could pick out some furniture from a warehouse and the items would be delivered to the house, no charge. Ray picked out a new recliner, the latest thing. The chair had a retractable footrest and a circle cut out of the arm where he could put his drink, just like at the movie theater. But Veronica is an antique collector and she wasn't going to like Ray's choices. One afternoon this furniture truck rolls up the driveway. Men start unloading all kinds of things. Giant ottomans. A Spanish-style sleep sofa. Big ceramic urns. And Ray's huge recliner. Veronica had no idea this furniture was coming, and she starts screaming at the men. The men said, "Lady, we just deliver the stuff." Veronica got on the telephone. Soon Ray came home and they had it out. Ray saw he had made a mistake. He told the men to reload the furniture in the truck. Everything but the recliner. I remember how he looked at Veronica. He dipped his face and glared at her. "That recliner stays right where it is."

But Ray had trouble getting used to the new chair. Half asleep, he'd stand up and forget about the footrest. He tripped on it. The sound of his weight crashing in the silent house late at night woke us up. Maria and I listened from our room. We heard Ray fall and swear. We heard him coming down the hallway, his shoulder brushing the wall, tipping the picture frames as he groped his way to bed. We heard the picture frames swinging on their hooks.

Mornings, he was rested, and I guess that's when he did it to Veronica. When else? Their bedroom door was locked while the percolator was chugging in the kitchen. By the time the coffee was ready, they were finished. Ray shaved and dressed and drove down to his office at the big warehouse south of Wilmington.

Once I helped with the inventory there. I sorted drawers of nuts and bolts. Industrial diamonds and tiny saw blades the size of my barrettes. Every morning before Ray went to work, he always tried to say something nice to me. He said, "That's a pretty dress," or "Snow today. You want me to oil your boots?"

Veronica said, "She can polish her own boots."

I saw him struggle to love me, but he couldn't get past Veronica. It was terrible to watch him try. Maybe I should have helped him take that step. I could have said, "Sure, Daddy, you can oil my boots."

I didn't like the taste of his good-bye kiss, since he had just swallowed his Maalox right out of the big blue bottle, standing at the kitchen sink. A taste like stale Canada mints. I cringed when he kissed me.

When Ray thought to call me "Peaches," did he know it was a whore's nickname? Ray calls my little sister "Merry Cherry." She swiped those halved cherries soaked in bourbon right from their tumblers. These sweet names seem sort of tragic, don't they?

Lying beside James Robinson I think of my life now and how I don't share it with anyone. Although I'm here in bed, on Ruth's side of the Castro, a strand of her hair looped on the pillow, I can't say I belong to either Ruth or James. Each of us is sort of on our own.

I think growing up must be like falling through a manhole. There's just enough room for one. Even when James has his finger in me, it's just a finger in me. I don't feel his heart and soul is behind it. Speaking for myself, my soul isn't touched. If the soul is a hopeless bystander in sex, why do they ask you to wait for your wedding night? Maybe after church blessings the soul wakes up and comes alive. How would I know?

Last year Maria and I both developed broken blood vessels. Spots appeared on our faces, right on our cheekbones in the exact same place. My spot was the size of a tiny pencil eraser; hers was a small red wagon wheel. Veronica made an appointment at the doctor to have our marks removed with an electrical needle. I was happy to get mine taken off. I climbed onto the Naugahyde table and rested my head on a pillow wrapped in a paper towel. The doctor stood over me. The needle felt like a little pinprick and then a small electric shock came afterward. It only took a second. I stood up.

Maria refused to lay down on the table.

Veronica told her, "That *disfigurement* won't go away on its own. It will be there forever."

Maria went around the table and stood on the other side. If the doctor reached for her arm, she jumped away from him. When he tried to push her down, she screamed. Patients in the waiting room heard her yelp and they fussed in their seats. I could hear their chairs bump the wall and the magazines slapping the coffee table. The doctor told our mother he wasn't going to force it.

That's one thing about my sister, she has her own mind. Maybe it's called "self-worth." *Ladies' Home Journal* said that most girls leave home because they don't have "self-worth."

I let the physician prick my face. I guess I would have sat down in an electric chair if Veronica said so.

After I got my needle, Veronica drove us home. Maria's broken blood vessel expanded until her cheek looked slapped. In a few months, her broken blood vessel vanished on its own.

James doesn't like me working for Ruth selling tickets. He calls me all hours from the Elbow Room. I have to leave my seat and go into Ruth's office to talk to him. Ruth grabs the telephone from me and screams at him. Now James expects *me* to *call him*, in secret, from the Sinclair station every hour. If there isn't a customer buying a ticket, I run across the street to the pay phone and dial James at the Elbow.

"Where are you?" he says.

"I'm supposed to be working the ticket window, but I'm talking to you."

"Where from?"

"I'm at the Sinclair, like I told you."

"You're at the Sinclair? How do I know you're not lying?"

James doesn't trust me when I'm not in his direct line of vision. He said he learned from his own mother not to trust a telephone conversation. His father had called home to say he was working late out at the mill. As he talked, she heard a diesel train sound its horn over the receiver. In the next instant, one second delayed, she heard the same horn right outside her window where the tracks passed in back of the house. That's when she knew her husband wasn't at the mill, he was right there in town. He was with another woman who lived just a few blocks north. Trains pass that slut's house first. His dad was getting away with something until that Great Northern engine told on him.

I see two customers waiting at my ticket window across the street. "I've got to go," I tell James.

"I don't believe you're at that Sinclair."

"Shit," I tell him. "I'm at the goddamn gas station."

"You lie."

"I'm not. Wait a minute—" I tell him. I drop the receiver. It clunks against the pedestal. I walk over to the gas pumps. I stand on the rubber hose and bounce up and down on my heels until the bell rings. Ding, ding, ding. The station is closed but a grease-monkey boy is working in a pit. He climbs out and rubs the back of his hand under his sharp chin. He sees me jumping on the hose. He shakes his head and grins. He's not bad-looking under that black gunk. I like his expression. He's finding something funny in this. Again, I jump on the hose, just for him.

I go back to the telephone. "You hear that bell?" I tell James. I don't wait for his answer. I slam the receiver on its hook. I cross the street and get back behind my window.

I'M AT THE TICKET WINDOW NIGHTS, but afternoons Ruth gets me dates. She forgets about the appointment with the "talker," and she tells me I'm supposed to meet my first trick Monday afternoon. "He's from Little Creek. He's not a kook," she tells me.

She leads me to a room behind the movie screen, where I wait in my baby-doll pajamas. Ruth gave me a pair of terry-cloth mules and told me to keep them on because the cement floor is cold and she doesn't want me to get a runny nose. I turn on the clock radio, but it's a woman reading a recipe for meringues. She says to beat the egg whites until they triple in volume. Then I hear the doorknob rattle. I get up and let the fellow inside.

"You're the new one," he says.

I guess it's written all over me.

I can see he's a white hat by the way his hair is shaved at the nape of his neck and in big naked horseshoes around his ears. James calls these nude circles "white walls." The recruit shows me his cash and then he puts it on top of the clock radio. He says he already spoke to Ruth and this is my tip, right? I nod. The money looks new, like he just came from the bank.

The recruit unlaces his suede desert boots. He tucks them together against the baseboard like he prizes them. He lifts his shirt and shows me his new belt. It looks like a snake biting its own tail. He opens his belt and lets the cobra buckle flop at his waist. He says he wants half and half. I know Ruth is probably timing me. She didn't say it should happen in a hurry, but I figure time is money.

I bring him over to the sink and run the warm water. I suds him up with Palmolive dish soap, the standard procedure. I'm washing this white hat extra good. I get some soap in the tip and he says, "Christ almighty, girl—" I guess it stings him.

I go, "Sorry." I dry him off with the towel and he's bigger every second that goes by. The soap didn't spoil it. I French him for a few minutes, thinking he might go off and that would be it, but he says, "Forget the rush act."

"Sure," I tell him.

"We're not having a race," he says.

I go back to it.

He pushes me onto the bed and I let him get on me. His tags fall across my nipples, still warm from his body.

I'm having a little trouble now. My heart's racing. My palms feel sweaty. I know what I'm supposed to do, but it doesn't seem so easy. Now that he's ready, my hole is too tight.

He says, "Hey, what's this?" He tries again. "I don't like it this tight," he tells me.

I tell him, "Shit, I'm trying."

"Hell," he says.

"Don't you believe me?" I say.

He doesn't want me asking him questions.

He can't get it in me. I'm just as surprised as he is. I know Ruth is going to be mad. I try shifting my hips. I'm concentrating, but my muscles are cinched shut.

"Shit," he says. "Now she didn't say anything about you having a cherry. I don't want to fuss with that. You still got your cherry?"

"I don't think so." I know I'm in for a bad report.

"Don't tell me it's honeymoonitis?"

"What?"

"Honeymoonitis. Brides get that. You don't have the same privilege as brides."

"Look, I'm real sorry," I tell him.

He's smiling, although I can see he's disappointed.

He rolls onto his back. He pulls my face down, but he has a dead rabbit. "Just finish what you started," he said.

He tells me to French him and use my middle finger. His asshole is tight, tighter than me. We see the coincidence and laugh. "Get that soap," he tells me.

"That Palmolive? You sure?"

I dot some soap on his ass until my finger slides in.

When he's finished, I tell him I could probably fuck him right now if he wants. I had a chance to relax.

"Maybe another time," he tells me.

He takes the cash from the radio and puts it right on the pillow. The money looks different against white muslin. Two tens and a five. That's more than two dollars a minute. I have to think of it like that.

I GO IN THE OFFICE to tell Ruth what happened. I tell her I was too tight. She would hear it from the customer next time he came back.

"That's a hysterical hymen." Ruth shakes her head. "That's disappointing news."

"It's a what?" I think Ruth must know everything about a girl's body, and maybe she found out I was deformed.

Ruth tells me, "It probably won't happen another time. It's the jitters. You should have had a little something beforehand to calm you down. Shit, why didn't I think of it? You turn out to be the nervous type, how could I know?"

She takes me over to the Elbow Room to celebrate my first trick. James is already there, so she doesn't broadcast it.

I get faced in twenty minutes. I go into the toilet and toss it up. I wipe my chin and go back out to James. He gives me the last inch of his drink. "Get back on the nag," he says.

"She doesn't want gin. She's turning green," Ruth says.

"She's fine. It's good for her."

The booze starts to erase my hard feelings. I'm in the Life now, Ruth is whispering. She looks at me different. James says Ruth is lining her own nest with every bit of flattery she hands out to her girls. But if you ask me, I think I have a lucky setup.

THE NEWS GETS OUT that the Paris has "fresh pink," and they're lining up. Ruth promises to take me along easy, and my next trick just wants to take pictures. Ruth tells me I don't have to flatback, he's just going to take some Polaroids. Rose Pearson won't let a trick take her picture, neither will Sharon or Peaches, so it's up to me. Rose says you don't know if you'll end up in someone's stroke book, and she doesn't want her picture to end up in the wrong hands.

I think it's just a picture. How can that be worse than when *we're* in their hands?

I take the Kodak trick back to a room. He snaps a roll and then he loads up again. Now he's saying, "Pull your lips apart. Let the pussy out."

I stand up and say, "That's enough of that." If he would just shut up. It's the mouth on some of these johns that gets under my skin.

Ruth tells me it's my turn at the peep window. I knew this was coming up.

Ruth says, "The *Goldfinger* routine is a breeze. You don't need much acting for that."

After that James Bond movie, Peaches was first to try it. Gold paint covered up her black skin. She disappeared all the way up to her hairline. Then she put on a blond wig. Rose says she looked like one of those statues they win at the Academy awards, one of those Oscars. I don't think it's the best thing for your skin. It's supposed to wash off with soap and water, but it takes some scrubbing. After I finish my act and take a shower, my pores are still glittering.

James said I looked like a lightning bug. He starts calling me "Bug." James doesn't mind me doing Goldfinger, but he never wants me to use Jergens or to stick that dust in my cunt. He says it's bad for my system.

Rose or Vanessa helps me get painted up. I dance in front of the windows, then I flop on the bed just like the scene in the movie when the girl is found dead. The act has to work up to a conclusion. It has to build tension, until the men are ready to shoot. That's when I bend over. They want to see my gold lips.

Then I get right into the shower. The paint swirls down the drain and I'm thinking I'd like to see the face on some prospector who finds this gold rinse water. He'll think it's the California Gold Rush.

I have some cash on me, and Ruth agrees to drive me to the bank to open my own account. It's after three o'clock; the bank is closed. I'm sure Ruth knows the regular banking hours, and she's trying something on me. I ask her to drive me back when it's open. In the meantime, Ruth has to cash me out, taking her carve-up from whatever I bring in. I have to trust she's giving me what I should get.

SINCE MY FREEZE-UP with Desert Boots in my early days, I've never had that problem again. I'm doing three to four tricks each afternoon, more at night.

James watches my routine but can't say anything since Ruth is in the driver's seat. She pays off Piers, who keeps riding James for debts James can't pay him. James never paid Piers for a suitcase of weed he was supposed to sell off in bulk, but which he divided into nickels and dimes. He did his own tidy business until it ran out. Piers expects James to fence enough items to settle that debt and another one since then. Even though he can't stop me, James treated me funny the first months I was working for Ruth.

"You smell like that chicken ranch," he tells me when I get in bed beside him. "Go take a shower."

"I took a shower."

"Well, you just get back in the shower and wash off those finger-prints."

He pretends I have cooties and ignores me while he watches Johnny Carson.

Ruth tells me to remember that we're paying *his* way. Ruth goes back into the kitchenette, where she's set up her adding machine, set-tling accounts for the owner of the theater. I wonder if she's figuring me in.

James says, "Listen to that. That's a miser. She's doing receipts dur-ing Johnny Carson."

I used to think sex was on his mind, but now I see it's money. Ruth knows all about that.

The other day I ask James, "Is that yours?"

"What's that?" he asks me.

"Did you drop that dime on the floor?"

"Where?"

"Right over there on the linoleum—by the Westinghouse. Is that *yours*?"

James walks over to the icebox to take a look. Is he going to bend down and pick up that dime someone left on the floor? Ruth and I watch him. We wait. I'm biting my lip to keep quiet.

He stoops over and looks at the shiny little coin. He sinks down on his heels. I hear one of his knees crack. He tries to finger that silver dime and pocket it. Just like Ruth and I thought. He can't resist.

The fact is, just a few minutes ago I nailed that trick dime to the floor.

I saw it in the five-and-ten, a real U.S. minted dime soldered to a tack.

When James realized the joke, he stood up and crossed his arms. Ruth slipped past him and tumbled outside. I inched past James, but he grabbed me. He threw me against the wall. The frying pans clanked on their hooks and the whole trailer shook on its blocks. He steered me against a doorjamb until my back was stabbing. I guess it was my kid-neys. I jerked away and jumped out the door. That's the first time James tried to hurt me and I guess the tide is still coming in.

Ruth was kicking the leaves and laughing her head off. Then we heard plates smashing. One dinner plate, then another. A big pop, then a wave of broken nuggets rolling across the floor, then another pop, another clatter of nuggets.

Ruth was grinning. Ruth's plates are heavy white china from a restaurant supply. They must have cost Ruth a little bit of money. Ruth is thrifty. She saves twist ties and rubber bands and cuts the rotten eyes out of potatoes. But as James slammed the plates, Ruth just stood there laughing. It was worth it to her. God, she must hate him.

WILMINGTON, DEL.

———

V ERONICA STANDS IN a tier of parochial school students at Sisters of Loretto Academy. The girls wear starched, bibbed dresses. For the class portrait, her jumper has been freshly pressed with a flat iron, its handle wrapped in an asbestos muff. Veronica stares directly into the camera, her innocent ten-year-old features contorted in a flirt. A new pencil dangles from a twine necklace, its point centered above Veronica's pelvis. Its glistening lead tip grazes her white bib, aiming at the tiny knob of her uterus, where I would grow. Her youngest child. The writer. The snitch.

I HAVE SAVED two passport pictures of Veronica, Karen and me. We were photographed together on separate occasions, once in 1955 for our residence in Italy when Ray worked at Fiat, and again in '64 when Ray took us on a business trip to Europe the summer Karen met Imran. Ray isn't pictured with our trio. He needed his own visa to come and go without us. Karen, Veronica and I are arranged elbow to elbow, one girl on either side of their mother. Veronica wears a cashmere sweater snug over her voluptuous shelf as she perches on a straight-back chair between us. Her two daughters flank her, organic props, weights, two poles of a magnet in which Veronica is a canceling, a reversing, force.

In the later photo, Karen has become as bosomy as Veronica. I can even see my own breasts poking unharnessed—tiny ice caps beneath my jersey. I brush my thumb over the tiny sepia square, fingering the hidden line of nipples. Our expressions from one decade to the next are almost identical. Here's the "littlest" still beaming; the stunning matriarch with her smoky eyes; the big sister staring directly at the aperture without self-conscious affect. The raised emblem of the official passport embossing gives these portraits a sad, historical implication.

T HE MONTH AFTER Karen disappeared, one of my classmates was killed in a wreck. There was a ceremony for the dead girl in the school gymnasium. The entire seventh grade filled the basketball bleachers to hear the principal's address. The junior high school color guard, in which the accident victim had been second twirler, presented individual, long-stemmed carnations to the girl's grieving mother until she had collected an unwieldy bouquet. The principal leaned too close to the microphone nozzle, which caused a piercing feedback and triggered exaggerated gestures from teachers who covered their ears with their rosters and lesson planners.

I wasn't paying attention until the principal announced my name. He asked me to come down to the podium. I didn't understand if I was being chastised for being inattentive, or if my assistance was needed, perhaps to carry the microphone stand back to the closet after the ceremony concluded. When I reached the lectern, the principal handed me a single carnation, a bloom identical to the untame flowers that the bereaved woman sorted in her hands. He invited the students to participate in a moment of silence for *my sister*, Karen Mitchell, and for the other girl, whose head had gone through the windshield of a Chevy Impala.

I waited beside the mother of the decapitated girl, tapping my carnation against my chin in shyness. The bleachers creaked as my classmates shifted their huge, dumb weight. I wanted the sagging planks to collapse and everyone to topple.

The instant that the principal dipped his face, signaling our moment of silence, I trotted away from the mother slumped in her public vigil. Running from the gymnasium, I dropped my carnation and tramped on it, ripping its golden head from the stem. The bloom skittered across the Hi-Gloss basketball parquet like a tiny doll's wig.

VERONICA'S HEART CONDITION and Ray's chronic ulcer were getting worse. Veronica kept her amber vial of nitroglycerine pills on her bedroom dresser, dead center in her cluster of Jean Patou bottles arranged on a mirrored tray. When I sneaked into her bedroom to spray some of the French perfume on my wrist, I lifted the smoked-glass prescription container and shook it to hear the tiny pills rattle. An unremarkable muted clatter, the same chalky resonance as baby aspirin. I saw her estrogen pills, which she had once kept on the kitchen sink until I started to swipe them. I thought they might add inches to my bustline. On the bureau with her medicines and scents, Veronica's ashtray was filled to the brim with lipstick-stained butts from her Kents. I emptied the butts into the toilet and wiped the ashtray until I could read its familiar warning, QUEL RIT VENDREDI, DIMANCHE PLEURERA—If you laugh Friday, on Sunday you will weep.

Ray drank Maalox right from the mouth of the bottle.

Veronica's obsessive-compulsive habit of checking the doors became worse. She went to the front door several times a day to test the locks. She stood at the picture window, hugging her elbows, as if she saw an apparition on the sidewalk. She looked like Blanche in *A Streetcar Named Desire*, who had shivered at the vision of a flower vendor dressed in black.

Those first weeks, Ray didn't want to stay in his office, and he drove his Econoline vans home, one after another, to do spot inventories in the driveway. He wanted to be with Veronica in case there was a phone call.

Only once had there been any information about my sister. A girl Karen had met at Grier School called Veronica one morning claiming that she had heard from Karen. She told Veronica what Karen had said: "I'm never going home. I have my own plans." But when Ray talked to the headmistress, she told him that the girl was a compulsive liar. There had never been any word from Karen. The "tip" was a prank phone call.

If I heard Veronica weeping while the television droned in the other room, I wondered if she was coming undone over Karen. She and Karen had often wept at television episodes of *Peyton Place* or *Dr. Kildare*, especially if one of Kildare's patients was a terminal case. When I heard her sobbing, I didn't inquire. It was such a helpless feeling. What could I do about finding Karen? I hoped Veronica was just reacting to a TV serial.

OFTEN, I CAME BACK to the house at dinnertime and saw the big black Lincoln Continental that belonged to Dr. Kerrigan, the family doctor. Ray's ulcer was under control, but sometimes the doctor indulged Veronica and stopped in to check her blood pressure. She got him to make a house call if she called him at the cocktail hour. I went into the house and found them in the bedroom.

"Where have you been?" Veronica asked me. "You never check in."

"I'm always here," I said to Veronica. "You just don't notice me."

"You make appearances," Veronica said.

I said, "Who does your dishes every night? You and Ray have to be Continental and eat at nine. I wash my dishes then I have to do *your* dishes two hours later. That's two shifts for the dishwasher. I'm like an Egyptian slave."

"You can't just be a slave? You have to be an *Egyptian* slave?" Veronica said, but she was pleased. If I was her Egyptian slave, then she must be an empress. She must be Cleopatra.

"You like my French cooking, don't you?" she said.

I relished any moment when Veronica pleaded with me for my approval. I crossed my arms and looked at the ceiling, making her wait for my decision. "Sure, I like your cooking. But you leave a mess."

Veronica used several mixing bowls and double boilers to make her French roux and sauces. She spent extra time to section green beans at opposite diagonals until each emerald spike looked like a De Beers creation. She sat me down beside her to teach me how to pare vegetables. If the new potatoes were larger than a walnut, she sliced them into opal half moons; she slivered carrots into julienne strips thin as yellow fuses.

"Is my mother all right?" I asked the doctor directly.

Veronica said, "My chest is tight."

"She'll be fine," the doctor said. His brogue seemed to creep in each time Veronica offered him some Dewar's. I saw their tumblers on the bedstand.

Then I heard Ray's footsteps in the front hall. He was singing "Rags to Riches," his wry theme every night when he came home from work. He did a good Tony Bennett imitation, and sang Bennett's two hits, "Stranger in Paradise" and "Rags to Riches," interchangeably. Since Karen's disappearance, his singing seemed forced. He came into the bedroom, his overcoat over his arm. He emptied his keys and loose change from his pocket onto the glass bureau top. He was going through two rolls of antacid tablets every day, and he crumpled the leftover silver wrappers so the doctor wouldn't see them. It didn't really matter, since there were chalky bottles of Maalox left out on the nightstand, but the doctor didn't ask Ray if he was following his "white diet." Potatoes, rice, pudding.

Veronica looked back and forth between the doctor and my father, taking drags from the stub of her cigarette, tinged Revlon pink. The doctor lifted the bottle of scotch from the bed table, knocking the rubber tubing of his stethoscope aside. He used the silver claw tongs to plop an ice cube from the crystal ice bowl into an empty tumbler, and he poured two fingers for Ray. The men stood at the footboard of Veronica's king-sized bed. She enjoyed a crowd of men, a retinue, a court. Sometimes even my stepbrother Alex would have joined her bedside vigil. He might have had a tiff with his young wife and had left her and his toddler son at their dinette table in the middle of a meal.

Alex's remarkable resemblance to the handsome model disturbed Veronica, and she couldn't always control her reaction to him. She struggled between opposite impulses—ingenue or matriarch. She was too hot or too cold with her son and could never find the right perch. Ray had learned to tolerate the intrusion, but Alex's presence added an edge.

Veronica had an eerie power over Alex; he sought her approval even as he tried to alarm her with his stints as a motocross champion or when he learned to fly biplanes. Finally, he established himself as a real estate speculator and construction tycoon. But none of his feats could erase what Veronica had told him from the very beginning—that his own father had never so much as laid eyes on him.

BEFORE KAREN DISAPPEARED, we went inside an abandoned house on Silverside Road. All its lights were blazing—the overheads, the table lamps, the porch lantern. Its furniture and knickknacks remained in their simple arrangements, as if the tenants had just stepped out to buy the evening newspaper or a loaf of bread. In fact, the police had taken the wife to jail for cashing stolen checks, but the husband had slipped out. The B&O tracks were just a hundred yards from the back of the house. Our churchgoing neighbors arrived to loot the place, collecting the scruffy furniture and houseware items to distribute to the needy. Women took the saltcellars and ripped the curtain panels off the window poles. Karen and I unpinned the lace doilies from the backs of the chairs, thinking Veronica might want them.

After Karen had vanished, I went back to the abandoned house. I thought she might have moved in and could be waiting for me there. The police had boarded all the doors and first-floor windows. Yet, on a second-floor landing there was a small porthole. A tiny velveteen house was glued to the circle of glass. It was a souvenir weather gauge like the one I had on *my* window at home. The velvet scene changes color when it's going to rain. The tiny velvet house glued to the *empty* house was a haunting emblem. I thought, These criminals have monitored the storms and sunshine just like I did. Indeed, it was the same sun metered out to all.

Yes, the sun still rose in the east, but east was not east.

Each morning, our streets were charged with sinister expectations that intensified all day until Ray came home at night.

When Veronica heard the garage door, she hurried to meet Ray in the mud room. "Any news?" she asked.

"Have *you* heard anything?" Ray said.

"Nothing."

"Nothing."

"*Anything* would be better than nothing," Veronica said.

After learning about Karen, our neighbors arrived with casseroles in the same way people bring covered dishes to a wake. Ray wouldn't eat casseroles. After growing up in an orphanage where everything was cooked to smithereens in stews and unidentifiable stockpots, he wanted his food separated on his plate. He would sit at the dinner table before an empty dish and with his index finger point to two o'clock, four o'clock, eight o'clock, directing Veronica where to place his steak, his potatoes, his green beans in compartmentalized heaps before him. Thank goodness Veronica had *me* to savor her cassoulet or pot-au-feu.

Then the neighbors stopped coming. I resided with my parents, but I no longer felt safe at home. I thought what had happened to Karen could happen to me. I recognized a mysterious "sister life" unfolding parallel to mine. I accepted its every nuance and encouraged its beautiful idea to emerge in any context I so desired.

During one interview, the FBI agent had said about Karen, "Sometimes a wallflower is in fact a wild seed."

The idea of a "contaminate seed" excited me. I imagined the contagion spore might have also invaded me and had already begun to flourish. Perhaps Karen and I were twinned in a pernicious mutation— little remnants of her soul had entwined with mine—like a grafted branch. Karen and I were *one*.

I tried to let go of my sister, but her hold tightened. An invisible root system thrived, just like the roots that had organized under our septic tank, expelling it upward until it warped the sod. I stood on the wayward hump of grass and bounced on my heels to make the hollow metal squawk. Ray called in the plumber to dig up the old tank. He hired landscapers to reseed the lawn. The grass thrived in a lush circle over the enriched soil.

HORSE FALLS
THROUGH ROOF

Each little ache or palpitation Ray or Veronica suffered was attributed to Karen's disappearance. I had no *physical* ailments; my repercussions from Karen's vanishing manifested in disturbing thoughts. I monitored random, natural deaths with scientific scrutiny. Walking home from the bus stop, my school friends went ahead of me. They weren't going to wait as I lingered at the carcass of a skunk or fondled a locust husk I found mucilaged to a tree trunk. When I looked up, my schoolmates had vanished; everyone had paired up for the afternoon. After Karen's disappearance, I was tinged by an unnameable taboo, and neighborhood kids ditched me. I became so self-conscious in my solitude, I created a spectacle.

I made relentless inspections and examined daily entomological catastrophes, the usual, common life forms that perished with little fanfare. I scraped snakeskin from the asphalt or picked at the dehydrated eyes of roadkill, peeling back the putrid layers of tissue. The rich stench was reassuring.

Then I loitered at a stream that snaked through the woods behind our house. The FBI had searched a beaver pool here when Karen was missing. I balanced on a few stepping-stones and searched the bottom gravel. I remembered the fairy tale "Girl Who Trod on the Loaf," about a selfish child who tossed a perfectly good loaf of bread into the water to get across a bog. For her unconscionable act, the girl sank away into the devil's abyss, her feet frozen to her loaf pedestal. Connecting the story of the marsh girl to my sister's disappearance was a curious gnawing fantasy. It was better to think of the fairy tale than to imagine what might have really happened to Karen. I collected salamanders from the stream and brought half a dozen home with me. I arranged them on a Limoges dinner plate to study them more carefully. With my fingertip I prodded their remarkable scaleless flesh as tender as pudding skin. To my horror, their porous spotted bodies dried up instantly, cementing the creatures nose-to-tail in a remarkable pattern around the rim of the dish. I couldn't scrape them off the china, and Veronica told me to soak the plate in my own bathroom sink so she wouldn't have to witness it. "What kind of hobby is that?" she asked me.

HORSE FALLS THROUGH ROOF was the surprising headline in the *Wilmington Journal*. At the local riding stables, a gelding had wandered up a ramp to a second-story hayloft; the planks were rotten and the horse crashed through the ceiling, skinning the meat off its shins. The photograph showed the long white tibia exposed from its knees to its pasterns. The horse had to be destroyed. Once, at Highland Stables, I had witnessed the humane procedure enacted. The veterinary assistant chased children away, but I sneaked back to watch the vet hammer a heavy metal pin through the bony socket above the horse's eyeball. The horse dropped where it stood. They needed a truck with a block and tackle to remove it from the courtyard. I thought it would have been more expedient to put the live horse in the truck first.

That same week, a neighbor's collie wrapped itself around a pole and died on its choke chain. It had not reversed direction to unwind its tether.

I was just keeping my eyes open.

A child two streets over had a metal plate inserted in his skull, necessitating that he always wear a helmet. The helmeted toddler pedaled his trike in monotonous circles. I began to look for this child whenever I walked up or down the neighborhood streets. The imperiled toddler had become my dark mascot. Then I saw the tricycle abandoned on the sidewalk, the peculiar helmet looped around the handlebars. I no longer saw his elliptical progressions, his furious pedaling, his threatened dome bobbing. I learned that the metal plate had caused a meningitis infection. The child "took a fever" and couldn't be saved.

Every week, Veronica drove me to the sawmill to collect wood shavings for the hamster cages at school. Ray knew the fellow who ran the operation, and I collected shopping bags of the golden bedding free of charge. The mill flanked the B&O tracks, and when trains rolled past, curls of pine shavings lifted in the drag and snowed down on us.

When we arrived one Thursday afternoon, police were stringing a yellow ribbon across the railroad tracks where a woman had thrown herself under a Chessie boxcar. Her body was torn in half, its two remnants covered by separate sheets. The twenty-six-car string had come to a halt, its huge Great Northern diesels still panting.

"Hurry up, hurry up," Veronica told me as I scooped the yellow shavings. "Don't gawk." But I wanted to see if the woman's body had been sliced straight up the middle or if she was cut across the waist.

The foreman at the mill told Veronica that the woman had been exercising her dog even in her suicidal temperament. He pointed to a small terrier, which in the aftermath still trembled on the hood of a police cruiser. An officer kept one finger looped under its collar. When the wind stirred the golden litter, the dog snapped at the air with furious aggression and choked on the shavings; its long tongue curled like a pink thong.

I craned my head and tried to see the severed woman.

"Why are you so morbid?" Veronica asked me.

Couldn't she see I did not think of death, *it thought of me*. Its parade was endless and never crested. Veronica was driving the Citroën when we met a migration of monarchs. The windshield was suddenly splotched with gold powder. Veronica started the wipers. I watched the creatures smeared back and forth, their polka-dotted thorax and feathered antennae ground into smithereens. On second thought, Veronica turned the wipers off. These throbbing specks were significant. Each daub of copper was part of a great chain of mortal events to which I was connected. I was linked to the girl in the crumpled prow, to the horse who fell through the roof, to the woman bisected by a boxcar, to the inscrutable masses of fauna, all sizes, that thrived or perished in hushed oblivion.

I suffered the razor edges of introspection. I experienced frozen trances of heightened perception in which time seemed suspended. At any moment, it happened. These "instants of clarity" could occur anywhere.

I was standing in the manure pile at Highland Stables, a dilapidated riding academy famous for its numerous citations from the Board of Health, where I worked every day mucking stalls after school in exchange for riding privileges. I breathed the strong ammonia rising from the soiled bedding, rich mountains of waste, an intoxicating anti-kitchen of steaming scents. There, in the hills of dung, I watched sunlight electrify spokes of golden oat straw. I noticed everything: the raw odor, the ribbons of steam curling higher, the gurgling fermentation, that miracle glimmer of urine-slick straw.

The juxtaposition of pure fifth and solar optics was thrilling. It wasn't kid stuff. I stepped into its yoke and shouldered the burden of *seeing* my surroundings. I didn't want to adjust or downsize its harness.

When I came home from the stables, encrusted in horse manure, Karen used to complain, "Your boots stink!" and she wouldn't let me keep them in the bedroom closet. She told me not to leave my hard hat on the floor with its sweaty browband; she had seen the cat pee in it. I no longer had to take orders from Karen, but I tried to imagine Karen without her own bedroom, without her own bed. Her precautions had given order to my life, and I was adrift without her daily comments.

The previous winter, Veronica drove Karen and me to the YWCA in downtown Wilmington where she had enrolled us in swimming lessons. She dropped us off and went to meet Ray at the Hotel DuPont for cocktails. It was snowing outside, and I thought it was because of the weather that Karen was reluctant to change into her bathing suit. The nippy temperature didn't encourage us to get out of our shetland sweaters. But in fact, Karen was frightened of undressing in the huge locker room with so many strangers, teens from other high schools and women of all ages.

I was anxious to swim and I peeled off my school clothes and stood beside my sister stark naked. Karen hadn't even removed her shoes. An attendant in a white uniform circled the open stalls, pushing a cart with a barrel of steaming swimsuits, all sizes, soaking in a bleach solution. The Y required all swimmers to wear these communal tank suits and return them to the bleach vat after each swimming lesson.

The attendant slapped a bathing suit on the bench next to Karen. "Here's a size twelve for you. Your little sister can wear a size eight."

Karen told the attendant, "I don't think we want to wear these bleached suits." She was remembering one summer when Veronica had laundered Ray's trunks and didn't rinse them. Ray put on his swimsuit and developed a serious rash from the telltale detergent. Veronica told him, "I thought you'd be going swimming, so why rinse them?" But Ray usually just lounged on the beach and didn't go into the water. Karen told me, "How lazy can she be to wash Dad's suit and never rinse it?"

The attendant stirred the mass of reeking nylon with a huge tongs. "You girls can't go in the water unless you put on a suit."

Karen saw I was already pulling my damp bathing suit over my hips. I was shivering in the cold locker room and wanted to jump in the heated pool. For my sake, Karen struggled with the moist, clinging tank suit and followed me out to the tiled enclosure where swimmers were splashing in the water. Before the swimming lesson started, there was a free period, and I paddled in the water with abandon. But the chlorine was so intense, my eyes closed up in five minutes. I screamed when my vision blurred and Karen's face became a smudged and fleshy mask; I couldn't make out her features. She pulled me from the water, scolding me for swimming with my eyes *open*.

We dressed and waited in the downstairs lobby for Ray and Veronica to retrieve us. My eyes were still stinging. All I could see were smears of neon from the Woolworth's marquee across the street. To soothe me, Karen bought a red Santa Claus lollipop from a canister at the front desk, from which all proceeds would go to a Shriner children's hospital. I stared at the sucker. Its glassy red bauble twinkled, exaggerated in my half-blind state. The candy warped the light with a kaleidoscope effect and it was just too beautiful to eat.

"Aren't you going to taste that?" Karen asked me.

Karen's eyes weren't blurred by the chlorine and she didn't see the miraculous gift she had given me.

WITH KAREN GONE, I was left vulnerable to my own reckless actions, like a bouncing ball without its backboard. Even worse, I was vulnerable to my *reactions*. Without her opposite, I was taxed by intrusive, around-the-clock reflections. My interior life took over.

Veronica noticed a shift in my moods. "You could try to crack a smile now and then," she said. "You could make an effort."

If I suddenly grew teary, she ripped a tissue from the box and handed it to me, but she didn't try to console me. She gave me the tissue because she didn't like tears; tears were physical evidence of my unhappy condition. I learned to quickly sear off my blubbering with my own interior insults, self-inflicted tomboy asides that I fashioned after the comic Don Rickles.

I snarled one-syllable ironies out loud, like *"Nice!"* and *"Perfect!"* when, of course, I meant the opposite. "So, shoot me!" I said, if I caught myself teetering in sentimental terrain or revealing too much. Then I heard John Lennon interviewed on the radio and I adopted his intolerant mannerism, "Oh *bloody* this, *bloody* that."

Only Ray's presence could crack my steely reserve. Ray was able to crack my shell. I might weaken, turn to mush and run into his arms. When he came home from work, I waited as he switched on the hi-fi and jammed a stereo album onto the silver spindle: *Jazz All-Stars with Sarah Vaughan*. He sat down to read the paper in his recliner. I wanted to climb into his lap. One time, when I approached him, he forgot that the footrest was extended. He stood up and crashed to the carpet, upsetting the lamp; the needle gouged the record.

KAREN AND I are very young, six and eight years old. We stand with Veronica outside the PennFruit Supermarket. We are wearing matching white sundresses in graduated sizes. Cool bleached-linen jumpers.

The three of us link hands and walk abreast, like a strip of paper dolls. Our tripled shadow spills across the concrete in a whimsical zigzag.

Then Veronica drops our hands.

R AY TOOK US to the same Cape Cod cottage every summer. Beach grass whipped in circles, stinging my shins; tankers steamed into the mouth of the canal; plovers trotted across the flats— their four-pointed tracks like jacks tossed in the sand. This panorama had always held up until the year we went to Cape Cod without Karen.

Without my sister beside me, usual summer delights seemed skewed and akimbo, like a gaudy beach umbrella ripped loose from its spokes. The "family vacation" seemed forced.

I no longer gorged myself on watermelon hearts Ray picked up at the jam kitchen. The kitchen used only the rind for watermelon pickle and there were tubs of fresh red wedges from the center of the fruit. Karen and I had raced to devour the icy chunks, holding them in our bare hands until the juice drizzled down our throats and over our tanned bodies, staining the sand pink at our feet.

Without Karen next to me, I only picked at the mealy hunks.

Veronica tips a shiny colander against her hip and walks into the raspberry patch like a goddess. Together, we pick the berry crop until the thorny half acre is pillaged—our odd jars and splatterware bowls mounded with fruit. I pull out the hem of my white cotton jersey and load up its hammock. I sample the fattest specimen, savoring its soft flannel skin before bursting its crimson bleb against the roof of my mouth. Its stain wicks deeper and deeper—

It isn't the same without Karen.

Between each Cape Cod vacation, the arctic sheet advances again.

I began to blame Veronica for what had happened to Karen. If she showed me a little affection, each instance made me suspicious. I'd rather invent Veronica's ulterior motives than ingest her placebos. Her every act of maternal kindness created its antigen in me.

Yet once or twice she went out of her way to please me. When I wanted bell-bottom jeans at the dawn of that fashion but I couldn't find them in stores, Veronica sewed the jeans for me, making the flared cuffs to my exact specifications. She worked through the evening at her Singer sewing machine. She measured my hips and drew her own pattern with a stick of chalk, marking crisp bolts of denim. She kneeled on the floor slicing a tiny blade across the heavy fabric until the pant legs ballooned according to my expectations.

That same winter, I was arrested with a circle of hoods, accused of "spending the night in a condemned building" where we had shared tabs of acid, rolled joints and tipped back a cumbersome jug of apple wine, sloshing its sweet contents. We tore through boxes of TastyKake Krimpets, and the cockroaches scrawled over the sticky wrappers. At the family court hearing, the judge scolded me for my poor school record, which he held up over his lectern, shaking its tissue pages. The report stated that I had been suspended from the high school for wearing "radical attire." I had insisted on wearing the bell-bottoms Veronica had sewn even though they weren't permitted in the dress code. I was pulled into the vice principal's office, and he told me to change into my gym clothes. I refused to remove my bell-bottoms. I told the vice principal, "I have a math test this period. I guess I'll have to miss it." I wouldn't change into my gym clothes and the vice principal sent me home.

When the family court judge implied I was a ringleader, Veronica rose from her seat and said, "Why are you picking on her? The criminals are sitting over there!" She glared at the older boys seated with their jaded guardians. After all, I was only one of five pot-smoking trespassers.

I was thrilled when Veronica stood up for me. Indeed, she rose from her chair and "stood up." I basked in her fiery protest, which proved her allegiance to me. She supported our youth movement; in fact, she had sewn my uniform—

But Veronica went on to tell the judge that she wasn't responsible for my disheveled appearance or for my obscene school record. "That's her own descent into hell," she told the judge.

RAY RECEIVED A PHONE CALL from the director of Highland Stables. The riding academy had decided to sell my favorite horse, Dreamboy, at the auctions. He might go to slaughter for Ken-L Ration. The gelding wasn't valuable and was no use in the riding school. The horse was "navicular," clubfooted in one hoof, and it had to wear special "banked" shoes that the farrier made to order. Did my parents want to purchase this horse with a clubfoot for three hundred dollars? It might save their daughter a lot of grief.

Ray paid the three hundred dollars. That seemed like a lot of cash to me. Certainly, this spontaneous gift, my beloved Dreamboy, was the most colossal example of my parents' affection for me.

In return for the horse's boarding fee, I would work at the barn every afternoon after school, organizing the manure pile. That would be an extra three hours a day that Veronica wouldn't have me underfoot. *Don't tell me she wasn't thinking of it that way.*

After I finished cleaning stalls and breaking up sheets of ice in the claw-foot water troughs, I saddled Dreamboy and rode out into the open fields. We galloped until sundown, when the last light skimmed the hillside. I reined in Dreamboy at the crest of a hill to watch crows returning to roost, the distant flocks sifting over the woods like black pepper. Then I maneuvered Dreamboy parallel to the setting sun to make our silhouette. I liked to imitate the familiar Frederic Remington bronzes of cowboys on horseback, lonesome figures of independence and steely self-reliance. I watched our dramatic shadow until it dissolved. I stayed in the saddle as long as I could stand the cold. The horse snorted plumes of frozen breath, but I didn't put him up in the barn until I was sure Veronica missed me. I waited as long as I could before I called to tell her I was ready to come home.

Ray later told me, "I figured if you had a horse in the picture, you wouldn't take off like Karen."

Ray invented other methods of keeping me near. One month, he paid me well to come to his warehouse after school to perform odd, unnecessary jobs like sorting drawers of bolts and screws or licking labels for file folders. I was certain he stirred up the bolts each night so I'd have more to sift through the next day. During my lazy agenda, he took me out for ice-cream drinks whenever I looked exasperated. I was of absolutely no use to him or to his secretary Grace, but for some reason, Ray wanted me to come down to the warehouse and be in his domain for part of each day.

I SEARCHED THROUGH Veronica's dresser drawers looking for an expensive Liberty silk scarf she said I had borrowed and never returned. I told her, "I gave it back to you last week, I'm sure I did." I stalled when I recognized the shelf paper lining the bottom of one drawer. There it was—the brown paper sheet on which Karen and I had inked our footprints months before. My slender track—just five little spots for the toes, a trim ball and crescent and a snip of heel—was paired with Karen's full footprint, a generous wedge of dark ink.

Veronica must have fished the sheet out of the wastebasket and used it to line her bureau. I didn't like seeing the contrast again. The footprint artifact seemed both a cherished memento and proof of our estrangement. Like a gravestone rubbing or like the much revered cave art that celebrates our first human link—I was in awe of it.

WHITE DIET

R AY'S STOMACH CONDITION accelerated and put him in the hospital for a week. When Veronica visited his room, she got into Ray's bed, pulling the sheet to her chin. She complained to the nurses and asked them to take her pulse and blood pressure. She asked for aspirin and ice water.

When I visited Ray after school, I found her lolling in Ray's bed and Ray sitting beside her in the plastic chair, his IV tangled up. I screamed at Veronica, "Get out of that bed!" She ignored my reproach and rotated her hip under the sheet. She was stretched out, her head propped on one hand like an idle sunbather.

"What are you doing?" I said.

"All right, all right," Ray said, trying to calm me down.

I tugged Veronica's arm until she sat up and found her pumps. When she had her shoes on, she hopped down and Ray got back into the bed, looking more than relieved to be lying flat.

The next day, I visited Ray alone. The same aluminum pitcher of ice water was sweating on the bedstand, his Chesterfield was propped in the huge Cinzano ashtray Veronica had brought from home. There was something foreboding, even fatalistic, about the colorful ashtray spilling untidy worms of ash on his bedclothes.

The whole ward was thick with cigarette smoke. Patients were allowed to smoke and had their names written on personal cartons of Winstons, Salems, whatever, which were kept at the nursing station. Nurses were supposed to monitor their intake, but they delivered new packs to patients whenever anyone asked for more.

After one week in the hospital with a bleeding ulcer, Ray's face looked blanched like a miner who never sees any sun. His eyes were circled with exhausted shadows. At fifty-three, Ray had a couple of exquisitely deep furrows running the width of his brow, lines so permanently etched they looked as if they were made with the tip of a trowel and set in cement.

Ray was back on a "white diet." Rice, potatoes, codfish, steamed chicken, everything pureed into starchy puddles on his plate. The doctor encouraged Ray to consume more milk products, but Ray wasn't a milk drinker.

I sat down beside Ray and handed him a wooden box. A wheel of cheddar cheese.

"What have we got here?" he said, smiling.

"It came to the house for you," I told him. "There's a note."

As always, whenever Ray accepted gifts from Karen or me, he said, "You shouldn't have spent your money. All I ever want is *a kind word and a smile*."

I grinned in compliance as I gave him the box of cheese; then I walked to the huge window that looked over the Brandywine River. I crossed my arms and massaged my elbows to subdue my rising panic during the transaction.

I listened to him unfold the envelope. The room was silent while he read the card.

The note said: "For Dad, please get well soon. —Your loving daughter, Karen." Karen had had the habit of looping her double "l's" like rabbit ears, but I had probably gone overboard in my imitation.

When I finally turned around to face him, our eyes locked, but his initial shock shifted into a brief ulceric spasm, then back to his ordinary warmth for me. He said, "Nice try."

I suddenly understood that Ray, in his difficult hospital routine, hadn't been remembering Karen. I had dredged it up again, reminding him that even in that private room, deep in the Pine Sol-scrubbed labyrinth of a Catholic hospital, when his innards were raw as a blister, he still had an unsolved problem.

He looked at me as if he were seeing one daughter transposed on his other daughter, as if it were Karen who stood sniffling before him.

VIRGINIA BEACH

(KAREN)

I T'S CHRISTMAS EVE again, my second with Ruth and James. The Paris is closed for the night. All the regular meatballs are home with the wives and kids. This afternoon, I found some Christmas cards in Ruth's desk, sample drawings by that polio victim who has to sketch with a pencil in her teeth. I addressed one of these cards to my sister. I walked to the post office. People were busy wrapping presents right there on the counter. They had their paper, their ribbon, they had their Scotch tape. I bought a stamp and put it on the envelope. Then I crumpled it up and tossed it in the trash can. What if they traced it back here?

Christmas at Bailey's Trailer Village is one of the loudest sights I think I ever saw. Cars on Shore Road slow up to look at the trailers lit up like satellites. It's nice to see some strings of lights when usually the place looks run-down and lonesome. Ruth put me to work twisting plastic evergreen garlands around the Expando awning. A full-sized Santa Claus sleigh sits on the roof of that old bilevel Pacemaker next door. Hope it doesn't fall through. You wouldn't see that in my old neighborhood.

Ruth found two electric angels. I put them in the window, but the sill isn't wide enough and the angels shiver off when the door slams shut. It's getting to be a joke, how many times I keep setting those angels back.

James went out to get a little tree. He took a hacksaw and walked a little ways up Shore Road where some scrub pine are growing on a traffic island. There was a flurry of snow coming off the Chesapeake Bay, just enough to have the cars leave black strips in the slush. James came back with a tiny pine tree, a perfect shape. "I took it right off the top," he tells me.

I can picture what he left behind—that poor tree without its better half.

James put the tree in a Budweiser ice bucket and tried to stand it up. Someone was knocking at the door. It was a state trooper. He came inside. His leather gloves smelled strong, liked he just oiled them. The trooper tells James that he followed his slushy tracks directly from the traffic island. The tracks led right up to our door.

"Brilliant," Ruth says.

"I'm giving you a citation for theft of ornamental landscaping on state highway property."

"Ornamental landscaping? You're saying those tree-size weeds are part of the DOT beautification program?"

"May I see some identification?" the trooper said. He took James's driver's license and copied the information on a form, then he ripped the top sheet of the citation and handed it to James.

"Since when is Shore Road a state highway?"

Ruth says, "That's Route 60, James. You know that. It goes on up the coast to Hampton Roads Bridge-Tunnel."

"Will you shut up," he tells her.

The trooper was looking at me. I was spreading butter on a slice of white bread and spilling spoonfuls of sugar on it from the sugar bowl. I folded it over and took a delicious bite. Butter and sugar are complimentary flavors. It's what James calls an "Irish sandwich," I don't know why. He taught me another one with potato chips and mustard on Wonder bread; that's a "white trash burger." I showed him the one I like: Miracle Whip, peanut butter and Red Delicious apples sliced paper thin.

Ruth told me if anyone ever shows up, I should make myself at home. I poured a big glass of whole milk. I took a big swallow and gave myself a milk mustache. Ruth eyed me like I was overdoing it.

"Merry Christmas," the trooper said as he stepped out. He saw the puny pine tree resting in the old Budweiser ice bucket, the Clydesdale horses circling with their frilly fetlocks. He nodded his head as if he could appreciate the idea behind it, even if James had stolen it. When he slammed the door, the electric angels fell off the windowsill.

Ruth and James have been sharing their dope and swigging eggnog since noon. I drink it right out of the carton before Ruth puts the rum in. Rum or not, it's too rich for my system.

James has the Yule Log on the television. The log flickers while the TV plays Christmas carols, but the Yule Log looks ridiculous on a ten-inch screen, like a flickering cigar.

James is getting drunk on that eggnog. Ruth tells me he has a bad history with that particular drink.

"When my kids were small, I bought them six baby ducks at Easter. James made a big punch of eggnog on Easter Sunday, and when he wasn't looking, my boys put their baby ducks in the punch bowl. You know kids. They wanted to see the ducks swim."

"That was a perfectly good quart of rum," James interrupts Ruth. "A whole fucking quart of rum ruined with duck shit."

Ruth says, "What does James do then? He takes those ducks out of the punch. They don't look too good—they're drunk. They're belly-up."

"Cross-eyed on *my* rum," James says.

"He buried every one of those poor little ducks in the sandbox up to their necks. It's just a row of yellow necks sticking up. The tomcat from the trailer next door is sitting there washing his paws. He's already chewed off one of those ducks' heads, right in front of my boys—"

James says, "Those ducks didn't feel a thing. They died of alcohol poisoning. They were basted." He stands up and stretches his arms. "You girls better watch out or I'll bury you up to your necks. Then I'll borrow someone's lawn mower—"

This is love talk. I want to know if he's talking to Ruth or talking to me.

We give James a tide clock for his Christmas present. Ruth and I went in on it together. The tide clock tells exactly what hour the tide comes in and when the tide goes out. Its face is painted to mark the rising and falling tide, with high at twelve o'clock and low at six. The half tides are marked in between.

James likes everything to do with the sea, but he only likes the water from *on deck*. He has to be onboard a carrier to enjoy the ocean. But since he did time in the navy brig at Big Portsmouth, he'll never be invited back on a ship.

Next, James gives me my gift. It's a big china cat, just like I said I wanted. It's just like the Pink Panther, the color of bubble gum with slitty jade-green eyes. I tell him I like it. But come on, a pink cat?

Ruth gets her steak knives and the magnetized rack that goes on the side of the ice box. James wants to show her how strong the magnet strip is and he tries to move a can of beans across the table.

At the last minute, we decide to go to midnight mass. James drives us to a fancy church over in Norfolk. We sit down in the back pews and listen to the children's choir. James is reeking from weed and from rum, and people slide farther down the pew, unhappy to see us sit down.

The collection basket comes along, passing into Ruth's hands, then into James's lap. I'm sure James is going to take something *out*. Fifty-dollar bills and twenties are left one on top of the other. Envelopes look fat, like wads of greenery are tucked inside them. James holds the basket under his nose as if he's sniffing a basket of fresh biscuits or crescent rolls. He puts a hundred-dollar bill in the basket and stirs it around.

I see the hundred and gasp. The congregation turns around to find me.

James is enjoying my surprise. "We don't chizz the lord on Christmas," he tells me.

Ruth is grinning. I see the churchgoers are shifting in their seats to look at us.

"No, we don't cheat Jesus on his birthday," James says.

James hands the collection basket to the next row. He's smiling a big smile. Giving God a hundred-dollar bill is his way of tossing off an insult. He's saying, "I don't need this hundred-dollar bill as much as you, God."

RUTH SAYS, "I'm going to buy a popcorn machine."

I sit up in bed. "Popcorn?" I say. "I love popcorn."

Veronica always makes popcorn for the TV movie, a big stainless-steel bowl of it. She holds it in her lap and rests one of the Baccarat salt-cellars on the arm of the sofa—a little crystal shaker with a sterling cap that holds just a thimble of salt.

Ruth says, "I need some candy or something in the lobby. Something legit. Just for looks. We don't have to sell the stuff."

"Well, I could eat some popcorn right now," I tell Ruth. "I'm just about starving. You two eat like birds. Well, I'm not a bird, you know."

Ruth looks at James. "Drive over to the minimart and get some Jolly Time for Karen."

He takes his time standing up. Then he gets his jacket and the car keys and walks out the door. He doesn't like getting bossed. Ruth walks over to her desk and finds my new supply of Ortho pills, a stack of little pink wheels with foil backing. She has hundreds of these wheels sorted and wrapped in rubber bands. Piers pinched them from some pharmacy supply in Richmond. Ruth says, "Here's your refill for your pills."

I've been taking one of these pills every morning for a year. Ruth says, "Girls can't bleed on business days."

I go off the pill for a week every few months, just to flush myself out.

I take the foil refills and put them away.

"These have been helping your acne, don't you think? It's clearing up." Ruth holds my chin and turns my face from side to side to examine my skin.

"I think you're right," I tell her. My complexion is smooth.

But next I get a sore throat. I can't swallow.

Ruth takes me to Emergency so the doctor can look at my tonsils. He twirls a long Q-tip at the back of my throat to get a gram stain in case I caught clap doing half and half.

Two weeks later, I get something else from a trick, blisters all over, tender burning spots. These sores bring a fever. Ruth gives me the big green bottle of Phisohex to wash the blisters. Then I use Ruth's compress routine for a couple days; it's not helping. Even James takes a rain check.

Ruth tells me all the girls went through this stage. "Ask Valerie—her sores were stubborn."

Ruth got after me to go back to work. I'm hardly on my feet and I've got a line of clients. I can't look at these guys without thinking what kind of secret rash they might pass on to me. What will I pick up next?

Monday afternoon, I decide not to go into work. I see Winn Dixie is hiring girls. I go in and talk to the assistant manager. He signs me up to hand out promotional samples in the cookie and cracker aisle. There's a special on Nabisco and they need girls to hand out Ritz crackers to the shoppers. He gives me a cocktail apron and puts me behind a card table. He hands me a little cheese slicer. I'm handing out cheese slices making chitchat with old ladies. I'm eating my own samples. One customer tries to brush crumbs off my blouse and I smack his hand.

I can't imagine doing this forty hours a week.

I step outside for a minute to mull it over. I find myself walking over to the Paris. I've still got the apron on. Next time I do the peep window, I think I'll wear the Winn Dixie apron and that's all. Men will like seeing the Winn Dixie apron on a naked girl. Their wives do their shopping at that store. The apron doesn't cover my ass. Cocktail aprons, nurse's uniforms, baby-doll clothes—costumes do a lot of the work for us.

ONE NIGHT I GET out of bed and go to the toilet. I try to pee, but I can't start the flow. I feel a sharp pain—like a hot marble is falling through me. I look at the bowl and see a skinny rope of blood, just a dribble, dissolving in the water.

Ruth tells me "You must have a clot."

I tell her, "Shit. I'm going to burst."

"You have a bruise," Ruth says. "That happens to the best of us. You'll have to change your routine for a while. No more banging, just French."

She gives me some sulfa tablets, big horse pills. But I'm in no shape to work and I stay in bed for two days.

In my sickbed, I dream about the white footprints. Ruth says I'm feverish. These dreams play with my head. It's my little sister. She's tricking me with these footprints, trying to lead me back. A man starts to chase her. He follows her white footprints on the asphalt. Her footprints are small. Her arch is high. "Leave my sister alone," I scream. He trails the white footsteps, but she's way ahead of him. The footprints dry up in the sun.

THE RCA COLOR SET

(Karen)

My name is Aunt Sarah
My skin is yellow
My hair is long
Between two worlds I do belong

My father was rich and white
He falls to my mother late one night
What do they call me?
My name is Sephronia

My skin is tan
My hair is fine
My hips invite you
My mouth like wine
Whose little girl am I?
Anyone who has money to buy
What do they call me?
My name is Sweet Thing
My name is Sweet Thing

My skin is brown
My manner is tough
I'll kill the first mother I see
My life has been tough

I'm awfully bitter these days
Because my parents were slaves
What do they call me?
My name is Peaches!

JAMES WANTS TO get rid of some stamps in North Carolina. We've already been to fourteen redemption centers in Virginia, West Virginia and into Maryland. James has got a friend at Isothermal who can unload some merchandise, and James wants to make a connection there. There was a hard freeze this morning. It's our first bit of real winter, and the heater in the Newport isn't going. This old nylon windbreaker, with its Clemson tiger paw on the sleeve, isn't warm enough. I need a new winter coat. I tell James, "I'm not driving all that way without a heater."

"It warms up once we get in Tarheel country."

"I'm an ice cube."

"There's a car blanket."

"You can't melt an ice cube by wrapping it up. That's how you keep it ice."

I know this because Ray told me about an icehouse where he worked as a kid. The place didn't have electricity, and they kept blocks of ice frozen all summer surrounded by bales of straw. When I heard that story, I thought of Veronica. Some people are like that icehouse— all wrapped up. "Wrapped up in herself" is what they call it. Coming into North Carolina on Route 17, men stand on the side of the highway tending oil barrels set over fires. James tells me these barrels are curing some boiled peanuts. James stops to get us some of these boiled peanuts, thinking it might warm me up.

I stretch my legs while James talks to the men behind the boiling drum. I look at the steam rising off the brine. The men are watching me. I'm used to it.

A man asks James, "Hey, is she your daughter?"

James watches who's talking.

The man says, "She your little sister? No? She a baby ball and chain? No shit?"

James is laughing with the men. They hear what they want to hear. See what they want to see.

◆ ◆ ◆

JAMES IS SUPPOSED to meet his friend at Isothermal at eight o'clock tonight. We walk into the Forest City S&H Green Stamp Redemption Center. It still has its Christmas decorations on the plate-glass windows, but I see the woman behind the counter has been cutting out a chain of hearts from red construction paper, getting ready for Valentine's. James looks at the big RCA color set on display. It's a twenty-four-inch screen, with Instant On, just like the others we've picked up in Virginia. We have two shopping bags full of S&H books with us. James fills out the form and hands it to the clerk. She reads the sheet and tells him she'll be ordering the set. It won't come in for another week.

"You'll be ordering it?" he asks her.

"That's right. This item has to be special-ordered. We had a few sets, but they're all gone since Christmas. It's not every day people walk in here and ask for that big RCA."

"I *walked in*, didn't I?" James says.

The lady looks nervous as she arranges a stack of flyers on the glass counter. I take one and read about a church supper. What they call a "bean supper." Slivers of frankfurter mixed in with the baked beans. There's usually cornbread. Maybe some carrot slaw. Bread pudding after. I'd like to ask if this bean supper is tonight.

"You don't have this exact model in stock?" James asks her. It's that sugar-coated voice he uses when he's going to sting you like a yellow jacket.

The clerk steps back from the counter and crosses her arms. Her eyeglasses have pink rhinestones that wink when she bobs her head. She says, "I'll be happy to order that RCA set. Is that all right with you?"

James tells her, "I'll just take this one here."

"That's the store model," the clerk tells him.

"The store model is fine," he tells her.

"Ya'll can't take that one."

"I've got my books right here. They're all counted. But you go ahead, count 'em if you want."

He follows the cord to a floor socket. He pulls out the plug and

winds the cord around his elbow and the crook of his thumb until he's
got it curled in a few neat loops.

The clerk tells us we can't take that set until we've signed a name
on the form. James comes back to the counter and takes the ballpoint
from the clerk. He signs a name.

The set is a big metal console with artificial wood veneer. A UHF
loop and retractable rabbit ears are hinged on the back. It's standing on
four short tube legs with chrome skid pads. It doesn't have castors like
some of them and can't be rolled out to the car.

James asks the lady, "You got a dolly?"

She shakes her head.

James sees she's got a bright green Craftsman dolly right behind
the counter. He walks over there and takes the dolly for himself.

The woman is dialing the telephone.

I'm surprised to hear her say, "Hello, Sis—" I was sure she was dialing her boss or the police. She starts to tell the story while it's happening. "They come right in here. That's right. He says he's come for
the RCA. That's what he says. His girl is Gina's age—"

James puts the set on the dolly while the clerk is talking. He's grinning. He's enjoying the fact that the clerk finds what he's doing a form
of excitement. He wheels the set out of the redemption center. I hold
the door so it won't scratch the TV screen. The woman is still on the
telephone as we are putting the RCA set in the back seat of the car.
James pulls the car blanket over the set. He puts the dolly in the back
seat. "I can use one of these," he says.

He straightens up. He laces his fingers behind his head and twists
his trunk, trying to unknot his back. I see the woman behind the
counter, still on the telephone. She must be saying, "Now they've got
it in the car—"

JAMES TAKES ME SHOPPING for a jacket. We stop at the Gaylords
and I look at the car coats. There are some nice imitation camel-hair
jackets.

James says, "One day, I'm going to put you in a mink coat."

"When will that be?"

"I'll surprise you."

"That *would* surprise me."

He lifts the tag on my cuff. "This is fifty-nine. That's too high."

"I'm not walking out of here without a winter coat," I tell him.

"You want to walk out? That your idea?"

I look at him. I see what he means. "Maybe I will."

"See that door there?"

"That one?"

He pulls my hand down. "Don't go pointing out your getaway door," he tells me. His jaw is tight. He smiles. His shelf of teeth are too white.

I turn back to the rack of coats and pluck at the sleeves.

"Look, I'm going over there to ask about their layaway plan while you take that exit."

"You're going to do what?"

"I'll go up to the Jewish piano and fill out a form for layaway. You wear that coat outside."

"You'll be at the Jewish piano? Where's that?" I don't see a piano in the store.

"I'll be at that cash register," he tells me. "When you get to the car, put the coat under the seat. Got it?"

I back out of the aisle, turn on my heel and leave the store. I walk over to the Newport.

The car is locked because we've got the RCA right there on the back seat. I guess James forgot it was locked when we started stealing *something else*. I peel off the coat and shove it into a ball. I kick it under the car, beside the front wheel.

I left my Clemson windbreaker in the Gaylords. I'm shivering. James comes out and gets into the driver's seat. I sit down next to him. He's studying the mirror.

"Are they watching?" I say.

"They're asleep," he tells me. "It's beautiful."

I open my door and reach under the car for my new coat. They treated the street that morning and I brush salt off the collar. "Good as new," I tell him.

"I used to say that about you."

"Say whatever you want." I insert my arms in the quilted sleeves and push the barrel clasps through the loops. I start to unpin the price tag from the cuff. James says, "Let me do it." At a red light, he takes my wrist in his lap and unhooks the tiny golden pin. "Thanks," I tell him, thinking he's being a help. What does he do? He jabs the back of my hand with the open pin. It's his kind of joke. He stabs me again.

I burst into tears, I don't know why.

I'm crying at the red light, holding my face in my hands. A police cruiser comes alongside. James is grinding his jaw under a fake smile. He tells me to shut up. The officer motions to James. James waits for the light to change, rides across the intersection and steers the Newport over to the curb. The policeman comes to my window first and leans down to look in the glass. He winds his wrist in a circle. I crank the window down.

"Everything okay, honey?" he asks me. I'm wiping my nose on the brand-new sleeve of my jacket. The officer is eyeing James.

"This your daughter, sir?"

"That's right," James says.

"Why's she so upset?"

"Got a bad grade at school," James tells the officer.

"Really? All those tears for your report card? That's a shame. You a sophomore at Beaver Dam?"

"Well, she ain't at Beaver Dam," James said.

"You're not a pupil at Beaver Dam? Now, where is it you go to school?" the policeman asks me.

"She attends school in Virginia," James tells him.

"I'm asking *her*," the officer warns James. "What you doing down here, middle of the week like this? It's not a federal holiday, is it?"

James says, "We came down to visit my sister. She's got that brown lung. She's got to have oxygen."

"Sorry to hear that. I guess she's been working at Burlington mill? There's not a factory girl who don't have it in some form. It's not just the old-timers." The officer walks around to James and asks for his license and registration. He tells James to remove the blanket from the TV set. "That's a big color set you have back there. You have the bill of sale on that?"

"That's my sister's. She needs it at her house," James tells him.

He's scraping his chin with the cardboard price tag of my stolen coat. He flicks it back and forth across his new whiskers; the little golden pin dangles from a piece of thread.

"That your hand truck?" the officer asks James.

"It's a nice one, isn't it?" James says.

The officer gives James his driver's license. He steps back from the door and stoops down to take another look at me. He tells James he can go on. But the officer trails us a few lengths back. He follows us onto the interstate. James decides not to meet that fellow at Isothermal and heads north again to blow off that cop. He's got himself another TV set to take back to Fort Knox. Even that booster Piers won't want it. After a few miles, the cruiser pulls off the highway onto a turnaround. I just know he thinks *I'm not who I am*, but he lets us go.

SHRINER NIGHT

(Karen)

Hendrick squeezes Clairol lotion onto my scalp and works the peroxide into my hair. His fingernails are so long and sharp I can feel them through his rubber gloves. All five girls, make that six if you count Hendrick, are at the trailer for lunch. Ruth has a "round-table" once a month.

The girls all agree I should go lighter.

Hendrick says, "You're golden blond already, so you can go plat-inum and get away with it." He works the smelly solution into the ends, piles my hair on the top of my head and removes his rubber gloves. He sets the Lux timer for twenty minutes. He takes his joint from the ashtray and lights it again, pinching the yellowed twist of paper between his pointy nails.

Ruth sets a bowl of macaroni salad in the center of the table, sur-rounded by quartered tomatoes. She serves us portions with an ice-cream scoop. Rose Pearson is standing at the counter slicing a canned ham. She scrapes the gelatin off with a table knife and licks the blade clean.

"I'm not wild about eating my lunch with that peroxide smell ru-ining the taste of everything," Rose says.

"She'll rinse it out in fifteen minutes," Hendrick says.

"It's burning my eyes," I tell him.

"What do you think? It's stripping your hair. It's got to be strong."

"You better watch out, he's burned his own hair twice. That's why he wears those scarves."

"He's just bald."

"Bald with tits."

I stare at the macaroni salad on my plate. The pimento slivers are bright and slimy. I pick them off.

"What's the matter? You don't like roast peppers?" Ruth asks me.

"Maybe not with mayonnaise."

Ruth digs the ice-cream scoop into the bowl of macaroni and serves me extra. She dares me to complain about it.

Ruth is giving her pitch about the Shriners. This is the fifth year the Shriners have come into Norfolk for their charity parade. Afterward, they rent the theater for a live show. They sell chances in a secret raffle, members only. The winner gets a blow job. He wins the freebie, but he has to get Frenched in front of the rest. He sits on a chair before the blank movie screen and takes his reward like a man. Hendrick tells me, "These bingo blow jobs have been happening this way for years."

Ruth says, "Karen might bring us an extra couple hundred if she does it. We can charge a dollar more per ticket."

Sharon licks her spoon and says, "Yeah. They'll pay more for an ankle-biter. Besides, I've done it twice. Rose has done it. Sheila did it before she moved to Miami."

"What do I have to do?" I say.

"Blow him in front of the crowd, that's all. It's a riot."

"Not so easy. Assholes start laughing. They try to distract your trick so he loses his hard-on. Remember that one guy who took forever?"

"They started to boo the poor bastard."

"I thought they were booing you, honey," Hendrick says.

"It wasn't anything to do with me. Remember that old one? Sixty-five. Seventy? He was a double shot."

Ruth says, "I thought you were going to kill him."

"He had to roll it around a spool and put it in his pocket."

I try to see myself Frenching a guy in front of rows of men gawking at me. "I'm supposed to blow this guy in front of all his friends? Is that it?"

"It's pedestrian," Hendrick says.

"What's my taste going to be?" I say.

Vanessa says, "Oh, listen to her, will you?"

"She gets a bonus, right?" Sharon says.

"You'll get a bonus—don't know what that is until we cash out," Ruth tells me. She's licking the serving spoon. Watching her makes my stomach flip-flop.

The Lux kitchen timer goes off. I see that these girls got together to convince me to do Shriner Night. I have to rinse my hair in the shower or it's going to get burned. I'm on my way to the bathroom when a man bursts into the trailer. It's the man who drives up to the Paris and leaves Vanessa each day. Each time Vanessa slams the car door, he's calling her "Bitch!" Then he peels out.

I try to get past this crazy freak and into the bathroom, but he pushes me into the icebox. He keeps walking.

His face is pinched up from drugs and from the need for more drugs.

He shoulders his way through the kitchenette, knocking things off hooks. He keeps coming. Vanessa says, "Wilson, you get the fuck out of here."

He doesn't stop. Wilson grabs Vanessa's wrist and twists it behind her back. It makes a sound like a curtain rod snapping. We all hear it.

"It's broke," Vanessa shrieks. "He broke it—"

The girls look back and forth. Wilson just broke her wrist like a breadstick. We heard it for ourselves.

He pulls Vanessa out the door. Ruth grabs a nine-inch skillet and swings it, but he bats it away. It crashes to the floor. He kicks it and it's airborne again. It smashes down. He's smacking Vanessa. Now her nose is bleeding. The sight of her blood pooling on her dimpled chin makes my macaroni salad rise back up my throat.

Hendrick tries to hide in the closet, but the door won't close. Wilson brushes James's tide clock off the wall. It smashes. Its glass face is shattered, but the needle is pointing to FULL TIDE.

The tides come in and out whatever happens here.

Ruth is back with a little gun. She tips it at Wilson. Ruth follows the two outside. I'm surprised to hear Ruth yell at Vanessa when she should bawl out Wilson.

Vanessa cradles her broken arm and sits down in the car. Ruth tells Vanessa, "You stupid cunt. You can't hide *him* from us. You can't hide *us* from him."

Wilson gets behind the wheel. "Vanessa don't need you," he tells Ruth. "She'll do better by herself."

"Sure, she don't need me. Trash always finds an empty corner."

Wilson puts the car into reverse and rolls it backward. Ruth is still yiping at him, waving the little gun.

Ruth comes back inside and sits down at the table. She puts the gun beside her plate and carves up her piece of ham. I should rinse the bleach out of my hair, but I want to hear what they're saying about Vanessa's boyfriend. But they don't say a thing. I lift the gun to take a look. I've never held a gun in my hand. Hendrick says, "Shit. Tell her to put that thing down." I rest the gun on the Formica, but something happens. I brushed the trigger. It goes off. A tight pop.

The room is filled with peppery mist. In an instant, my eyes are burning. The girls scream and run out of the trailer.

Ruth shoves me outside. My lips are stinging like it's hot sauce. Everyone is coughing.

"That's a tear-gas revolver, idiot," Hendrick tells me.

"Your trailer's a disaster," Rose Pearson tells Ruth. "You won't be able to go in there for days."

We walk over to the neighbor's Spartan and she lets us wash our eyes and faces in her sink. Poor Rose Pearson can't open her eyes yet. The gun was pointing at her.

Ruth doesn't say a word. I wish she would say something.

"In a few minutes, we'll go in there and open all the windows," she tells me, as if she forgot I'm the one who pulled the trigger.

The neighbor won't let us stay warm inside her place because she has a canary. The bird might keel over from the tear-gas smell. We stand on the gravel drive lighting cigarettes. Rose and Sharon want to get their car keys from the trailer.

My scalp is itching now. It's on fire.

Hendrick tells me, "Honey, you better rinse your hair or you'll lose it all." Ruth leads me back inside the trailer. It's reeking like a nest of skunks. We crank the windows open. She props both doors. "Just get in the shower," Ruth says. Rose Pearson tiptoes into the kitchen and grabs her purse and her car keys.

"That food is wasted," Rose tells Ruth. "Maybe you can rinse the ham, but toss that Creamette salad."

I'm inside the shower rinsing the bleach from my hair. Ruth leans in to tell me, "If your hair is ruined, Hendrick's got those wigs."

When I get out of the shower, the mirror in Ruth's bedroom holds my attention. My hair is white as cotton, like clumps of cosmetic puffs. My forehead is raw and sore from the Clairol solution, like a sunburn.

Everyone's gone back to work. I see James in the kitchen. "What the fuck happened in this place?"

"I shot the gun by accident. We opened all the windows."

He's holding the cracked tide clock and hasn't turned around to look at me yet. He sees the dirty dishes from the girls, their cigarette butts with pink lipstick on the filters. He's trying to collect a roach stub from the milky glop on someone's plate. I'm thinking I should have hidden the tide clock and got to those dishes before he saw the mess.

James turns around and looks at me. His eyes are squinting as if he's looking at a floodlight. I think, Shit, he can't be going blind from it. A sneer crosses my lips. It's out of my control.

"Who you smirking at?"

"Not you," I tell him.

"What'd you do to your hair?"

"I went lighter," I say.

"Looks cheap."

"It's platinum."

"Is this Ruth's idea?"

"Hendrick did it."

"You doing that Shriner Night, are you?"

"Ruth says I can make a bonus."

"Well, you aren't doing it."

"I guess I am," I tell him.

James whacks me. He punches me until I'm on my knees. I get up. Down I go again. He kicks my ass with his pointy boot. I can feel my pelvis humming, that triangle of bones I never notice until they're getting pounded.

I'm saying, "Stop it, stop it," but he's dragging me out the door. My loafer comes off. He pulls me around behind the trailer. He unlocks the door of the Alum-a-room shack. He throws me inside. He tosses my shoe in my face. It's going to give me a fat lip. He shuts the door. I hear him push the S-hook through the hasp. The shack is pitch-dark.

"Let me out," I scream at James. My voice jumps around the metal room like it's disconnected. He's standing right on the other side. Leaves crunching under his feet. A minute later, I hear the Newport's engine catch; the flywheel has a telltale screech. I figure James is gone. I'm just about freezing with my wet hair. Seeds of light sprinkle across my shoulder. The two windows are shuttered on the outside. Maybe I can crank a window and spring the shutter, but there's towers of S&H boxes. I shift some cartons and a toaster oven falls off the top. Its metal grills slide out and crash at my feet.

Ruth will come home before *The Tonight Show*. That's at least eight hours from now. If I start screaming, the neighbors will discover Fort Knox. There's at least eleven TVs stacked in here. They'll find me like a piece of stolen property. I'm not interested in being sent home yet.

These items will bring James Robinson back, eventually. Or Piers will show up after his shift. He'll have to let me out. Maybe the electric company is reading meters this week, but I won't meow. They'll send me back to Wilmington.

My eyes adjust to the dark. The dark isn't a bad thing. Tiny basting stitches of light leak in through the door seam.

SATURDAY NIGHT the Paris is closed to normal business. The ticket booth is shut, its pleated aluminum awning pulled down and locked. The felt board says NO SHOW TONITE.

The Shriners use the side exit to enter the theater, keeping two men at the door to watch for outsiders who might try to crash the secret meeting. Inside, the houselights are up. Almost a hundred men sit in the forward rows, smoking and trading pint bottles back and forth. If they've had a long day riding in their parade, raising money for crippled children, they don't look any worse for it.

Ruth walks onstage. She's wearing a nice dark suit, all business, like the time she went to the small claims court. "This is our fifth year together," she tells the Shriners.

They whoop.

"We've got two films you've never seen. We have the new one with Sherry Templeton." Ruth crooks her finger and calls me onstage. The Shriners applaud as I walk up the stairs. I'm wearing one of Ruth's bikinis straight from the office hamper. I'm balancing in Sharon's three-inch spikes with the brass toe shields, but they're a size too large. Ruth introduces me with my business name. "This is Cindy," she says. She unhooks my halter top and lets it flop open. The men call out my name and tell me what they think of my bustline. Ruth says, "These don't need Playtex. These don't need Invisible Support."

A Shriner brings out a big glass fishbowl full of ticket stubs. He tries to mix up the stubs, but his hand is too big for the mouth of the bowl. He nods at me. I insert my fist and swirl the tickets.

The man cups the bowl in the palms of his huge farming hands while I dip my fingers in. I pull up a ticket stub. I give it to Ruth. She reads it, "Number N759. 759."

We look at the audience. The men crane their heads around searching for their winner.

He doesn't make a peep.

Ruth announces the number another time. We wait. She talks to the fellow holding the bowl. Ruth tells me, "That one chickened out. Draw another one."

I reach into the fishbowl a second time.

Ruth reads the number. A man stands up. The audience screams at him. I can't tell if they admire this fellow or despise him. The men are making a peculiar racket, like a barnyard before a thunderstorm. The winner walks onto the stage. He's in his thirties, I guess. He has a gut on him. He takes off his shirt and unhooks his belt, pulling it through his pant loops. He lets it slap the stage. He presses the heels of his hands together before his bare chest, until his muscles twitch and jiggle like Mr. Universe. He stirs up quite a ballyhoo.

He waits with his arms at his sides until everyone hushes up.

He says, "I'm ready to do my duty for the Noble Fraternal Order of the Mystic Shrine."

The audience cheers.

The man pulls his trousers off, one leg at a time. He keeps his briefs on. He sits down on the folding chair. I straddle his lap. We face one another, but I don't *watch* his face.

He squeezes my breast like it's a Spalding Pinky. I squeak from the pain. Ruth tells me to hush. She says I should let him feel me up all he wants, it will prime his pump and I'll be doing less work. She says, "Ride his lap for a few minutes first."

I let him play patty-cake on my tits. Then Ruth and the Shriner with the big hands leave the stage together, like old friends.

The Shriners start pitching advice.

"Show us your progress," someone says.

The winner pulls his dick out of his briefs. It's standing up. I figure out that this guy's a plumber. His pals are screaming, "Crank his auger—crank it, crank it."

I get off his lap and down on my knees. I start sucking his dick. My lip is still puffy from when James whacked me with my loafer. Ruth told James that if he locks me in the shack again, he'll have to find another hamper for his booty. "You want to discipline your girlfriend, just don't use my Alum-a-room," she tells him.

I tell Ruth, "He can't stop me from working." But I see she's not thinking about me. It's something between her and James.

I'm doing my job and these rows are stone quiet. They hush as if *they* can feel my lips. Then they wake up. All at once, they're relieved it isn't happening to them. They start saying oddball things to distract my trick. I'm working my tongue from the basket to the tip. I'm Frenching him with all my wits, but he's taking his time.

The men are raising a rumpus, but I hear somebody shrieking in the back of the room, long honking cries, like he can't stand it. These screams remind me of home, our house was in a flyway. The cries remind me of my sister.

They had been laying foundations and framing houses all summer. Maria went into the new development and tried to cross a floor joist like a balance beam, inching across the open basement, from one side to the other. I guess she slipped. I heard her screams and followed them up the street. I found her swinging from an I-beam, dangling six feet above the new concrete. If I hadn't come up there to coax her, God knows how long she would have had to hold on.

I reach up and hug her shins and tell her, "Let go, I have you." But she won't release the I-beam. Her fingers are white as asparagus. I tell her, "One, two, three—"

By the time I talk her into it, this meatball will pop. It's a game in my mind while I'm Frenching the Shriner.

The audience is chanting, "Shoot, shoot, shoot." I bring it there, wipe my mouth and sit back on my heels as his cock explodes. Ruth told me the audience wants to see it for "proof of purchase."

When I turn around, I see a police officer walk down the aisle. Was he waiting all that time? The Shriners notice the cop and they stand up in a big wave. They see it's only *one* cop, all by himself. He can't collar all of them. They sit down again and start stomping their feet. They chant "Sherry, Sherry—" They want to see their porn queen. They forget about me. Only a few men start to file out, thinking of their wives and children.

Ruth talks to the policeman. Hendrick flicks on the projector and cuts the lights.

The Paris is licensed for triple-X films, but not for live acts. The police come in once a week to "visit" Ruth. Ruth says it was just a matter of time until I was introduced in the routine. They know she's got windows and rooms in back. They might shut us down on individual nights, but we're open the next day. Business as usual.

Shriner Night can't go by without a little police supervision.

The officer waits for me to get dressed, then he drives us to the station. Sharon and Vanessa, with her arm in a cast, were working rooms during all this, but they did a vanishing act. I see Sharon's car parked at the minimart as we drive past in the cruiser.

At the police station, they take my picture against a chart that says I'm five feet five. They roll my thumb across an ink-soaked sponge like the one I use to moisten S&H stamps. I show them the fake driver's license James gave me months ago. It's a perfect replica. My weight and the color of my eyes are true, but the name says "Cindy Stevens." I used to think maybe this girl, "Cindy Stevens," is dead, and it made me nervous. James said that's an idea I got from the TV show *The Fugitive*.

James says this girl "Cindy" isn't dead.

She doesn't exist.

Sometimes when he wants to get under my skin, James calls me this name. He reminds me I don't have any right to complain. He calls me "Cindy" like I'm not a real person.

Exterminators are marching around with silver canisters of chlordane and it's hard to breathe that stink. It turns out they are delousing the night court and we can't get a hearing until the next morning.

Ruth says, "We'll come back tomorrow."

"Let me see about that," the officer says, "you might have to be our guests."

"Look, that bug poison might start up my asthma. I'll bring Cindy back down in the morning." Ruth makes it up as she goes along.

The officer puts us back in the cherry-top and drives us to Bailey's. It's all in the family.

I notice a new billboard where the Marlboro Man had been just yesterday. It's the Yardley Girl holding a bar of English Lavender soap. I'm thinking about the raffle winner and how I might like to wash out my mouth with that pretty pink cake.

When we pull into Bailey's, I see James standing in the door of the trailer. I get out of the cruiser and wave to the officer. I hold out my arm and wiggle my fingers until I'm sure James sees me acting cozy with the policeman. Ruth takes my sleeve and steers me past James, who I haven't slept with for a week, not since he locked me in the Alum-a-room. I wash up in the bathroom, but my thumb is stained. Ruth sees it and says, "Well, that's a nice trophy." Ruth pushes me into her bedroom. She slides the lock. This lock is as weak as an eyelash, but she's making her point. She tells me to get in the Castro.

I get in bed and turn on the set. Johnny Carson is holding a baby lion. He leaps up from his seat. The lion is wetting his desk. Ruth is sitting on the edge of the Castro using an emery board on her callused elbow. She smears Pond's cream in the palm of her hand and rubs it over the red knob. We hear James banging around the trailer, tugging drawers loose in the kitchen.

"I guess he's mad," I say.

Ruth says, "Let him crash things. You have to stand your ground, honey."

James starts banging on the door.

Ruth ignores him.

"Shit. I'm looking for my car keys," James tells Ruth.

She lets him into the room. He sees his key case on the dresser. He grabs it, tosses it up over my head and snatches it in midair before my face. He smiles at me, a tight evaporated line, not really a smile at all. He dips his face one inch from mine and says, "Ever notice how you find something in the *last* place you look? Sweetheart, where are they going to find *you*?"

I HAD MY HEARING at court. The chlordane was making the bailiff nauseous, so the judge took us into his office. The judge took Ruth's cash. It was something like a one-time fee. He made it a point to show me a form with some scribbled lines. "Okay, Cindy, you're on the books. Congratulations."

"Thanks," I say.

"It's official. Caught in the act," he says.

Ruth says, "What she have there? 'Lewd and unnatural?'"

"Shit. Is that what it says?" I ask.

The judge looks at me again. "Cindy, you're new to *me*, but you're in the Game for a while if Ruth had you doing Shriner Night. That's for pros, honey, so I guess you're not still on the baby bottle." The judge looks at Ruth. "I don't know, Ruth, these new ones are getting in just under the wire, but not by much."

"Oh, she's older than she looks. She's all baby fat," Ruth says. "Cindy needs to diet."

I didn't like my weight being put out there like that. But Ruth was dishing it just to get us out of there.

The judge assigned me to a social worker, Betty Diggs. Ruth nodded her head and pulled me out the door. "This turned out good. Betty Diggs is one of ours. I bring you downtown for your interview with Betty. Once. That's that. She'll write her reports every week and turn them in."

"We pay her something?"

"Well, she's not the United Way. Of course, she gets a whack of our weekly pull. She had Rose Pearson and Ronnie before her. Now she has you."

Ruth tells me no one wants to shut us down because of the navy. There'd be a mutiny. The only time we have to lay off is when Easter comes around, and sometimes on Independence Day. The Fourth is a holy day for the military. Easter week they start busting every goer from D.C. to Charleston. Southern Baptist influence, James says. We lay low from Palm Sunday until the next weekend. That week, navy families come from all over, proud moms and aunties swarm onto the base wearing their bonnets.

"Easter we slow down? That's funny. Bunnies never slow down."

Easters in Wilmington, Maria and I sorted out the black jelly beans from our Easter baskets and put them in the garbage disposer, grinded them up. Once Ray gave Alex a giant chocolate egg with a pair of regulation dice in the center. Maria and I got peephole eggs, little domes crisscrossed with handmade sugar ribbons. These peephole eggs had miniature flower buds and fondant mushrooms. Tiny figurines—milkmaids and kittens—were glued to the floor inside the egg with edible sugar-cement, and the peephole was constructed like the sugar lens of a periscope.

Those peephole eggs aren't really much different from the peep windows at the Paris. They're the same thing, aren't they? It's a make-believe world, it's all pretend.

VANESSA DOESN'T COME IN to work for two days. Her landlord finds her body in the apartment. She's curled on the bathroom linoleum, but the toilet is gone. It's been unbolted from the floor. The police think her boyfriend Wilson has smashed her head with the toilet tank and he's trying to hide the weapon. But they find the toilet in the next apartment. Wilson sold the commode. It was a brand-new unit. American Standard. Solid porcelain. The landlord hears Wilson is selling the toilet, which isn't his to sell, so he comes up there. He sees Vanessa OD'd. There she is, without a pulse, who knows for how long, while Wilson is trying to pull down some cash for that toilet.

The police are sending her body to her parents in Connecticut for a funeral. Ruth calls us into the office. She says we can have our own service. She lights a hurricane candle on a little dish. The girls start crying. I can't force myself. When they go back to work, Ruth pinches the wick and snuffs the flame out. She tosses the hunk of wax in her desk drawer. "I'm saving this for the next one of you who can't see the writing on the wall." She's warning me about James. That's just scare tactics. I tell Ruth, "I'll never end up like Vanessa because I'm not like Vanessa to start out."

"Oh really?" Ruth says. "You and Vanessa are more alike than you think. You and Vanessa could be sisters."

JAMES WAITS FOR ME in the hall. He tugs my wrist and pulls me onto the bed in the "kids' room," where he's been sleeping the last couple nights.

"I've missed you, baby," he tells me. His cigarette is burned down to the filter, like when he's been thinking too hard and forgets he's holding it. He pinches it out in the Lincoln Monument ashtray, right at the president's feet. That president figurine sits in his chair with his wounded eyes watching us have a fuck.

"What are you smiling about?" James says as he starts to screw me.

"Lincoln," I tell him.

"You didn't want to suck that Shriner, did you, baby? You didn't have to take that ride to jail, did you?" He stops pumping his hips and looks me in the eye.

"I don't see *you* giving me crazy money," I tell him.

He says, "Ruth went too far. She's wasting her inventory on that mob of rednecks."

I don't like being called "inventory."

James buries his face in my hair. He whispers, "Squeeze my gloots, baby." I hold his ass, pinching his muscles on either side. At first, I didn't know what he was talking about when he tells me "Squeeze my gloots," but he explained it's his gluteus maximus. His "gloots." These words aren't exactly enriching my vocabulary, are they?

Veronica used to make us look at the Oxford English Dictionary. We had to stand there for a few minutes leafing through the tissue pages of that giant dictionary balanced on its own pedestal stand in the living room. Each page had a year's worth of big words and definitions. When Veronica played Scrabble, she'd ask Maria to verify her spelling. "Find 'quiddity'" she told her, "is that two *d*'s?" or "Look up 'stick-to-itiveness.'"

Maria said, "Stick-to-itiveness? Isn't that too many letters for Scrabble?"

"Look it up anyway," Veronica said.

My sister would look up the word and read it to her. Veronica always had the correct spelling. Veronica told us that her teachers at Sisters of Loretto had been amazed by her spelling skills. Each year, she won the spelling bee.

Words aren't everything.

James is past the "no return," and I lift my hand to study my inked thumb, black as a date, then I grab his ass again until he shoots.

After that, he's got his attitude back. Mr. Important. He tells me, "Ruth's trying to make you star of the line. You want to be star of the line? That's full time without full pay. Where's your common sense?"

"Who made you boss?" I say, pulling the sheet around my hips. "Are you doing payroll now? Tell me when that is—"

He whacks me square across the mouth. The roots of my teeth hum, but worse, this time my lip is split. In an instant, it blows up like an Oscar Mayer.

Ruth comes in. They start screaming over my head. Two vultures fighting over raw meat. Ruth tells James, "You bust her face and she has to sit out. I'm not giving her sick pay." Ruth looks at me. "Don't sit there, stupid. Put ice on that mouth right now."

That mouth. *That* ass. *That* slit. I'm just one of everything I've got. Inventory.

I get up to get some ice.

WALTER CRONKITE IS GIVING the daily body count for the VC and the NVA. He's telling us how many Americans were killed in action and how many were wounded in action. He's saying "KIA" and "WIA." These abbreviations pick up the pace and lessen the blow. Cronkite says, "Don't these begin to sound as familiar as RSVP, IOU, SWAK—"

James watches the war pictures every night on the evening news and again right before Johnny Carson. He can't get enough. It's like he wants to be in the jungle, walking around with a knife in his teeth.

Ruth tells him, "You're watching that war with the volume too high."

Ruth sets out a stack of bills on the Formica table. She gives me two hundred dollars for Shriner Night after she takes her "indoor money," the larger slice. I don't bother to ask how much that is, the two hundred has all my attention. James is leaning against the sink eyeing me like I'm a racehorse who just placed. I once heard Piers say he owned "part of a horse."

James said the only part of a horse anyone needs to own is the "nose."

I never understood how someone could own "part" of a horse until I started living with James and Ruth. I know what part of me they fight over.

I tap my bills on the tabletop, making a thick wedge. "What are you looking at with your tongue hanging out," I tell him. I'm lisping from my fat lip, but I'm all cheek as long as Ruth is standing next to me.

Ruth says to me, "Put that somewhere. It don't grow on trees, you know."

I have a secret hiding place where I keep my money. I found a motel Bible at a sidewalk sale. A hundred books were spread on a blanket. The Bible caught my eye. I bought the book for a dollar and took it back to the trailer. I cut a big square hole in its pages with a Wilkinson single-edge blade. I put my cash in the slot and shut the covers. I collected the pages I cut out and threw them away at the minimart, so James wouldn't find them and figure out where I had made my stash.

James saw the motel Bible on my bed and told me, "That's not the legitimate book. The only real Bible is a King James Version."

"King James?" I thought he was making it up. He walked away and came back with his own copy. Right on its cover it says *King James Bible* in crinkly gold letters. He opens it up. "Here's something for you to think about," he says. "Proverbs 23:27: *A whore is a deep ditch.*"

"Since when do you need the Bible to find your insults? I guess you must have finished that paperback *Five Hundred Jokes for on the Job and in the Office*? Now you got to look in that Bible?"

"*A whore is a deep ditch,*" he reads it again. He's happy with himself. He walks away.

I paper-clip my wad and put it in my motel Bible.

When Ruth says, "Money doesn't grow on trees," she's just saying, "Put that cash in your motel Bible."

In Wilmington, we had a *money plant,* a big silver bush with shiny "coins" all over it. It's pretty showy. The wind stirs it around and the pods make a tinkling sound, like loose change.

"This means we're going to be millionaires," my little sister told me.

"It's lucky," Ray said, "because we didn't plant it here, it just showed up on its own. It's a good omen."

The next year there were *two* money plants. One right next to the other.

WILMINGTON, DEL.

K AREN HAD BEEN missing for more than one year. I watched the 1966 New Year's Eve countdown on national television. As the ball sank, I wondered if Karen was in the huge crowd crushed into Times Square. I searched for her in the sea of mirth-makers, but faces were lost behind snowing confetti.

At the recent Christmas holidays, I arranged extra felt booties for my toddler nieces and nephews, but the tiny socks ran across the mantel like an ellipsis. I sorted through the Christmas decorations—large gold accordion stars from Turin, music boxes, the spice balls, a precious Battersea enameled angel—until I found Karen's stocking, the letters of her name sewn in tiny glass beads that glittered in the firelight. I hung her stocking above the hearth.

"What are you doing?" Veronica said.

"It doesn't look right without hers next to mine," I said.

"You're making things worse," Veronica said. "Take it down."

I unpinned Karen's felt sock from the mantel. I tugged my own stocking from its place of honor beside the gorgeous Battersea angel. On second thought, I propped it against the hearth, not wanting to call attention to it, but not willing to forfeit my whole Christmas for my sister.

On Christmas Day, the telephone jangled three times and stopped. I picked up the kitchen wall phone and listened to the dial tone. I was certain that the three distinct rings had been a message from my sister. I hovered around the wall phone waiting for it to ring again. It never happened.

◆ ◆ ◆

TWO DAYS LATER, I received a Christmas card, a pencil drawing
by the paraplegic artist named Ann Adams. The greeting-card artist
sketched Christmas scenes without using her hands. She clenched a
drawing pencil between her teeth and shaded her art work with tiny
movements of her chin. She sent stationery samples to households on
marketing lists hoping people would mail back a check. The card was
oddly crumpled and accordioned as if it had been caught in the sorter
or plucked from the trash bin.

There was no signature after the greeting, *Joyeux Noël*, but the
handwriting on the envelope was my sister's, I was sure of it. The double *l*'s were Karen's typical loopy ears. I saw these distinct rabbit ears
in our last name, Mitche*ll*, as it appeared on the envelope addressed to
me, but I didn't tell my parents my suspicions. The postmark said
"Norfolk, Virginia."

Norfolk, Virginia. So that's where she is, I was thinking. I went
into my father's desk drawers to find the AAA map of the Delmarva
Peninsula. I found the city named Norfolk just a bit north of a huge
splotch called Dismal Swamp. The juxtaposition was disturbing, and I
vowed to retrieve Karen from that forbidding landscape.

I stayed home most of the school vacation waiting for Karen to ring
again. To kill time, I read novels. I stole *The Tight White Collar* from
Veronica's bedstand, a novel by the author of *Peyton Place*. I read a
scene in which a woman refused to make love to a man until he had
washed his hands. Was washing up before sex as routine as washing before dinner? What would a man use his hands for in sex? How would he
touch her?

One morning, the electric company came to remove a big hemlock
on our street that had grown too close to a transformer. Our neighborhood association wanted the tree to be saved, and the whole thing was
lifted by crane and set down in another location.

When the crew dug up the tree, its network of roots was *larger* than
its canopy.

I watched the workers extract the tree, using a chain saw to cut
through its resistant root ball. I followed the giant tree swinging from

its cable as the crane maneuvered it out of my sight. I saw the gaping hole where the tree had been removed, its remaining roots sheared, left scattered in the frozen marl like severed fingers. The excavation some-how echoed what had occurred in our family.

WITH KAREN MISSING, I was abandoned to face my adolescence on my own. I felt my waist cinching in, my hips flaring. My nipples hard-ened into hot stems or swelled like puddles of warm Karo beneath ten-der burning coins.

I felt a sudden, crashing identification with Hollywood's lovelorn starlets. I became especially obsessed with the tormented bombshells Tuesday Weld and Natalie Wood.

Natalie became my role model; Tuesday was surrogate for Karen. Natalie played voluptuous teenage characters who battled selfish ma-triarchs. She was a hot, brimming daughter—half open wound, half harlot. The common denominator was always an unsympathetic mother who drove Natalie into cheap arrangements with men. I recog-nized Veronica in every case. I imagined how Natalie might act out a scene with my mother. Who would win?

With Karen gone, I tested several new role models. I was fascinated by the gritty Cockney waif, Rita Tushingham, in *A Taste of Honey*. I weighed her fate against the plight of the cheeky debutante, Tippy Walker, in *The World of Henry Orient*. Both these girls were lost in the new, tilting hemisphere of men, and just like me, these girls were slighted and ignored by their own maternal sources.

But it was Natalie who seemed to reach out. It was Natalie above all. After watching her in *This Property Is Condemned*, I went to my bedroom and closed the door. I pulled out a manila envelope from be-neath the braided rug where I had been hiding newspaper clippings about Karen since the first weeks she went missing. The serrated mar-gins of the tear sheets had already started to yellow. There was Karen's picture in the *Wilmington Journal*. Her face in the *Philadelphia In-quirer*, boxed—GIRL DISAPPEARS FROM MT. PLEASANT NEIGHBOR-HOOD. The headings were sensational. "If it bleeds, it leads" was the rule of thumb in my college journalism course, years later.

I had used pinking shears to cut out Karen's picture from her junior high school yearbook. Her eyes looked straight into the camera. Only a slight downward turn at one corner of her lips suggested a note of anxiety or discomfort.

When Karen disappeared, I refused to get my picture taken for the yearbook. As my class lined up before the photographer and a woman handed out combs to everyone, rattails for the girls, tiny black pocket combs for the boys, I hid in the drama closet. I had become known as "the missing girl's sister," and I feared that my face might appear in the school publication matched to that caption. There were always a few of us, our names listed under the heading "Unpictured."

I found an article about a physician who had used local anesthesia to operate on himself. Using a mirror, he had removed his own gall bladder while taking notes on the procedure. Medical officials called the physician "a nut case." But I identified with the doctor. He was researching his own stamina for self-discovery, seeking his own limits real or imaginary. My curiosity wasn't a healthy or comforting trait. The hungry ache of "wanting to know" might be as dangerous as amateur surgery.

NIGHTS, I STARTED to have disturbing nightmares about Veronica. I dreamed she was riding her misshapen bicycle in elliptical circles around me. As I walked up a dream street, my mother steered her grotesque contraption, tilting in and out of my path. I was trying to join my sister on the opposite curb, but our mother pedaled the twisted two-wheeler back and forth in hideous synchrony each time I tried to cross over, keeping me caged in her sinister circle until Karen gave up and turned her back on us.

IF VERONICA WAS FEELING upset about Karen, it came forward in her spur-of-the-moment house calls from Dr. Kerrigan. He arrived to give her more "mood pills" and to take her blood pressure. She seemed to engage his tenderness during the gentle procedure. The doctor propped her elbow and inflated the arm band, pumping the little bulb; in conclusion, he patted her hand. She had medical supervision, but I had to sort out my own feelings. Veronica even suggested to Dr. Kerrigan that it was *I* who drove Karen away. She said I was "bossy, athletic, cheeky, with the duplicitous nature of Shakespeare's Puck."

"That would be annoying," the doctor said.

"She got right under her sister's skin," Veronica said.

I felt my eyes stinging, hurt by her accusations. But I was secretly relieved that Veronica seemed certain Karen had run off and wasn't in fact murdered.

Perhaps in contrition for her public reprisals of me, Veronica bought me a houseplant and placed it on my bureau. The diminutive shrub was an ornamental pepper plant with tiny crimson fruits—real miniature chiles, like inverted Santa hats. I was relieved Veronica was ending her tirade against me with the exotic little bush. I fingered the leaves of the plant and examined its fiery baubles. I accidentally rubbed my eyes with my fingertips. The oil from the peppers burned fiercely. I rubbed my eyes again, only making things worse. I ran through the house screaming, "You tried to blind me! I'm blind—"

"You're not going blind," Veronica told me. She led me to the kitchen sink and filled a shot glass from the tap, a pretty crystal jigger that doubled as an eyecup.

If she had known about the dangers of the noxious little houseplant, she might have warned me.

SOMETIMES, VERONICA WANTED a specialty item for dinner, and she sent me on foot to buy a small jar of capers or a tiny corked bottle of saffron fronds at the elite Hearn's Market.

I saw the pyramid of Hearn's cakes as I entered the market. Perfect, individual geometric servings of rosewater cake were set on paper doilies and displayed in a glass case like a prize exhibit at a museum. At a customer's request, a clerk arranged the cakes in glazed white cardboard boxes and tied the boxes with tartan ribbon.

At the start of Karen's adolescence, Veronica had encouraged Karen to stop eating sweets. But I couldn't resist the treats, and I stuffed the sponge cake squares into my mouth and washed them down with whole milk. I drained my tumbler, leaving a white velvet coating on the glass, in which a few pink crumbs were imprisoned as proof of my indulgence.

The fact that Karen's very last words to me identified these Hearn's cakes drove me crazy. Despite her program of abstinence, she had asked me if I wanted her to bring me a sweet.

◆ ◆ ◆

I WAS MUCKING STALLS and riding horses at Highland Stables. There I met a girl named Colleen, the sixth daughter in an Irish-Italian family. Her father ran an excavating business and owned enough equipment—backhoes and big earth movers—to fill a football stadium. Ray said her father might be with the "organization" since his wife was from a prominent Italian family. Her siblings pronounced her name with a speed bump, C'leen, as if her family had too many names to remember and had shortened Colleen's by one syllable.

Her slurred tag evoked thoughts of toppled purity, and was irresistible to me.

After hours, Colleen and I stayed late at the barn. The horses were stabled and rats started to come out of their nests. The rodents trotted the length of a huge sign nailed across the doorway—RIDE AT YOUR OWN RISK—and jumped into the zinc feed troughs. As we disturbed a busy cluster, they leapt at us in a spirograph of red eyes. I pulled Colleen to safety inside the tack room, and we locked the Dutch door. We took our breeches off for rounds of strip poker. Fully stripped, I stood in front of the potbelly stove. Its concentrated heat rolled up my naked hips and buttocks until I was glowing. I sat astride an expensive Steuben jumping saddle, wearing only my dirty socks, my feet tucked in the short stirrups. The slope of the hunt seat tilted my pelvis forward, and Colleen rocked the smooth leather pommel until I had an orgasm. Then it was her turn; she mounted the built-in sawhorse and sat on the saddle where I'd left a wet smear on the golden calfskin.

At dark, we were again dressed in our breeches and stood by the front gate waiting for our parents to collect us. We ducked in and out of a huge forked oak and never said a word about our illicit half hour together. My skin still tingled, scorched from the fierce stove, and by an interior coil of heat that caught me off-guard. I was relieved when Veronica rescued me from my secret mistakes, and I was glad to hear her car approaching. Veronica practiced the European habit of tooting her horn at every switchback and blind spot. I recognized the unmistakable bleating of the Citroën as it snaked the wooded hill, and I walked right out into the middle of the street, letting its cleansing high beams wash over me.

◆ ◆ ◆

THE AFTERNOON when Karen disappeared, I sat at the kitchen table writing my detention homework. I wondered if writing would always be punishment, rehabilitation, reprieve.

At the junior high school, I was fined for defacing my English text when I penned my own confessions along the margins of "Evangeline." I had a crush on my pretty teacher and tried to get her attention. "Don't mark the text," she told me, biting off her consonants, which teased me to go further.

Next, we read William Cowper's "The Castaway," to which I added new lines at each stanza break. Cowper wrote, "We perished, each alone: / But I beneath a rougher sea, / And whelmed in deeper gulfs than he."

"We perished, each alone" seemed a perfect maxim and irrefutable, but I raised my hand and pestered my teacher. "Isn't life solitary for its full duration, not just at its conclusion? I mean, aren't people lonely from the cradle to the grave?"

I watched my teacher's tiny Adam's apple pulse in her ivory neck as she swallowed once to clear her throat. She told me, "We're here to discuss only what's printed in your English text."

For scribbling on school property, I received one week of detention, during which I wrote to my teacher a series of lyrical regrets on ruled paper folded into accordions.

I was sent to the school psychologist. My English teacher claimed that I was too precocious to have straight *F*'s. What could be the problem? The psychologist administered several tests, including the famous "square peg in round hole" examination. He timed me as I inserted bright geometric blocks in corresponding slots on a gypsum board. He told me that my intellect did not correspond to my performance. I was not achieving my potential. "Why is that?" he said.

"You don't know?"

"In your own words," he said.

"You don't know about my sister?"

I blamed my problems at school on Karen's disappearance, shyly at first, and then with full license. But I couldn't accuse Karen for my academic flops, could I? Throughout my student career, I was labeled a "troublemaker." Even as early as the second grade, I couldn't sit still through a lesson, and when the teacher couldn't stand it, she *tied* me to my seat.

Each morning, she tethered me to my chair with her extra scarves, wrapping my waist and ankles in pastel chiffon shackles.

The grammar school had tried to enlist Veronica to come in to class to help curb my hyperactivity. She volunteered only once, to teach a French lesson.

"*La clef est* sur *la table. La clef est* sous *la table.*" Veronica stood at the front of the room holding a car key above and then below the palm of her hand. Her hollow gold charm bracelet tinkled as she turned her delicate wrist back and forth.

I was a loner, and by the time I entered junior high school, Karen's disappearance had branded me an "untouchable." I had not been instructed by guidance counselors in ways to manage my celebrity. Teachers offered their two cents, summarizing the situation like this: "Karen had not developed any self-esteem." These teachers glowered at me, suggesting I better get cracking. I better figure out ways to secure some self-esteem of my own.

It occurred to me that "self-esteem" should be divvied up between siblings, awarded and ensured ahead of time the way citizenship is awarded by right of birth or like a key to the city is presented to someone who hasn't yet proved what he might do with it. Why must self-esteem be earned? My cockiness came from insecurity, not the other way around. Yet, if *I* was cocky, Karen had seemed passive, retreating, disappearing. Our tentative grip on our self-esteem made me write things down; it made Karen run.

EACH YEAR ON VALENTINE'S DAY, Ray came home with several flat, satinette boxes from the "Ladies Foundations" department at Wanamaker's. There might be a silk slip or lacy negligee for Veronica, a baby-doll nightie or a robe for Karen. For me, it was always the same, a Days of the Week panty set. It was a running joke. I always received the Days of the Week. Once, Ray came home with Days of the Week in

French: LUNDI, MARDI, MERCREDI in black lettering embroidered at an angle across the shiny pastel nylon.

After Karen disappeared, Ray didn't remember to stop at Wanamaker's. Veronica teased him and threatened to go shopping on her own for a little post-Valentine pick-me-up. She told him, "You can't just forget a tradition. What's come over you? I'll take Maria along."

I went with Veronica with the understanding that she would buy me a ring. I could have my choice of any semiprecious stone. My birthstone was ruby and that, of course, was too costly.

In the jewelry store, I looked at a velveteen tray of glass rings. Imitation emeralds, imitation rubies. Nothing looked interesting. The salesman returned with a different tray. Centered on a velvet scarf was an opal the size of a cocktail onion. The milky stone reflected the overhead lighting, refracting multicolored sparks—pinks and purples and greens like a daub of Nesselrode ice cream.

"Opal is *Karen's* birthstone," I told my mother.

"Does it really matter?" Veronica said.

"Opal is for October. Karen was born in October."

"How is Karen going to know?"

"But I'll know."

I picked up the ring and pressed it onto my ring finger. The fourteen-karat gold band was nicely chill and quickly warmed up to my body temperature. I struggled between two distinct poles of feeling: the luxurious sensation of wearing a moderately expensive trinket against cresting waves of panic for accepting my sister's rightful birthstone. It was as if I had stolen from Karen not only an item of jewelry, but everything, every entitlement of her birth.

Her place at the table.

Her shelf in the bathroom vanity.

Her hand mirror left blank unless I inserted my own face in its empty oval.

Her daily horoscope, "Libra," and her first dibs on everything else she could no longer claim for her own and which I adopted, pushed aside or read out loud in her absence.

I never took the ring off my finger.

I started to have terrible thoughts. I imagined chopping off my finger after the second knuckle. Whack! The knife comes down. Neat and clean. The dismembered finger wriggles off the breadboard.

Still, I wore the tainted opal. At night, I held it before my face, its milky glimmer still visible in the dark. "This is *your* ring," I whispered, when I stared at the luminous, soapy bauble. "Yours if you want it."

THE UNDERGROUND

I N THE BLANK after-school hours, I was sharing a sixty-cent tube of Testors with Colleen, Melvie Hirschon and Tony DelRose. Melvie squeezed a golden button of glue onto the bottom fold of a lunch bag and handed it to me. Tony DelRose took the paper bag from my hands and squirted *more* glue into the sack. He told me, "It's got to be a big hawker."

The boys waited for me to insert my face in the brown paper collar.

I pretended to sniff the Testors, making sure I didn't breathe anything. Carbona stain remover, Everblum dry-cleaning solvent "for serious spot jobs," whatever it was, my charade was quickly sabotaged by the tricky vapor. The icy fumes rested on the back of my tongue. I felt its velvet cinch tighten until my head floated on a weightless stem, like a paper dahlia.

Those winter afternoons we prowled the shabby warehouses at Diamond State Vending, searching the aisles of jammed candy dispensers and pinball games. We tried to jimmy cigarette machines to dislodge quarters. Canvas sacks of change lined the floor of the office where a bookkeeper ran the coins through a sorter. I chatted with the woman as the boys filled their pockets. Even if we *all* filled our pockets, there was never a dent in the mounds of silver. The bookkeeper didn't seem to care what we took; it would be less work for her.

Tony DelRose was stealing cars and driving them from Wilmington to a garage in Hyattsville, Maryland, just outside D.C. He knew I wanted to find my sister, and he told me he'd take me with him any time I wanted. Tony DelRose was an apprentice to his cousin, Richard Orsi, a ringer up in Philadelphia. Orsi was at the top end of an established routine; Tony DelRose was working his way into the game. He acted like a hotshot as he explained the operation to Colleen, whom he courted on weekends, tucked in the back seat of her tiny Corvair parked on the knoll at the landfill. Colleen said the smell along the top ridge at the landfill was almost too distracting when he made love to her.

Tony DelRose pinched late-model sedans right off the suburban streets of Wilmington. He could get into a car, tickle the electronics and roll it away in a few minutes. He was in Washington by sunrise, before people woke up and found their vehicles were missing from their driveways. No cruisers were alerted until long after Tony had his packet of cash and was sitting on the Metroliner eating a creme horn, on his way back to Wilmington.

Tony tried to get Colleen to come with him, but she wouldn't get in a stolen car unless Tony could convince *me* to come with them. I was crucial to his plans with Colleen.

"You still want to go to Norfolk? To see your sister? I'll take you."

"That's right," I told him. I kept the Ann Adams picture with me at all times, unfolding the smudged greeting card now and again. I studied the card's blank interior, then placed it back in the envelope. I studied the envelope's wavy cancellation marks, and the "rabbit ears" in my last name.

Melvie said, "You don't even have her address—"

Tony said, "Look. We'll do it any weekend, okay? You say when."

THURSDAYS, VERONICA WAS at her Kiwanis bridge club until four o'clock. We might have used Melvie's house, but Tony didn't like it there. Melvie's living room was paneled with tongue-and-groove mirrors, uninterrupted except for two seamless windows where the outside landscape tumbled in.

I imagined Melvie sitting with his parents in the mirrored room. They must be pleased by their family portrait to subject themselves to such repetitive scrutiny. In one corner, a baby grand piano was multiplied in the converging mirrors until the place looked like a showroom at House of Organs. It wasn't just the mirrors that upset Tony; he didn't like the mezuzah tacked to the door lintel or the framed photographs of the Holocaust that lined the fireplace mantel. Melvie's family didn't flinch at the pictures of the death camps, but seemed to want to absorb them, the way trees can grow new bark over sharp knots of barbed wire where it cuts across the trunk.

Veronica had enough trouble sorting through her personal history with Curtis Pettibone, and she didn't bother to explain world events to us. Once, after Karen and I had had air-raid practice at Silverside School, we went home and asked Veronica, "What's an A-bomb?"

Alex was seated beside her and answered for Veronica. He told us, "The A-bomb is a hoax invented by schoolteachers. While you kids are crouched under your desks, they can have a cigarette in the teachers' lounge."

Melvie's parents had engineering degrees and worked at the Du Pont Experimental Station, testing nonstick chemical coatings or any number of new plastic discoveries.

"Plastic is Jesus," Melvie said. I liked hearing him take the name of the Lord in vain.

"Your mother is a scientist. Mine is always playing bridge," I said.

"Bridge is a variation of whist."

"What's whist?" I said.

"Whist is a variation of bridge." Melvie was doing his intellectual tap dance just to tease me.

Tony DelRose looked in the liquor cabinet for something to round off the Testors. Glue evoked a headache if we didn't cultivate a little buzz from something else. Tony pulled out a bottle of Glenlivet scotch, but the seal was untouched. "Don't break that open," I told him.

Melvie shoved the bottles across the shelf and found a liqueur called Chartreuse in the back of the cabinet. I sipped the green syrup, which smelled alarmingly familiar, like Karen's Jean Naté "After Shower Splash." Even when I was stoned, Karen was an echo.

Melvie had to go to a music lesson. He was studying classical piano. I took guitar lessons once a week. My guitar teacher was an insurance salesman who moonlighted teaching accordion and guitar. He had an angry skin disease that affected the backs of his hands and fingers, all the way up to his second knuckles. Sometimes his fingers were so blistered he steered his car using just the heels of his hands. He was socially crippled by his psoriasis until a doctor suggested that he become a music instructor to overcome his self-consciousness. Facing students would force him to adjust to his affliction. His high school students called him "scab fingers," but no one quit his tutelage. If he tapped my knee to regulate the tempo, his flaming condition was a distraction, but soon I learned the chord changes for "Blowin' in the Wind." Next, he showed me the banal strumming for "If I Had a Hammer," his raw fingers a rosy blur.

We waited for *Shindig* to come on the TV. Until then, we watched Merv Griffin. He was singing a duet with Gloria Loring, whose long blond hair fell to her waist.

"Shit. That's a bleach job. That's not natural," I said to my friends.

Tony pulled his nose out of the sack and squinted at the TV screen to study the torch singer's long fake hair. "Looks okay."

"You like it? That bale of straw?" My own hair was reddish brown. Ray called it "chestnut." CHESTNUT was never listed on any hair-care product the way others were emblazoned: FOR BLONDS, FOR BRUNETTES, FOR LIGHT AUBURN. I couldn't find a product that said FOR CHESTNUTS.

Colleen said, "You really should go blonder. I'll do it for you."

Veronica's Citroën turned into the drive. She was early. We stood up with awkward, hitching limbs like a row of teen Frankensteins. We fell out the kitchen door and trotted stiffly around the house, trying to regain our balance. We watched Veronica collect packages from the trunk. She pinched a new carton of Kents between her legs while she sorted her purchases. The sight of the carton nested high in the crotch of her lemon-yellow stretch pants made the boys visibly nervous, and we turned away. Colleen started for home. I walked the boys across the backyards until Melvie split off.

Then it was just me and Tony walking out of my neighborhood.

I sat down with Tony on his aunt's sofa. Tony's parents had abandoned him to his divorced aunt and he had little faith in the family system. He had had several minor arrests. He drove his aunt's car. He drove his aunt's car *drunk*. His freedom upset Melvie, whose family was intact, his dinner hour and curfew planned and negotiated in democratic family meetings. Melvie carefully monitored his private humidistat in his own pristine moral climate. His candor and honesty were by turns compelling or irritating to me.

But I had become addicted to the scent of Tony's DEP hair gel, a salon myrrh edged with the remarkable sweetness of fresh sweat. He kissed me. His full, moist lips reminded me of the anatomy satellite at school, where I had learned about the "epithelium," and the erupting "goblet" or "chalice" cells in mucous membranes that make a kiss *wet*. He opened his pants and pushed my head over his lap. My lips brushed his zipper and I felt its golden teeth still warmed by his heat. He was teaching me to French him. He wrapped my hair in his fist and I learned not to scrape the shaft with my molars and not to nip its engorged head.

I remembered what I had seen Karen do to Imran, and how she had squared her shoulders each time she was finished.

That winter, Ray was hospitalized again for his ulcer. I took the bus downtown after school, but it delivered me too soon for hospital visiting hours. I could wait in the hospital lobby or hang out at a seedy tobacco emporium called the Underground. I was attracted to the little boutique because alongside the tobacco it sold homemade candles, incense sticks and antiwar buttons and posters.

I met the shop's proprietor, who lived in the basement rental on Ninth Street. The shop wasn't zoned for residential occupancy, but I could see a brass bed through the beaded curtain that separated the shop space from his living quarters. A woman had worked in the shop —perhaps she lived there too—but when I asked about her, the man said, "She's gone back to the Cascade mountains in Oregon."

"She went to the mountains?"

"They weren't going to come to her."

"Oh," I said. "She sold me some incense. I forget the name of it."

He leaned on the glass counter and looked at me. "Let me guess— the sandalwood buttons, right?"

"Yeah, that's it. They burn longer than the sticks."

"Who are you?" he said.

I told him my name, and he said, "I think I recognize you. Honey, I'm Walter Stackhouse." His eyes didn't budge from me and I had to look away.

On the bed in the other room, I saw something with a long wooden handle. It might have been a crutch or prosthesis, but it looked like it might be a rifle. In fact, it was the sanded neck of an electric guitar. Walter dabbled in musical instruments. He resurfaced guitars with his own trademark "gator finish," an acrylic shellac that checkered and blistered significantly upon drying, giving the guitar its scaly gator appearance.

He sold these "gatorized" guitars to local rock musicians. Walter walked around the display case. I saw he wore western boots and he had a lanky cowboy gait, a habit of thrusting his pelvis slightly forward of his trunk as he leaned back on his bootheels. I liked how it looked.

Before I visited Ray, I waited in the shop, examining the curious items in the glass display cases. Next to an array of smoking paraphernalia, there were rows of scented candles, packs of Tarot cards, antiwar bumper stickers arranged in a colorful fan and a sprinkling of political buttons. One spool of circle stickers repeated the phrase WAR IS NOT HEALTHY FOR CHILDREN AND OTHER LIVING THINGS. It was a classic remonstrance of that era, but its forced naïveté annoyed me.

I read the sticker out loud to Walter Stackhouse, " 'War is not healthy for children.' Well shit, no kidding—"

Walter looked at me hotly. "That sticker says it all. I was just over there. You don't need a dissertation on that war," he said. "I can describe that jungle in twenty-five words or less."

I said, "You were over there? Really? I guess you would know, then."

I'd been coming to the store for several days while Ray was in the hospital. One afternoon, Walter came around the counter and stood behind me. He wrapped his arms around my shoulders, pinning my arms to my sides. He dipped his face to the nape of my neck. I felt his hot breath, a humid cloud filtered through my loose hair. I thought his embrace might just be brotherly affection, until he let go. There was something lewd in the way he released me. An unpromising touch that registered and lingered.

I BOUGHT A PACKAGE of colored pipe cleaners from Walter and twisted them into animal shapes, which I left on Ray's hospital tray. Ray was disturbed by the purchases I made at the Underground. He saw the Zig Zag cigarette papers I had allowed to slip out of my purse.

I occasionally rolled cigarettes and sometimes I had pot, but I kept them for their suggestion—that I routinely practiced an illegal activity.

I bought a pack of Tarot cards from the display case and laid them out across Ray's hospital bed with no idea how to read them. I enjoyed the drawings, which forecast specific events. A letter left out on a table meant that "someone was coming to visit." A pitcher of water and two glasses meant "there would be gossip." I read the booklet that explained which pictures meant death or love or betrayal.

Ray called them Gypsy cards, and he told me, "I don't like you shopping at that opium den." His eyes narrowed as he listened to me bubble and croon about Walter Stackhouse.

"He was in the army, but now he's a conscientious objector."

"Stackhouse, is it?" The word sounded menacing on my father's lips.

"Walter," I told him.

The next morning, Ray left his hospital bed and took the elevator to the lobby wearing only his linen service bathrobe over a scanty hospital johnny; he walked the city block to find the little shop. The Underground was closed when Ray visited, but Walter Stackhouse later told me he had seen a man in a blue hospital gown cup his hands and press his nose to the window in order to see into the dark shop. "He looked like death," Walter said.

Ray must have seen the beaded curtain that led to the back room. Walter's brass bed was covered with a rumpled Amish star-burst quilt that had belonged to the girl who went home to Oregon. The quilt wasn't exactly the same as satin sheets, but Ray didn't like seeing a bed. "That's the straw on the camel's back. That place is off-limits." I ignored Ray's warnings and continued to loiter in the shop. One afternoon, I brought Tony DelRose and Colleen. Tony purchased a box of Asthmador capsules. The capsules were meant to be placed in a holder and burned like incense to clarify air. Instead, Tony divided them up among the three of us and we swallowed several capsules and waited for the hallucinogenic effects. The powder was 60 percent belladonna—deadly nightshade.

As I rode the bus home by myself, the chemical started working. I weaved up the street from the bus stop and stumbled into my house. I

was unable to greet Veronica, who stood in the kitchen holding a rubber basting bulb. The utensil was alarmingly, unreconcilably disgusting. I couldn't be sure if it was the drug or my common sense that made
it seem so. Veronica stopped what she was doing and eyed me as I stag-
gered through the kitchen. The bulb dripped on the linoleum. "What's
wrong with you?" she said, but she didn't press me for an explanation.
She seemed unwilling to learn more. She turned back to a veal roast to
suction its sizzling juice with the basting bulb. She didn't follow me
down the hall to my room. She let me fight that poison on my own.

I stayed in my room and heard chattering voices, saw double images. Brushing my hair in front of the mirror, I saw two others standing
behind me. *Me* and *me* and *me*. I was talking to myself, hearing the
same identical phrases in a trio of echoing voices.

Two days passed before the Asthmador was cleansed from my system. I wanted to tell Walter about my ordeal, but when I entered the
shop again he was having a high-pitched telephone conversation. I
heard Walter repeat several phrases with insistent emphasis on the
word "tonight!" before he slammed the receiver down. I was certain
Walter was discussing drugs or stolen property. I wiped a glass countertop with a rag and pretended not to hear the rise and fall of the conversation. Then two customers came in to buy tobacco, and I took the
key off its tiny hook and unlocked the humidor for them.

That evening I stayed in the shop until after dark. I didn't like to go
home to Veronica with Ray still in the hospital. Walter gave me a
broom, and I swept the gritty linoleum until I had collected all the
wayward curls of cash-register tape from along the baseboards. When I
finished sweeping, the air was dull from the rising dust. Next, I took
the Windex and washed the plate-glass window, careful not to scrub
the street number, TWENTY-NINE, which was stenciled backward on the
inside glass. I wasn't ashamed of doing these chores for free. Once, I
had even lugged Walter's sheets and towels to the coin laundry. He told
me to make sure I banged the cardboard box several times to rid it of
roaches before putting the folded towels in; roaches zipped and skated
over the washers and driers oblivious to the rattling spin cycles. I
adopted Walter's chores as if they were mine, hoping he'd let me stay
in the shop as long as I kept busy. I began to pilfer food from my

mother's pantry, and I arrived at the shop with fresh Bosc pears Veronica was saving to poach in wine for her bridge luncheon. I took every one before she could stop me. I arranged the gorgeous fruit on the glass counter above the boxed cigars. "Try one," I told Walter, and I watched him bite into its creamy globe.

I put the broom in the closet and looked around for another duty. Anything to keep me there at dusk, to let me hang back in that neutral zone of loneliness which was not as grim as the emptiness of home.

Walter came up behind me. He said, "I'm closing up, honey."

"Oh, I guess it's late. Sorry," I said, embarrassed. He was standing behind me. He gripped my waist the way someone might hold my hips if I was leaning over the rail of a ship or reaching into a wishing well. I had never been held at the waist, quite like that, and it disturbed some center of gravity I wasn't conscious of until it left me.

He turned me around to face him. Then he kissed me. More shocking than his kiss was the snap of the light switch as he reached over and flicked off the overhead fluorescent.

Walter walked me through the beaded curtain.

I think I always knew this was going to happen.

I wasn't frightened. I was wondering about the level of my skills and how they would be tested. I felt a crosscurrent of anticipation and a humble reverence for his astonishing beauty when Walter pushed his jeans down and kicked his feet loose from their tight cuffs.

He lifted an unfinished guitar from the faded star-burst quilt and propped it against a chair. He peeled open the sheet and I got in bed. He climbed in beside me. "When do you get your period?" he said.

"Excuse me?"

"When's your next one?" he said.

"Oh, I just had it."

"Beautiful."

He kissed my neck. I tilted my head back as he bit my throat. I saw the headboard. I screamed.

Its leg span was that of a silver dollar—a remarkable spider frozen on the headboard, just two inches from the available tarmac of my forehead. The spider wiggled its pedipalps, exhibiting amorous or territorial behavior, who could tell? I shot up. I scrambled to the foot of the bed. I could never forget the malevolent thrumming of the spider trapped inside my plastic shower bonnet when I was small.

"Stupid girl," Walter said as he squashed the spider and cleaned it from the headboard with his sock. He jerked my arm and centered me on the mattress. He pushed my skirt over my hips until I heard the zipper snag. He gathered its hem at my waist, a woolen truffle.

I was a virgin.

The tiny vermeil curtain, contrary to popular belief, was still intact after thousands of hours in the saddle, after whole summers riding bareback in just my Speedo swimsuit. I wondered if we would *hear* the hymen snap, like the beeswax seal on a jam jar. Then, I thought of two proven procedures for removing a Band-Aid—you can tear the adhesive off in a stinging instant, or slowly tease it off. Each method has its discomforts.

I yelped just once with Walter's first thrust. It was instant, like when the wind tugs a white sock from a clothesline and carries it off.

That must be that, I thought.

Then, Walter fucked me while I searched the ceiling. I was certain another spider might emerge from the ancient crown molding. "Look at me. Look at me," he scolded. I locked on his eyes. He studied me with the intensity of someone threading a needle. I started to notice Walter's excitement and its effect on me.

At first, I protested when he touched me, repelled and teased by my own curiosity until my conscience was freed. With Melvie or Tony DelRose I might never have dropped my guard. I monitored a hot kernel of pleasure as if this disembodied seed, a tiny navy bean of fantastic sensation, had nothing to do with me. I didn't think of the spider on purpose; it crept into my imagination, a thrilling aspect, not an impediment to my sexual fantasy, my triggering climax. Walter rolled off me, his muscles smoothed and languorous. I saw he took familiar comfort in a ritual still new to me.

I stood up and felt dizzy as I looked for my panties.

Ray must be eating his white dinner: creamed corn, baked haddock, Junket rennet custard or butterscotch pudding, which he always saved for me. He must be wondering why I was late. I picked up my underwear from the floor. The panties said TUESDAY, but it was Thursday.

I pulled them on and felt the first shocking residue, a hot spill soaking into the pink nylon crotch panel. I found my jeans, knocking over Walter's boots. I arranged the boots, toes together, at the foot of the bed and walked out through the beaded curtain. Walter had locked the dead bolt with his key and I couldn't leave the store. I looked for his keys on the counter, but they must have been in his trouser pockets. His pants were on the floor in the other room. I walked back through the beaded curtain.

WHEN I ARRIVED AT Ray's hospital room, the tiny pink washer of my hymen was insulted and stinging, and I couldn't stay seated beside him. I imagined my next episode with Walter Stackhouse. Our lovemaking would get easier, the way a cashmere button hole "gives" a little each time. I stood up and went to the window. Despite my physical discomfort, I was feeling giddy from my indoctrination, which I reasoned I had carried through fair and square, and I could take credit for something.

Ray seemed worse than the day before. His ulcer was bleeding again. It had been a momentary scramble when the hemorrhaging couldn't be controlled, and he looked like he'd been through it. His new bleed might have happened when I was in bed with Walter Stackhouse. I was reluctant to face Ray from my new perch, a peculiar suspended animation after the sex act. I thought Ray might recognize it. I turned around and forced a smile, like a disheveled child starlet captured in a tawdry freeze-frame.

Ray looked at me twice. Did he see the difference in me?

NOFUCK, VA.

(KAREN)

I'M ANSWERING the pay phone in the Norgetown, taking numbers for Russell Stover when I meet Horace McDade, a black quartermaster right off the *Independence*. His ship is in port after six months in the South China Sea. She's getting refitted for a new assignment after that Gulf of Tonkin emergency. Horace says he's glad to be in home port for 9 billion reasons. One of those reasons is me.

"Oh, sure," I say. I've heard it before, you know?

Horace was seeing Peaches; now he comes to see me.

Ruth doesn't like blacks hanging around the Paris office. White clients come to the Paris because they don't want hit or miss with outlaws trolling the bricks outside Naval Base Norfolk. Ruth says hookers get windburn. They get raw blisters from walking blocks in their high heels. Men don't like paying for girls with their dirty Band-Aids oozing.

Ruth says a hooker will bring her john back to a flop where she has a trick baby waiting in its bassinet. It's bawling. Clients don't want to spend money on an exhausted Donna Reed. Ruth's girls don't have babies. She gives us Ortho wheels like it's Pez.

Horace is tall and handsome, high-waisted like the fighter Muhammad Ali, but without the fancy back-and-forth. No matter how nice-looking he is, Ruth doesn't like Horace dating me.

But Horace is into me. He takes me to the Cape Henry Lighthouse and to the Chrysler Museum. He wants to show me the nude paintings, but the museum is closed each time we show up. Once I thought I saw the Newport behind us; maybe James had trailed us. After a while, Horace sees he doesn't have to take me to these recreation spots, and he brings me to a friend's apartment where we make love. Then we go to the Boulevard Room, a jazz spot in the neighborhood.

I've been coming in late for dates with my regulars, so Ruth gives me all the nuts, these meatballs who bring their own ideas in a shopping bag. Or they want water sports. Ruth says, "We got Mr. McTinkle. Karen, it's your turn."

I still can't get the hang of it. Ruth makes me drink a pitcher of iced tea and hold it. I tell Ruth, "I can't piss on command."

Ruth says, "You will or you'll burst."

I start having trouble. The doctor at the clinic calls it "bladder spasms." He says it's on account of these clients banging me. I talk my tricks through a nice hand job, with lots of Jergens. I try to finish them before they climb on me. I'm doing this meatball from Langley. I'm using *two* hands. He stops me right before he shoots. He hands me a souvenir penknife that says WILLIAMSBURG, VA. It's a trinket from a tourist shop. He wants me to stick him. "Shit. Stab yourself," I tell him.

Ruth didn't screen this weirdo. She has to do "damage control" and she takes me out for dinner. She says, "You want a sirloin at the Charcoal Corral?"

I tell her, "You think I want steak after that stabber?" I tell her I want "catch of the day." Maybe a plate of fried clams, enough to feed an army.

Ruth takes me to Neptune's, right on the water. Last week she took Valerie when she had a bad character.

WHEN JAMES LEARNS about Horace, he tells Ruth she's losing control of her business. He says, "Karen's running wild."

Ruth tells him, "I don't care what Karen does after she's finished work. As long as it's off-premises."

Horace's tour is up in three weeks and then he starts work at the Firestone Tire Center. He wants to bring me onboard before he's discharged. He gives me an authorized Naval Base Norfolk pass with my name printed on it. "Cindy Stevens."

I've been Cindy Stevens at jail, in the emergency room, and I write Cindy Stevens at department stores so they'll send me perfume samples and chances for a Caribbean cruise. It doesn't look funny anymore.

I tell James, "So, I'm getting the grand tour of the *Independence* just like Linda Bird Johnson."

James grabs my official pass to the supercarrier and pulls it up to his face to read the small print. He flicks it on the countertop. He starts banging through the kitchen cupboard, slapping down a cereal bowl and filling it overflowing with Grape-Nuts. He stops. He lifts my chin with one knuckle to read me the law. He says, "You climb on that bird farm, we're through."

I can't decide if James feels more jealous about me or about my invitation to board the *Independence*.

He pours milk over his Grape-Nuts and stirs it around with a spoon. "You get what I'm saying?" he says.

I nod my head up and down and then side to side. I'm saying yes but really I'm saying no. It's my silent "Screw you."

James pitches the bowl of cereal at me, but the mush hits the refrigerator and slides down the laminated *Head of Christ*.

I get a rag and start to clean the Grape-Nuts off the *Head of Christ*. I guess it's bad that it's the *Independence*. She's famous. Horace tells me his ship had a big role in the Cuban Missile Crisis, and it just came back from six months in the South China Sea in support of Viet Nam operations with embarked Air Wing 7.

I'm mopping up the milk, but I'm telling James, "Horace says they got a Navy Unit Commendation for a record seven thousand sorties, day and night strikes."

James says, "Seven thousand sorties?"

"I guess that means fourteen thousand takeoffs and landings."

The MPs probably wouldn't let James step foot on a carrier just to tour it. James is still angry about being kicked. He wasted his best years in the service. Ruth says, "James went down in flames," but she doesn't mean he's a hero.

"Seven thousand strikes," I say again. Now I'm being mean.

James tells me, "What about you? How many takeoffs and landings you log with those white hats?"

I say, "More than you can see from shore."

James looks crushed that I don't recognize his sore feelings about his military status.

I tell him, "James, no wonder those boys are trying to have their fucks with regularity—if they're heading right back into that. You don't want to be in that war, do you, baby?"

He pinches my arm until I squeak. James can't stand it when I show him pity. Pity is worse than stealing from him.

HORACE DRIVES ME out to Sewells Point to show me the piers. Everything is rat-gray. Rat-gray whether there's a war on or not. War is the whole point for this whole setup. We drive up Willoughby Bay past the Naval Air Station heliport. Those big camo'ed choppers are lined up like a row of grasshoppers, their rotors folded up. He shows me the parade deck where they have official band concerts. "Sometimes there's a wedding," he says.

I imagine how a bride would look on that parade deck, next to all those helicopters.

Before we board the *Independence*, we have a hamburger at the Tradewinds, a club right on base. Everyone stares at Horace McDade, but they're really watching me. I'm wearing a new Villager skirt, gold herringbone, and a new mohair sweater. Penny loafers with silver dimes. Mohair looked nice on the store mannequin, but when James touches me all over, it comes alive. Hairs float up my nose from the static electricity. I smooth my collar, but the hairs get in my mouth.

Horace is grinning like the cat who ate the canary.

"What are they staring at?" I say.

"*You*, beautiful. They're looking at you."

Horace is getting a kick out of sneaking a pro in here. He's black and I'm white as snow.

"How am I doing?" I ask the quartermaster.

But when he brings me onto the *Independence*, my heart starts pounding. The flight deck is several stories high, like a mountain cliff ready to break away from shore. The height is getting to me.

There's a crew on deck resurfacing the tarmac. James calls these boys "deck apes," "purple shirts," but Horace greets them, "Afternoon, men." He tells me to walk on the other side so I won't get my shoes tarry. Technicians are inspecting the catapults and testing the cables that snag the jets so they don't keep rolling and nose right into the drink. The men are cheerful to be out in the air, like Ray acts when he does yard work on Sundays.

Horace tells me, "Come on, let's go belowdecks. I'll show you my cozy spot—"

"I don't think so," I tell him. "This is as far as I go."

"Come on, Cindy. I've got our afternoon planned—"

I tell him, "I'm not going down in its stomach—what do you call it? Glory hole? No thanks."

"Honey, what's the problem?"

"Can't move an inch," I say. My knees are rubber. I can't lift my feet. The soles of my shoes are frozen in place. Horace pulls me over to the hatch, a huge dark horseshoe. I can't leave the broad daylight of the flight deck. I'm not really thinking about the *Doria*. I'm not thinking of that little girl in the crumpled prow and the cabin where my sister and I might have died in our sleep. I don't try to remember it. It crept up on me all of a sudden.

SINCE SHRINER NIGHT, Ruth doesn't mother me. I'm on my own when James goes crazy. "Let the feathers fly," Ruth tells me.

I sit on the toilet, but I can't pee. I look at the toilet paper and there's a tiny red star on it. A red star. That's all that comes out.

I walk into Emergency and describe this star I keep finding.

"A star?" the nurse asks me.

"That's what I'm saying."

They push me down in a wheelchair and roll me up the hallway. It's an operating room as bright as a ballpark. They put me in stirrups.

A doctor says he's going to "aspirate" the clot. First he has to "stretch" me with these six sterile metal rods, one right after the other. He holds up the first one. It's like a shish kebab skewer. The last one is as big as a mop handle.

In the recovery room, I'm hooked up at both ends. They've got a drip going. They want something going in and something coming out. A catheter tube runs pink for an hour and then it's clear. They want to see me use the toilet on my own before they'll let me go home. A social worker comes in. She's telling me about a shelter where I can recuperate. When I say "No thanks," she loses her temper. "Why do you girls refuse to face facts?" She asks me, "Where did you get these bruises?"

"These here? These are old."

She touches a yellow square on my thigh, big as a slice of sandwich bread smeared with French's mustard.

When that bitch is gone, I hear James coming down the hall. His voice is sweet as sugar as he cuts through the red tape. He comes into my room and pulls my IV needle free. He goes around to the side and starts wiggling the catheter tube. "Ouch," I'm saying, but I'm glad to have it out. I find my clothes folded in a plastic bag. I get dressed. He drives me back to Bailey's.

AFTER WORK, I GO WITH Sharon Martone and Rose Pearson to the Elbow Room. Since Ruth has stepped back, I don't like to go home to James. When the girls leave, I wait for Horace at the Elbow until they close up—sometimes it's 3 A.M. I sit at the bar and eat cherries and orange slices they use for Manhattans. When those are gone, I start nibbling the martini onions punched on toothpicks. Penny says, "Shit. If you're starving, go over to the Seventh Wonder, don't eat all my fruit."

I'm always going to pay a price for staying out late. I try to time my rendezvous with Horace when James is flying blind and too drunk to do battle. But sometimes if I wait too long, he's awake and got his second wind.

I'm sitting in the Boulevard Room with Horace. The music is loud. Horace has his nose in my ear so I can hear him talk. I guess this is what James sees when he steps into the place.

James shoves the table aside. The table is a cable spool and it keeps rolling down the aisle. Horace stands up, but James shoves me out to the car. The whole house screams at a white couple making a spectacle in that smooth spot.

James has a handful of my hair and he leads me to the Newport. He shoves me in and he gets behind the wheel. He takes the back of my collar and smashes my face into the dash. He says, "You into Sambo?" Whack. "You want to suck that shitstick?" Whack. "Where's Peaches—you doing three-way with that Hershey slut—"

Horace comes out to the car. He yanks the passenger door, but it's locked. James pulls away slow and smooth, like he's driving a pumpkin. Horace starts trotting along. James speeds away.

At the intersection, I try to unlock my door, but the plastic knob pops off. I pinch the threaded stem until my fingertips are cut. The lock snaps open and I jump out. James steers over the curb and onto the sidewalk where I'm running. He drives right into me and I roll off the hood. I hit the sidewalk pretty hard. My canine tooth punches through my lower lip like when you force a shower curtain on a hook. I sit up on the sidewalk. I push my tooth back through the torn spot.

I WAKE UP. I'm freezing. I'm *blind*.

I touch my face all over, like Patty Duke playing Helen Keller. My eyeballs feel like Penny's onions under my fingertips. Shit, it's freezing. I could use my Clemson jacket—what happened to it? I'm wearing just my bra and panties and my penny loafers.

SILVER STITCHES SPILL over me. I guess it's daybreak. Clock radios and toaster ovens keep falling off these stacks. All James's booty is toppling onto me. I've been screaming, but the next-door neighbor is in the reserve; maybe he's gone for the weekend. I scream until I'm hoarse. I'm sore all over. I guess I'm pretty banged up. I sit down right where I am to take my inventory.

I WAKE UP. I open my eyes. I *think* I open my eyes. It's dead black.

I PULL MY PANTIES DOWN and take a pee. Ruth keeps russets in here but there's only one left in the sack. It's growing eyes, but I nibble the potato until it's gone. I scream to the next-door neighbors. "It's me, Cindy! Are you deaf!"

Nobody shows up. I scream my real name just to try it.

SOMEONE TAPS ON THE DOOR. It's James. He hisses through the hinges, "Shut up, Cindy. You're in there till you shut your mouth."

"Where's Ruth? She's going to find me."

"Ruth's in Greensboro."

If he's telling the truth and Ruth went to visit her kids in Greensboro, I'm never getting free. "Let me out," I say.

"I decide when that is," James says.

• • •

Bright red seeds dissolve along the door seam. It's sunset. I slept another whole day. I'm numb and shivering. Even my guts are frozen, like shit in an ice tray. I might just have to do it like an animal.

I don't know what time or tide it is when I hear the hasp scratching. The door opens. I squint in the daylight. It's Piers. His coveralls are shiny with weeks of ironed-in grease. He's gleaming like a bowling trophy. He wants some of his TV sets, but he finds me. I fall into his arms like a baby.

"This ain't right," he tells me. "Shit. It ain't human."

"You come for the TVs?"

"Forget the appliances. Nobody's seen you for two days."

The shack smells like piss. It's embarrassing.

"I bet I look like hell," I tell Piers.

"I guess you're not entering a contest," he says. He finds my loafers and tucks them under his arm. Piers leads me down the alley between the Ventoura and the double-wide next door. I start whimpering like a dog rescued from the pound. Piers covers my mouth with his Boraxed hand.

He sees James in the kitchen pulling his jacket off the hook. He's on his way out here. Piers pushes me into the cab of his pickup. He throws it in gear, but James is at the passenger door tugging both my ankles. He's got my knees. The door crashes open and shut. I'm sliding out. I hold onto the gun rack. A Winchester falls into my lap. Piers takes the gun and points it at James. "Get your rat paws off her."

"Since when do you keep it loaded, Mr. Safety-Conscious?" James says.

Piers flips the rifle over and starts banging James with the butt end. James squeaks and falls out of the truck. I tug the door shut. We pull onto Shore Road. I turn around in the seat and see James on his knees, trying to get some air back in his lungs. Piers looks in his rearview. He asks me, "What crawls on all fours in the morning, two legs at noon—"

I say, "Snakes just slither, right?"

"That's right, honey. They slither from the cradle to the grave."

I spent almost three days thinking about this exact minute. The minute I leave Bailey's for good. But when I see James crumpled on the driveway, I want the sweet part of James to stand up and leave the bad half on the ground. Like in those Warner Brothers cartoons, when it shows a mouse go off to heaven and its soul leaves its body—a smoky outline rises up, propelled by little wings at its shoulders and cuffs—that's the angel leaving its human remains in a heap.

PIERS GIVES ME HIS lumberjack shirt from the well behind the seat. It smells like motor oil and that Borax powder. He tells me that's the standard smell. "Peterbilt No. 5."

He drives down Shore Road and over Lesner Bridge into Great Neck and farther. We come down a rural stretch. Cows. Miles of electric fence. He turns off the road at a farmhouse and some shabby outbuildings. Two goats are tied to a clothesline runner. The sign says TIDEWATER PRAISE ASSEMBLY SPIRIT-FILLED CHURCH.

I tell Piers, " 'Spirit-filled' sounds like creme-filled donut."

Piers says, "You're just starving."

A bulletin board says MORNING RENEWAL: 10:00. EVENING BELIEVERS MEETING: 6:30. VIBRANT PRAYER MEETING: 8 P.M.

The parking lot is empty.

I don't like the looks of the church-farm and I want to go back to Ruth's.

Piers can't decide if he should get me washed up before giving me to the pastor. He says his girlfriend might have some clothes for me, but if he brought a naked girl home to his girlfriend, she would probably get the wrong picture. He says he's sorry.

"Hey, it's not your problem," I tell him.

Piers says, "You won't hold it against me if I leave you off?" He tells me to wait in the truck while he goes to find someone. He goes inside a tiny ranch house beside the barn church. Its front door is gouged as if a huge dog has sat there pawing to get inside. I look around for this dog, but I can't see a sign of life except those goats trotting back and forth on their clothesline wire. The ranch house looks run-down. Someone has left a broken dinette chair out on the carport. The chair has a lemon-yellow vinyl seat, but one of its chrome legs is bent like it's kicking in a chorus line. It reminds me of the beat-up props we use for peep windows.

"I don't like the looks of this place," I tell Piers when he comes back. I point out the busted chair. "And you see those claw marks on the front door? That must be a big dog."

Piers nods his head. He says, "Those scratches? That's just the soulless spooks trying to get inside."

"Don't talk about ghosts. It gives me the creeps."

Piers chuckles. "The pastor's coming right out. He's on the telephone."

"Who's he talking to? Collect to God? Is he trying to send me home? If that's the case, I'll go back to Ruth's. Maybe I can stay with Rose Pearson. She told me—"

"Honey, this place is better than Ruth's. Ruth can't solve your problem."

"My problem is James." I like saying it when James is nowhere in sight.

Piers tells me, "James is your symptom. If it isn't James, it's going to be his look-alike."

"James is my symptom? Piers, who's *your* symptom? What's *her* name?"

"Shit, girl, does your mouth come with an oil can? Just let Deacon Lauer help you out for a while, okay?"

Deacon Lauer comes over to the truck and helps me get down. Under the lumberjack shirt, I'm just about as naked and filthy as someone in that billboard for the War on Poverty.

I can see this deacon thinks I'm important to him and he's important to me. He puts his face into mine. His eyes are fierce blue like hard candy. He's puffed up about his church role. Getting a whore off the street. How often does he get the opportunity?

He says to Piers, "A Shirley Temple hooker, now that's a modern-day shame." He's talking like I'm not even standing here. He's calling me a "hooker"—who does he think I am? I tell Piers, "Hey, tell him I didn't hook. You ever see me take a corner anywhere in Norfolk? I was never on the bricks one single time—"

"Oh, hush," Piers says. He gives me my loafers, knocking the heels together first. A twenty-dollar bill falls out. I guess I had one of those in the toe and forgot. It gives a bad first impression, I guess.

The preacher picks up the money. He takes my hand and pinches the back of my wrist. The skin sticks together in a tiny fold where he's plucked it.

"Yessir. See that? She's dehydrated," he tells Piers. "She needs to go to the hospital."

"Look, I'm not going to any hospital," I tell him. Since that time I was peeing stars, I never want to go back. I use James's sugary voice and I'm telling the deacon, "No, I don't need a doctor. But, hey, you're right, I'm dying of thirst. Just give me a glass of water. Maybe you have some Red Rose? I'll drink any kind of tea. I'm not fussy. Piers can tell you—"

MAP

OF THE WORLD

———◆———

1968–70

THE MUSEUM
OF CHILDHOOD

———

COLLEEN WANTED to bleach a strip of my hair to match a vampire's bride we had seen on an episode of the soap opera *Dark Shadows*. She mixed two glasses of gin and lime Kool-Aid, and we drank it too fast. We stumbled into her bathroom, and she draped a bath towel over my shoulders. She separated a clump of my hair with her fingers, but when she tipped the bottle of color stripper, its applicator tip came unscrewed and spilled peroxide across my scalp. She had to bleach my whole head. Afterward, my frizzed hair stuck out on each side like the crisped wingspan of a bird caught on an electric fence.

Tony and Melvie showed up. Tony had just tilled a new Continental, a huge black "doctor's car." It had only four hundred miles on the odometer and he was anxious to get the bugs out. Ever since my private deeds with Walter Stackhouse, my desperation to leave Wilmington had been getting worse. I couldn't bear living at home like a child, still in sheep's clothes, after I had learned what to do from Walter. I felt different. Feeling different made me feel *guilty*, especially when I remembered standing next to Ray's hospital bed in my drenched panties. My immoral act had catapulted me from childhood, like a slingshot shoots a peach pit.

Just as Karen had climbed down the fire escape to meet Imran, I had entered the same turnstile when I walked through Walter's beaded curtain. Since then, I didn't belong at home. Now, when I watched Veronica primping before a cocktail party, my secrets stirred up until I was dying to blurt them. I wanted to tell her men loved *me*.

Tony asked me, "Your getaway car—like it?"

"Perfect," I said.

We piled into the hot sedan.

I went on impulse without even packing a suitcase, without my hairbrush or toothpaste, and none of my Days of the Week panties, nothing, just like my sister had done.

I wasn't trying to mimic her, but when Karen lived at home with me, we had sometimes had accidents in tandem, double incidents in which we both did the *same* thing at the *same* time. Silly things, like lifting telephone receivers at the same instant; flushing toilets in quick succession; or dropping phonograph needles onto identical 45s, stationed at either end of the house: Mary Wells singing "Two Lovers," her breathy, heartbroken voice enriched from two sources.

I cracked one of Veronica's precious Canton platters as I washed it in the kitchen sink at the same moment Karen had shattered a handblown lampshade, a rare specimen of Sandwich glass—a precious antique. We walked from opposite ends of the house in unstaged solidarity to face Veronica and admit our careless mistakes. We found her eating horehound candies, a forbidding medicinal smell which I will always associate with making a confession. We approached her chair, each of us holding out the shards of the rare heirlooms. It was a giddy feeling to stand abreast of my sister as we leveled the broken parts before our mother.

Veronica told us that artisans had endured great hardships in order to produce these beautiful specimens that we had carelessly destroyed. "For instance—this little mirror in its hand-carved rococo frame? To make its gold filigree, real gold dust was mixed with powdered *lead*. This lead eventually paralyzed the craftsmen—" She paused until we nodded our heads up and down in appreciation of the artist's sacrifice.

As Tony sped away from Wilmington, I imagined the museum of my childhood and everything in it. I pictured the Limoges dishes wrapped in green flannel, the silver teaspoons, their bowls nested tightly together. I remembered which pieces were lost from the place settings and smiled. Was I one of these?

Melvie asked to be discharged at the next intersection. When he saw that I hadn't followed him out of the hot car, he panicked. He stood on the traffic island, shaking his delicate wrists as if he had just washed his hands and couldn't find a paper towel to dry them. Watching his panic reaction, I felt a stony sensation. I knew that when Melvie was dismissed—there goes all reason. I climbed into the front seat to sit abreast of my friends. Tony passed out cigarettes and we lit them with the automatic cigarette lighter, fighting over its glossy teak button. I punched through the radio, finding chart-busters. The hit "Secret Agent Man" was especially haunting. "There's a man who leads a life of danger . . . Everyone he meets he stays a stranger—"

I was closing in on my sister. From my seat in the stolen limousine, I felt our lives converging, weaving tighter, like zipper teeth locking. I imagined that my every reckless act from that minute on was a stepping-stone to our reunion. In my flight, I could meet my sister halfway in neutral territory.

Tony stopped to buy king-size Cokes from a drive-through Burger Hutt. A girl passed the drinks through the window before asking for the money. Tony couldn't resist taking advantage of the youngster's inexperience, and he drove off. I heard the girl's wounded shriek as we pulled out of the lot.

Entering Baltimore, we hit traffic. Tony weaved through the congested lanes with a little too much abandon. The speedometer crept up to a hundred miles an hour. I whipped around in my seat and saw six pulsing cherry-tops in a blistering row behind us.

We left the expressway and plowed down an exit ramp. Tony drove over medians, climbed onto curbs, bisected traffic islands. At a tangled intersection, we shot into a stream of oncoming traffic. We were hit on the left. Another car struck our tail, and we were clipped a third time. The hood ripped free and slammed down on the other side of the street. The car was totaled in an instant. Colleen went limp between us. A sudsy, vermilion spray surfaced on her lips. She had bitten through her tongue.

We squeezed through an opening in the accordioned chassis and ran away from the pileup. We went down an alley and stopped before an American Tourister factory. A big neon suitcase blinked on and off at the entrance. I stood still beneath its pulsing glow.

My friends had disappeared. I was suddenly alone beneath the blinking suitcase. I looked up at the sign and watched the neon fork left and right to create a throbbing, bright cherry valise. I remembered what the FBI had asked Ray, "Did Karen take a suitcase?"

I walked back to the intersection.

The police swarmed over the wreck like worker ants on a plate of cake.

Blood expanded in a green-black sheet down the front of my shirt. It dripped from my forehead and from my right biceps where the car window had sliced across the tight crab apple of muscle. An officer said, "Is this a stolen car?"

I said, "Is that a stupid question?"

"Were you riding in this vehicle?" he asked.

"Is that a dumb question?"

THE TIDEWATER
SPIRIT-FILLED CHURCH

———

KAREN WALKED INTO the Tidewater Praise Assembly Spirit-Filled Church, too weak to stand up. Piers cupped her elbow, and they followed the deacon into a basement guest room below the Spirit-Filled Chapel, an old farmhouse gutted to make a giant room.

Her basement room was next to a large kitchen with a six-burner restaurant stove and piggyback ovens. Women shared kitchen duties and Karen would be expected to pitch in. The deacon said his congregation had monthly camp meetings and "feasts," for believers who came from other counties as far west as Roanoke and Wytheville. On the chipped Formica counter, Karen saw a mousetrap set with a spoonful of crunchy peanut butter.

Cheap reproductions of Jesus hung on the walls of the whitewashed room. It wasn't the familiar *Head of Christ* she'd looked at for two years, but Jesus with a lamb tucked under each arm. Jesus grinning madly with a full row of Pepsodent teeth. There was one casement window up at ground level, but tufts of grass screened the daylight.

The deacon showed Karen the bathroom and a new toilet that flushed *upward* to the septic line. He explained that the purchase and installation of the "flush-up" commode was voted on by members of the congregation. Karen was glad to see a toilet after peeing on the floor of the Alum-a-room shack. But she couldn't stand up much longer. She curled on the cot, pulling its stale sheet over her shoulder. Its cotton hem showed an aggressive patch of mildew, a dense sprinkling of black dots. She was too tired to worry about a little mold.

Piers stood over Karen. "I never want to see you back at Bailey's Trailer Village. You hear what I'm saying?"

"You don't have to worry. Good luck with your RCAs."

"Will you shut up—" he whispered. He kissed her once and left her in the basement room.

That first evening, the deacon's wife brought her into the ranch house and drew her a bath. Karen helped the woman remove the water-logged baby toys that had been left in the tub. Karen was pleased that a baby lived in the house. When she drained the tub, she told the woman, "I haven't seen a bathtub ring as bad as that since I used to chase my sister through the dust."

The deacon's wife dotted iodine on Karen's weeping sore where her tooth had punched through her lip. Karen went into the "Swap Shack," a room inside the church lined with boxes of donated clothing and other worn-down items. She found some pull-on slacks made of poly-ester fleece. The natty fleece looked like the lambskins in the Jesus portraits.

Karen sat down to dinner with the deacon, his wife and their little toddler. She recognized the three remaining lemon vinyl chairs. The deacon borrowed a folding chair from the church hall to make room for Karen. She ate her food and tried to answer their questions. Was she baptized? Did she get submerged, or was she drizzled with water? The drizzling kind wasn't as good as getting dunked.

Her plate was full—grits, cornbread, some kind of chewy ham slice, a pitcher of buttermilk and sliced tomatoes with dribbled bacon grease. She had trouble swallowing the salty mush.

In the morning, she mopped the linoleum in the church and scrubbed the miracle flush-up toilet, which was used by the congregation before and after daily services. Deacon Lauer made her stop working to hear sermons in the chapel. He brought her into the spirit-filled hall for morning renewal and for the evening prayer meeting. It was a circus. She watched young men in glossy rayon suits stand up to give impromptu speeches. The members responded with shrieks and bois-terous "Hallelujahs." She was surprised at the noise level, when Veron-ica's Catholic church was whisper-quiet.

"Ever hear of a church mouse?" she asked a woman seated beside her. She pressed her ears with her fingertips as the loudmouth youths screamed about Satan, but she saw she offended the believers and she dropped her hands in her lap.

After listening for an hour, Karen thought she really wouldn't mind having some Pepto-Bismol. Her stomach wasn't right.

On the third night, she was awakened by a noise. She looked up to find a man crouched at the casement window above her bed. A second face crowded the window. The faces bobbed there for a few seconds, like the moon and its pale after-flash. Then they disappeared. Karen jumped up and ran to turn on a light. By this time, the men had come down into the church basement and were standing in her room. She recognized one of the men from the revival meetings. Karen had seen him speak at the eight o'clock Vibrant Prayer Meeting and again at the Morning Renewal. He had been introduced to her as a subdean or some kind of field preacher. The congregation treated him like a celebrity. He had recently been arrested for giving sidewalk sermons and was jailed for disturbing the peace. When he was released from jail, he started preaching again even before he was off the courthouse stairs. He was arrested a second time. He had chanted and ballyhooed about Jesus until his voice was gone.

Standing beside the field preacher was a pimply teenager, maybe his son or a nephew. James had sneered at these revivalist types preaching on the traffic islands. He called them "sky pilots." Jehovah's witnesses often came into the Norgetown, interrupting Russell Stover's transactions on the telephone. JWs banged on the door of her trick pad while she was with a client and left pamphlets and maps with directions to the local Kingdom Hall on the washers and dryers.

Rose and Peaches wore crosses on neck chains. James told Karen that whores get the Glory if they spend any time at all in jail. "If you can't do the time, don't do the crime," James told her, as if falling into God's hands was like landing in jail.

The two men standing at the foot of her cot told Karen that they were there to "save her."

"No kidding," she said.

"You've been corrupting sailors on their way to Nam. And those Langley pilots, who only got a fifty-fifty chance on a *good* day."

Karen sat down on the cot and cocked her head in disbelief. The subdean was mixing in God and country. She'd heard everything now.

The subdean locked his eyes on Karen the way a dog watches its dog biscuit. *"Ye have sinned against the Lord: and be sure your sin will find you out."*

She remembered James reciting from his King James Bible, *"A whore is a deep ditch."* She tried to bolt, but the man twisted her wrist.

"Though your sins be as scarlet, they shall be white as snow; though they be red like crimson, they shall be as wool."

Karen said, "And how are you going to do that?"

"With God's love manifested in us."

The young boy said, "That's right. *I seek not my own will but the will of the father which hath sent me."*

Karen shrugged her shoulders.

Together, the men pushed her back on her bed. She struggled but couldn't get up. The subdean looked as if butter, no, as if lard wouldn't melt in his mouth. The pimply kid watched in nervous respect for his elder. Again, the man began pitching: *"Mercy is seasonable in the time of affliction; as clouds of rain in the time of drought."*

He quoted the Bible directly as he penetrated her and just as immediately found relief. He was as worked up from preaching to her as if he had been talking smut. But when the young kid took his place, he forgot his Bible lessons. He was making it up as he went along.

Karen drummed his chest with her fists, but he tugged her arms out straight.

She smelled the Gold Bond camphor rising from their trunks where they had dusted themselves with the medicated powder. The men thought her whore germs might be controlled if they applied it beforehand. It was just two of these talcum-powdered spiritualists, but it was two against one. Flatbacking these Jesus stylists, she wanted to tell Rose Pearson and Valerie, if she ever saw them again, that she did it *missionary for the missionary.*

She shoved the youth off the bed. He stood up and pulled on his trousers. He cinched his belt. He said, *"She does not take heed to the path of life; her ways wander, and she does not know it."* He looked at his elder for approval.

Karen said, "Oh, shut up. Go suck on Mary's tit."

Her dirty mouth was a reminder to them that they were out of their league, and they left in a hurry. Karen went to the flush-up toilet and lost her dinner. It wasn't the piggyback sex, but her daily fare had again been grits with red-eye gravy, and it was impossible to digest. She rinsed her mouth and got dressed in the same fleece pants from the Swap Shack. She put on her loafers.

On her way out, she noticed the mousetrap had been reset with a chunk of potato salad. She lifted the trap with kitchen tongs and dropped the whole thing in a hamper. She tried the door at the top of the stairs. The knob wouldn't turn. Her assailants had locked her in, worried that she might spill it to the deacon. She turned around and went to the other end of the church basement. She climbed out the bulkhead.

There wasn't any moon. She followed the lane divider on the county road. She could follow the yellow line anywhere—to Miami, New York, California, any of those exotic locations—or she could walk the line all the way home. She had heard about drunks weaving up the center line of a rural highway and sometimes getting hit. James told her that these crazy drunks get cold and lie down on the asphalt, which is still warm from the heat of the day. Karen sat down on the pavement and flopped back. The yellow line met her crown and began again at her feet. The snaking streak on the blacktop reached out from her native source and connected her to every pitiful option—every tar-paper shanty, trailer park or ranch house along the way.

But the road hadn't warmed up during the day. She felt the cold enter her spine and she stood up again.

She kept walking. The cleats on her loafers lisped, a comforting metallic chirp. There wasn't a single car until a police cruiser rolled up behind her. When its floodlight snapped on, her shadow shot up like a tall black paper doll.

She sat down beside the officer.

"Now where do you belong, Miss Midnight?" the officer asked.

AT THE STATION HOUSE, she explained, "I had a fight with my boyfriend, so I took a long walk."

"Your boyfriend should know better. Are you ready to go home?"

"Sure. I'll go home from here."

"Officer Richie can drive you home, honey. But sometimes your folks don't want a cruiser pulling up in front of the house—"

"That's right, they'd sure hate that."

Karen was told to fill out a form with her name and telephone number, from which the officer could contact her parents. Before she was finished writing, she asked the officer if she could use the bathroom. She walked to the other end of the hall. She walked out a side door, leaving just her fake name, Cindy Stevens, written on the form.

At a pay phone, she struggled to remove the dime from her loafer. The dime was wedged tightly in the leather slit and she couldn't get it out with her fingernails. She found a penny on the ground and used it to dislodge the dime. The procedure had a startling echo—as she pried the coin out, she realized that she had had this dime in her shoe the whole time she was working for Ruth. She could have used it before now—why had she waited? When the dime popped out, she thought of James and her rejection of him.

She dialed Peaches's number. She wasn't surprised when Horace picked up.

Karen said, "I'm at a phone booth. I don't know where."

"Sugar, I thought he was gonna kill you. You get away now and don't come back to Virginia Beach. Never come back to Bailey's."

"I was thinking I could come over there. Maybe you can put me up?"

Horace was silent.

She didn't ask again.

Horace told her, "There's too much shit happening here."

"Well, I guess."

"No can do," he said.

"Well, that's that. Tell Peaches I say 'Hey.' "

Horace clicked off. She pictured Peaches in Horace's lap.

Karen dialed the operator and asked to place a collect call to her brother Alex. Karen didn't have the number. The operator told her she would have to hang up and call Information. Karen dialed Information, but she didn't have a pencil. She tried to remember the sequence, but the seven numbers ran together. She called Information again and tried to scratch the number with a pebble on the stainless-steel tray under the telephone. Again she failed. By the third try, she recited the correct number to the long-distance operator. When the operator put the call through, Karen was sobbing from her efforts.

She pulled herself together. When Alex answered, she asked him, "Well, how's everything with you?"

Alex went blank. Karen heard nothing on the other end but a remote mechanical whirring, like a distant eggbeater.

"How's everything?" she asked him again.

After a second he said, "Is it you?"

"Yes," she told him.

"Is it you?" he asked her again.

His stunned and repetitive query mimicked her own confusion. *Yes*, she was his sister but not the same sister. The exchange made Karen so uncomfortable she almost slammed the receiver down.

"Alex, do you think you could drive down here for me?"

"Sure I will." He didn't hesitate. "Where would that be?"

"I'll be at the Cape Henry Lighthouse."

"You're where?"

"I'm just outside NoFuck. You must know this spot?"

"Shit, Karen. That's a famous military resort. Every boot knows about NoFuck."

Alex told Karen, "I'll be there by sunup. Sit tight." He hung up the telephone. He dialed Ray's number, but he clicked off before the first ring. He wanted to tell Veronica about Karen himself. He dressed carefully. He buttoned his collar tabs and took more time brushing his suede jacket.

ALEX DROVE OVER to the house and used his key to let himself into the sun porch. He walked into the living room and waited beside the tall clock. He heard the mechanism crunch its gears as the minute hand advanced one notch. Veronica was going to be upset with his news. He decided to pour her a scotch. He stood at the liquor cabinet and sloshed an inch of booze in a tumbler. The telephone call from Karen was a form of power that he would use to draw his mother to him. But he worried that Veronica might link his disturbing news with the messenger who brought it to her bedside. He immersed his index finger in the glass of scotch and sucked his fingertip.

Ray came up beside him.

"Karen called me," Alex said.

Ray touched Alex's shoulder and turned him around to face him. "You're saying Karen telephoned *you*? She called you? I guess she didn't want to talk to her mother—I guess she was thinking—"

"Who cares *who* she called? She's waiting there right now," Alex said, shrugging away from Ray's hands.

"Well, come on then," Ray said.

They walked back to the bedroom to wake Veronica. Ray stood back as Alex tugged his mother's wrist until she sat up, blinking. "Now what's wrong?" she said.

Alex said, "Karen's coming home."

Veronica perched on the edge of her tousled king bed and panted like a bird after it hits a plate-glass window. Ray thought that her arrhythmia had started up and he went to find her nitroglycerine pills, her Librium.

Veronica whispered to Alex, "Why is she coming back here?" her voice hot and thready with fearful ire.

Alex shook his head, mimicking her annoyance. He tried to convince her that he didn't know why his stepsister was returning. Seeing Veronica's display, he wondered if Karen was crazy to want to come back.

Veronica said, "But you talked to her. What did she say?"

Alex remembered Karen's tentative voice as she allowed her bond with him to reemerge, her typical sweetness clearly audible in every halting syllable. He couldn't admit his fondness for Karen to Veronica, and he saw that his scheme to control this episode was backfiring.

Ray came back into the room with a full glass of gin. He gave Veronica two pills and waited until the tranquilizer had smoothed her facial atrophy. He massaged her shoulders and rubbed the frozen triangle of muscles across her back.

Alex crossed the room and sat down in an armchair. The news had not rejuvenated his bond with his mother but merely tested it further. Ray tried to reassure her, but Veronica's eyes were wide and unreceptive, like flat black buttons on a rag doll. She was in shock. At last, she flopped against the pillows. She fell asleep. It was the middle of the night when Ray left with Alex for Virginia Beach.

Within the hour, Veronica was awakened by a telephone call from a hospital clerk in Baltimore. Veronica was woozy from her tranquilizer and gin infusion. She lifted her highball glass from the bedstand and drained its melted ice. She asked, "Who is this?"

"This is Bill Martin at Emergency. Is this Mrs. Mitchell? Mrs. Mitchell, the resident surgeon requests permission to operate on your daughter—"

"Karen's in the hospital? Is she hurt?" Veronica asked him.

"I'm sorry. The patient's name is Maria Mitchell. In police custody—" the voice said.

"In custody? Oh, it can't be *her*. You must mean the other one."

The clerk named Bill Martin explained that her daughter was in Baltimore on a stainless table after a Hollywood-style crash-up with two other teens. He told Veronica that the girl needed some stitches along the crown of her head where it had met the dash. She needed a double track of sutures on her right arm where the batwing window had cut across her biceps. It wasn't serious, but the sutures might leave scar tissue, perhaps some railroad tracks across her forehead.

Veronica asked the hospital clerk, "Can you hold on for one moment, okay?" She put the receiver down and went to check my bedroom. My guitar was tipped against the footboard of my bed. I was meticulous about my instrument and I wouldn't have retired before replacing the guitar in its case. The bed was unmade, the sheets rumpled. Veronica walked over to the four-poster and smoothed the Wamsutta with the palm of her hand to test its temperature. The sheets were cold as silver.

K AREN WAITED FOR ALEX at the Cape Henry Lighthouse. She was wearing the same Swap Shack clothes she had worn for three days. Everything she owned was still in the trailer at Bailey's. She had left behind her jewelry, her mohair sweaters, her ceramic cats and her motel Bible with seven hundred dollars in cash. All she had with her was half of a rattail comb she had fished out of the wastebasket at the lighthouse. She pulled the broken comb through her bleached hair so often its teeth plowed distinct rows in her dirty crown. She tucked the comb behind her back when a car turned into the parking lot. Alex steered right up to where she was standing. As Ray got out of the car, he saw Karen hide something. He came up to her and tugged her arm out. He took the broken comb from her hand and looked at it in shock.

"What did you think it was, a funny cigarette?" she said.

Ray laughed at her jab. He deserved it.

He took Karen in his arms and squeezed her. "I'm so glad about this," he said, resting his chin on her head as he hugged her. He was having trouble finding words. He let her go and pulled out his pack of Chesterfields. They each took a cigarette. He saw her puncture wound swelling her lower lip and he found the small Red Cross first-aid kit he kept in his glove compartment. Karen sat on the fender of the car as Ray dabbed her chin with a Mercurochrome sponge-tip applicator. It was an oddly paternal gesture, and she submitted to her childlike role.

Ray wanted to buy her breakfast and Karen directed them to the Seventh Wonder Diner. None of the girls would be there at that hour in the morning, but Karen almost wished that James would show up, just so she could rub something in his face. She would be safe because

James was a matchstick compared to Alex, who had been a soldier and a motocross champion, not to mention Ray, who had cut his teeth on "dead killed steel" at the open hearth.

Each time Karen looked down at her plate to stab her waffles, Ray stole a peek at her. She was sixteen and wasn't a child anymore. Ray searched her face to see what was left of her baby looks. Her dimples had retreated and her features were newly chiseled; her smile seemed forced, as if she were testing muscles she hadn't used for some time. He recognized she'd been working. Her ghoulish skin tone, pale as paste; her huge blue eyes that didn't rest on his face for more than an instant here or there. She reminded him of local whores on Market Street in Wilmington, girls he passed year after year, driving downtown to his warehouse. These Wilmington girls knew his car, his face. When he rolled past them, they didn't bother to make eye contact or throw their hips since they knew he wasn't cruising for their business.

Ray told Karen, "We thought we had lost you for good."

Karen ate her breakfast and felt sick. She had a four-hour drive and at the end of it was Veronica. She was thinking of the phrase, "There's light at the end of the tunnel," but she saw only Veronica's icy cameo at the end of this tunnel.

She wanted to tell Alex about the preachers who had raped her. Their Bible talk still reverberated in her ears. But she couldn't discuss *that* when Ray and Alex were still trying to adjust to her bleached white hair.

"It's like straw in 'Rumpelstiltskin,'" Ray said. Of course, Karen knew he was joking to release the tension he felt, but she remembered the fairy tale. The troll was like a wicked pimp and the heroine was forced to sell her soul.

Halfway home to Wilmington, Ray had to stop the car so Karen could get sick on the shoulder of the highway. Her breakfast came up. She apologized to Ray for wasting the money.

"It's nerves," Ray said. He opened the glove box and found a new bottle of Maalox. He broke the seal and handed the bottle to Karen. "I can't drink that," she told him.

He tried to get her to accept the medicine. When she refused, he swirled the bottle and took a long swig of it himself before putting it back in the glove box.

MAP

OF THE WORLD

———

VERONICA WAS SITTING at the dining room table with two large silver bowls lined up before her. She was sorting rose petals as she sometimes did to make potpourri. When Karen looked again, she saw that Veronica was shelling pistachios. The shells were dyed a harsh red, but the interiors were creamy white like the ruffled undersides of climbing roses. Veronica's fingertips were stained vermilion up to the second knuckle.

Finding her mother shelling pistachios confused Karen. She tipped her face in her hands and began to weep.

Veronica told her, "I've been waiting for hours. Going crazy. I had to do *something* with my hands to kill time." Veronica's face was alarmingly stilled. Karen saw that Veronica needed more time to defrost—the way an ice sculpture melts imperceptibly, sinking on its pedestal, its gradual transformation invisible to the naked eye.

Karen took a few tight steps toward her mother.

Veronica stood up. She turned to face Karen squarely and said, "For two years I didn't know if you were dead or alive." Her diction was chilly and metronomic.

Karen couldn't defend herself. Yes, she had let her mother think she was dead.

Veronica said, "Would it have killed you to call the house?" Veronica plucked Ray's sleeve, tugging him into the den. She shut the door after them. She told Ray, "I have *more* news. Now the baby one is in trouble. She's run off just like her sister."

◆ ◆ ◆

FROM THE HOSPITAL, I was transferred to a cell in the city jail where the vice squad made their evening deliveries. Colleen was sitting there. She stuck out her tongue to show me *her* stitches, a zigzag row of sutures across the pink wedge. The spiky knots were driving her to distraction. They tickled the roof of her mouth like spiders. Tony had been picked up too and was waiting at a different jail downtown.

With our blinding Clairol hair, Colleen and I didn't look much different from the working girls in the cell, card-carrying prostitutes that Baltimore Vice collected on a typical Friday night.

In the morning, an officer told me I had a telephone call. He walked me to a desk and handed me a receiver; the phone was in constant use and its plastic earpiece was remarkably hot. A dressed-up jailbird was using the other phone, talking to her pimp about her heavy fine.

Ray heard my voice and said, "You're okay." It wasn't in the form of a question. He told me the news about Karen.

"She came back?"

"Your sister's here. *Where are you*? I could have used your help with Veronica. Where did you disappear to?"

His query was a familiar one. I was always grilled: "Who are you? Where do you belong?"

RAY WANTED TO DRIVE to Baltimore. Veronica grabbed his elbow and said with alarm, "You can't leave Karen here with me. Take her into Philadelphia first. Cheltenham will do her intake today."

"Cheltenham?"

"I called the State Hospital in New Castle, but it's more red tape. It would take forever to get her in there."

"You contacted the State Hospital? That place is almost condemned—"

"I covered all the bases—why not? Cheltenham *expects* her. She can be admitted this afternoon."

"We can slow down," Ray said.

"She's going in today," Veronica said. "It's all arranged."

"She goes today? No discussion?"

Veronica didn't say the next word.

"I guess you're digging your heels in?" He didn't see how he could swing it the other way.

Ray always said that we pay for our sins in a lump sum payment at death's door, or we get nibbled to death with the installment plan. He seemed to think he was always paying. He took his car keys from the table and told Veronica, "We should sell tickets to Margaret Mead."

Veronica said, "This family doesn't need an anthropologist, it needs a dog officer."

Alex took Karen into the kitchen. Karen said her stomach was fluttering. Maybe a Coke would be good.

Karen looked out the kitchen window into the backyard. Along the creek, forsythia bushes were swelling into bloom, their branches clustered with yellow stars. Loose whips of the willow trees were a bright, stinging green. Spring again. The new season didn't soothe her but had the opposite effect. Karen told Alex, "Nothing changes. You'd think I was exactly where I started from when I walked out this door."

VERONICA HAD PUT AWAY all of Karen's clothing when Karen disappeared two years before. Some of her coats and sweaters had been donated to Goodwill, but who knows what had happened to the rest of it? When Ray looked in the attic, there wasn't any box or barrel marked with Karen's name. Ray told Karen to take whatever she needed out of her sister's drawers. Karen went into the bedroom we had once shared. On the wall above rows of china horses was a huge color poster of the Monkees. The juxtaposition of the stylized pop group and the little prancing horses looked entirely innocent to Karen, and she couldn't imagine how her little sister could be in trouble. Ray pulled open a top drawer. "Go on," he said. "Your sister won't mind if you borrow something."

Karen refused even to browse and pushed the drawer in.

Veronica came into the room. She had packed a Pan Am zip bag with fresh underwear, stretch pants, sweaters, a couple of acetate "shell" tops and a nightgown from her own wardrobe. "These should fit you. They're loose on me," Veronica said matter-of-factly.

Karen went into the bathroom and changed out of the clothes she had taken from the Tidewater Spirit-Filled Church Swap Shack. She pulled on a pair of Veronica's lemon-yellow Capri pants. The snug trousers were something Ruth's girls might wear to strip for the peep window.

Ray thought that Veronica's icy mood might have crested and waned since he had agreed to take Karen away. He tried to bring Karen and her mother together. He stood between them and opened his arms like a statue of St. Francis. "Come on now," he told them, trying to herd them closer. Veronica lifted her chin. Her fiery green eyes were lit with a brittle fury that made him flinch. She wanted her innocence confirmed in advance of any truce-making.

Veronica reminded Ray of everything she had endured in her lifetime. "My own father locks me up. Summers I'm shipped off by rail and subjected to the fancy of whatever predator rode the train. Then, it's the model. He finds his carnal diversions until I'm left out in the cold with two of his 'love children.' Next comes you and I'm saddled with a new set of daughters. Before you know it, these daughters are ferried off by drifters or demons, living in vice dens or riding in stolen car rings—"

Ray tipped his head as she reeled off the familiar litany. But in his natural affection for his daughter, he had called Karen "Peaches," as if nothing had happened in two years and she still deserved her pet name.

"Oh, please—" Veronica said when she heard his endearment.

Ray didn't give up until Veronica had made one small gesture of contrition. At Ray's insistence, she put her lips to Karen's cheek without the typical pressure or application of a kiss.

She told Ray, "You better get going. That officer in Baltimore said there's a strict window of time if you want to get Maria out of jail today—"

KAREN CRADLED THE PAN AM bag in her arms and looked out the car window. After driving for a few minutes, Ray told her, "The gap is too severe. Wounds are too deep. Your mother needs a little more time."

Karen nodded. It didn't come as a shock.

Ray said, "Veronica's very frail, her heart—"

They passed the familiar sign that said WELCOME TO WILMING-TON, THE CHEMICAL CAPITAL OF THE WORLD, and on its reverse side said THANK YOU FOR VISITING WILMINGTON, THE CHEMICAL CAPITAL OF THE WORLD.

"Thank *you*," Karen said as they passed the landmark.

Ray had often brought us into Philadelphia on business sojourns, into U.S. Steel, to the refinery complexes at Marcus Hook or to the big Scott Paper plant. At Scott Paper, we climbed a scaffold to watch machines cut toilet-paper rolls. Ray thought that bringing his little girls with him on sales trips was good for business. His daughters looked sweet in their matching dresses and Mary Janes. One year, a photographer came to his warehouse to take a Christmas picture for the company. He put Karen and me on a hydraulic lift truck strung with popcorn garlands. Ray sent the picture out on a complimentary calendar.

"Your sister's in jail," Ray said.

"For what?"

"She got in a stolen car with those juvenile delinquents. They cracked it up."

"I never spent one night in jail myself," Karen told Ray. She wasn't trying to earn points, but she was pleased her close calls hadn't come to that.

"Yes. Now Maria's in for some red tape," Ray said to Karen.

"I guess she was running away?" Karen said.

"Nothing like that," Ray said.

"So what was she doing?"

"She says she was looking for you."

"Oh, yeah? What took her so long?"

"I'm just saying your sister wasn't running away from home. *Looking* for something is different from running away."

Karen remembered what Dr. Benvenuto had told her two years before. He had said, "If a mother-daughter relationship is flat or unhealthy, it's most often engendered by the mother herself."

Dr. Benvenuto didn't accuse Veronica by name, but he was implying that Veronica was, indeed, the mother he was talking about. She imagined that her little sister must have met the same roadblock.

The doctor had told Karen to *trust* him. He explained to her that his name meant "Welcome" or "Good to see you." Karen should think of him as "Dr. Welcome." Karen didn't like a gimmick when she saw one, but the doctor had assured her it was his real birth name.

"I don't need a psychiatrist. I'm not crazy," she told Ray.

"Of course you're not crazy," he said.

"Is Maria crazy? If the house was on fire and we ran off, they couldn't call us crazy," she said.

Ray looked at Karen and wondered how she had come to that point, the point of thinking that her home was like a burning house. And now his youngest had fled. Was she feeding the blaze or escaping it?

"No one says you're crazy," Ray said.

"Once I go in this hospital, when do they let me back out?"

Ray knew that these upscale mental hospitals will admit anyone who's willing to pay the stiff fees. If parents want their kids locked up, they don't need any reason. A child stays in as long as you could throw the cash.

Ray told Karen things would seem better tomorrow.

Ray stopped at the White Horse Tavern, where he often took respite on his business trips when he needed a booster. Ray called it his "filling station." It wasn't even noon. He ordered a Rob Roy for himself and asked Karen what she wanted. At the Elbow Room she might have had a real drink, but sitting with her father, she ordered a cola. Ray had brought Karen to the White Horse before when he dragged her along on his sales trips, but the familiar tavern looked especially dreary in the daylight. Its dog-eared equestrian motif looked threadbare and depressing. The woodwork showed several frescoed layers of grime entombed in several applications of shellac. Dust and cobwebs gauzed the decorative saddles and bridles hung over the backs of the booths. Karen saw the worn path in the garish fleur-de-lis carpet where waitresses tramped back and forth to the register to ring up drinks and cash out.

After Ray finished his second Rob Roy, he was feeling better. They got back in the car and drove into Center City Philadelphia. When Ray stopped at a red light, a vendor walked up to the window. He hawked a stack of fresh soft pretzels threaded on a wooden dowel. Pretzels used to be Karen's favorite treat, and Ray bought her one. She hardly nibbled its doughy loops. She licked off some of the salt and held the nude golden knot in her lap for the rest of the drive.

CHELTENHAM INSTITUTE WAS established two hundred years ago as the first psychiatric hospital in the nation. Its site no longer qualified as a country location. The inner city had encompassed its perimeters, but many of its original buildings were intact. Its core structure was a solid stone Greek Revival mansion with a Roman dome and cupola with lantern windows. The front entrance, flanked by two-story Doric columns, was elegant and oddly quiet, like a ruin.

Ray drove through the gates and steered around the circle drive. He might have been a father delivering his daughter to a coming-out ball instead of committing her to a nuthatch.

"Daddy, don't put me in here."

Ray's buzz had already worn away, and he flinched when Karen asked him to reconsider.

Ray squeezed her hand. His stomach was tearing up, and when he parked the car, he reached into the glove box for his bottle of antacid. He drank the medicine and stared at the hospital grounds. For several moments, they sat side by side in the car, until Ray had swigged all the minty chalk left in the bottle.

Ray walked Karen under the porte cochère and up the flat marble front steps. It reminded Karen of the hotel in Paris where she had slipped out for trysts with Imran.

Inside, the lobby stretched like a huge ballroom, with high ceilings, prismed chandeliers and antique tapestries of unicorns and griffins. The airy room was elegantly appointed with upholstered wingback chairs, love seats and gleaming tables arranged in individual clusters for intimate conversations. There was a small session in progress at one end of the room. Perhaps a family had come to visit one of its members who was in residence at the hospital.

The obscure tendrils and cartouche of the Persian carpets curled in familiar, dizzying patterns, just like the rugs at home, but there were no medical personnel. Karen saw nothing that implied that this was a house for the sick except for one small display case of hospital

memorabilia from the eighteenth century. An original sign said: CHEL-
TENHAM INSTITUTE. FOR LUNATICKS AND PERSONS DISTEMPER'D IN
THE MIND. The exhibit showed handblown medicine vials, antique
straitjackets of yellowed canvas and other baroque medical utensils
from the hospital's early years.

"Daddy—" Karen said, "let's leave."

Ray fell dumb. He could not forfeit Veronica's favor for his daughter's desperate wishes.

Dr. Benvenuto had been summoned, and he greeted Ray and Karen
with the ebullience of a table captain on an ocean liner. He had interviewed Karen after her sexual promiscuity in Europe, and again after
her balky months at Grier School. He had followed her highly publi-
cized disappearance from home as it was first documented in the local
papers, and, of course, early that morning Veronica had reached him on
the telephone. The intake exam could be waived until the following
week.

Karen would be immediately integrated into North Unit, the ado-
lescent treatment wing.

The doctor asked Ray to his office to sign paperwork.

A nurse had materialized beside Karen, and she waited for Karen to
get her bearings and say good-bye to her father.

Ray kissed her once and walked away with the doctor.

Karen watched him leave, and she felt the pleasing expectation of
being released from her family obligations. She had felt like this when
James Robinson had zipped her away from Wilmington in his Newport. Karen followed the nurse down the hall. It was a relief not to face
her father and watch him struggle with his feelings. She could taste his
chalky antacid on her lips after he kissed her.

The nurse, named Tommie, took Karen's Pan Am carry-on and led
Karen away in the opposite direction from her father. She was a tiny
West Indian woman. Her white uniform was hand-pressed and smelled
of Renuzit, a familiar, in fact a compelling, scent. Karen recognized it
was the same starchy smell of Piers's coveralls. Karen was taller than
the nurse and could have shoved her, turned around and trotted
through the lobby and out the door. But Karen altered her stride to keep
in step with the smaller woman. Together, they weaved through high-

ceilinged hallways, past office pods and into long corridors lit with sconces.

"You're going to feel better soon," Tommie said. Her comment seemed to promise both an immediate elevation of comfort and an implied hope, even a tentative, sunny prediction for the long-term outcome.

Karen's stomach was upset. She pressed the back of her hand to her lips. The nurse recognized that Karen was going to be sick and pulled her into a staff lavatory. Karen retched, but she had nothing in her stomach. It was just her bucking diaphragm.

Tommie gave Karen a cone of chilled water from a cooler. She sipped it and rinsed her mouth in the sink.

At the door of the teen ward, there was a glass kiosk with a pass-through slot, like the ticket cage at the Paris Theater. An aide on the other side put a key in the drawer and the drawer rolled out. Tommie picked up the key and unlocked the heavy oak door to the unit.

Karen remembered her days and nights in the pitch darkness of the Alum-a-room and felt a ripple of panic, but the hospital was illuminated by an uninterrupted grid of institutional fluorescents. She'd never be locked in perpetual night. She walked into the controlled environment without any prodding.

North Unit's large common room was empty. Tommie told Karen that the other patients were "in school" in another part of the building. Karen was greeted by three attendants, but no one had the typical appearance of medical personnel. They didn't prod her about why she had arrived at this particular junction and displayed a practiced indifference, like tellers in a bank. In Virginia Beach, tellers had changed money for her every week, giving her fifties for all her small bills so that she could fit more cash in her motel Bible. These tellers never asked her, "Where did you get a wad like this? Flatbacking?"

An attendant named Gary examined the contents of the Pan Am carry-on for materials not permitted on the unit. He removed a manicure set in a vinyl sheath—a nail file, scissors, toenail clippers and a bottle of nail polish the same color as Veronica's fingers after she had shelled the red pistachios. Nail polish was considered a flammable accelerant and she couldn't keep it. Karen was allowed to have a squeeze bottle of hand lotion, just like the bottle Vanessa had used in her act for the peep window.

The attendant told Karen that if she wanted to light her cigarette she would have to come out to the common room to use the mechanism attached to a center pole by the nursing station. Gary showed her a little metal box, like an electric pencil sharpener with a recessed coil in which a cigarette could be inserted. She could light her cigarette, but the slot was too tight for her pinky finger.

Gary said, "On occasion, a patient goes through a phase when she wants to hurt herself. You know?"

Karen nodded.

He told her, "She might find a tin can lid or break a drinking glass. Or she might burn herself with the tip of her cigarette. You ever feel like that?"

Karen was still banged up and sore in her joints from her days in the Alum-a-room shack. Her lower lip was tender where her tooth had punched through. She remembered the time James had repeatedly pricked her with a safety pin for no reason. She might have told this attendant that she didn't have an inclination to harm herself when other people were doing a pretty good job beating up on her.

The attendant smiled at her. He seemed to know that she wasn't the type. Girls coming off the street are different from the ones sent from home. He sorted through the clothes in the Pan Am bag. Karen watched attentively, seeing these items for the first time herself. "Oh, what's that one?" she asked him.

He lifted out a pretty blue cashmere sweater. The sweater was almost new but was missing one button. The buttons were tiny sterling silver knots, precious baubles that would be hard to match at the five-and-ten.

Tommie took the sweater from Karen and held it up. She said, "We can fix this easy. We'll just move the top button and put it in the middle. We never button the top one, do we? I've got a thimble and my kit. I'll do it on my break."

Tommie had used the plural form, "*We'll* just move the top button." Karen was charmed by this tiny surrogate, who was not Veronica. Not Ruth.

Later, she watched Tommie use her stitch ripper to remove the top button. Tommie snipped the proper length of thread and tugged her needle back and forth through the cashmere placket until the sterling knot was aligned with the middle buttonhole, where it was needed. Karen felt relief in the consoling silence of a good deed. The nurse looped her thread several times around the button stem for extra strength and tied it off.

VERONICA HAD TAKEN a Seconal and was asleep when I returned from jail, where I had spent the weekend. I sat before my father at the kitchen table. "When can I see my sister?"

"She's in Philadelphia for a while. She's in the hospital there—"

"I can't believe she's not dead."

Ray stared at me across the table. I was dirty. I was bloody. I asked Ray sheepishly, "Please. Can I watch *The Monkees*? It's coming on—" My request triggered a round of distressing laughter from my father, as if my innocence both wounded and amused him. I feared he might rouse Veronica.

Ray looked at me. He couldn't get over what I had done to my hair. It was stripped and even lighter than Karen's. Could his daughters be sullied in exactly the same way? Ray still had envelopes of our baby hair in his desk, coils of natural filaments. Karen's baby hair was silky and golden; mine was a deeper sorrel.

He touched my stitches at my temple, then fingered a parched swatch of my bangs. He asked me, "Why did you do this?" He seemed to be talking about my hair expressly and not about my exodus with Tony DelRose in the stolen Continental.

"Please. Can I see the show?" I begged him.

Ray said I could watch the TV show.

I went to shower. I carefully shampooed my scalp with Phisohex where the sutures erupted. After I had bathed, I came out to the den in my fluffy bathrobe and slippers to sit nose-to-nose with the big Zenith. I got as close as I could to the Breck-rinsed mop-tops whose antics already seemed conventional and contrived, but I didn't care. A few hours earlier, I had been huddled in a concrete cubicle that had swelled beyond its capacity, and it still wasn't capped as it held sixteen business girls, all sizes.

Ray came in to give me my week's allowance. He handed me twenty dollars.

I thought he was going crazy. "Are you giving me a raise? Why?" I said.

"Just for being *you*," Ray said. He tried to convince himself I wasn't changed from yesterday.

K AREN'S PRIVATE ROOM on North Unit was furnished with a built-in bed and heavy chairs that couldn't be pitched or stacked. The window was protected by a heavy-gauge screen like the kind in a monkey house. Her private bathroom had a shower stall without a curtain rod or pulley so she couldn't rip her sheets and make a "Fieldcrest noose" and hang herself. Karen stayed in her room for two days, but when she stood in line at the cigarette lighter, she met a girl named Sharly, a willowy teenager who had been pulled off the street. They paired up in group therapy and sat together for the weekly psychodrama, hoping to melt into the background where they wouldn't be asked to participate. When they were alone, Sharly asked Karen, "You holding?"

"What?"

"You got any flake?"

"That pimp dust? Not me."

"I'm just asking."

"I'm answering."

They laughed at the awkward moment between them. They sat down together in the common room to sightsee. Sharly was a "cutter" and had marked her arms with numerous slits, the way a baker scores a pie shell. Sharly explained her "bracelets." When she cut her arms, her interior pressures were dispelled, each anxiety spur was anesthetized by her secret act. Sharly told Karen that a bloody wrist gets an immediate reaction. All her gauze wrappings defined her unhappiness better than words. "Words are useless, you'll see."

The staff tried to enact "milieu therapy," and the tone and ambiance of the unit was always being tempered and controlled. There were only one or two truly psychotic patients, and their mysterious habits sometimes upset the environment.

Someone drank a quart of antifreeze on a recent visit home, earning him the nickname "Prestone" after his stomach was pumped. A girl named Margaret Dixon thought she was a wolf or its immediate descendant. All day, she prowled up and down the hall, sometimes breaking into a lupine trot. She had quite mastered the stealthy gait of that predator.

Karen asked Tommie, "Was she *raised* by wolves or what?" She thought of Veronica who had raised her, and she wanted to tell the nurse that there are wolves and then there are tigers.

Tommie told Karen that the wolf girl had a twin sister who had strangled in the slats of a trundle bed they had shared. The surviving twin was never the same. Karen thought of the two girls on the *Doria*, how one was killed and the other spared. Whatever the starting block, the wolf girl had adopted the furtive, lurking mannerisms of the feral canine.

On weekends, the wolf girl's father came to visit her. He couldn't communicate with his daughter, who wouldn't stop prowling, and he threw up his hands. He came over to Karen and Sharly and started conversations. Soon, he spent his visits seated with Karen and Sharly, often bringing them candy boxes.

His name was Bennett Dixon, a man in his late fifties who was always well dressed in a cashmere overcoat and wing tips polished to a buttery bronze sheen. He enjoyed Karen's company and sometimes whispered remarkable suggestions in her ear. One afternoon, Ray arrived and found Bennett sitting beside Karen. The men shook hands briefly and Bennett moved off to find his own daughter.

Because Sharly had been hustling in Philadelphia, Karen opened up with her. They traded stories. Details merged, and once or twice Sharly claimed she had seen the same meatballs as Karen.

"They're all the same," Karen said.

Karen confessed to Sharly that she must be pregnant. Sharly tapped Karen's belly. A small dome above her pudendum was hard as an orange. Something was growing there. "That's the name of the story," Sharly told Karen.

"I know," Karen said, pleased to tell someone.

"Is it a trick baby? Or you think it was your James?"

"It must be James. I guess those pills Ruth gave me were stale."

"Do they get stale?"

"I guess they can. I used foam with clients. You'd think between the pill and that Ortho foam I'd have been more lucky."

Sharly said, "I don't think luck has much to do with it unless you were doing leprechauns."

"Ruth didn't do much business with midgets."

Sharly said, "One time, I went onto that circus train. You know, it comes into the city one week every year? That's a roach trap on wheels, I'll tell you. It's filthy. That's when I find out dwarves are hung. You'd never think it could be true."

Sharly took Karen to her room and lent Karen her smocked peasant blouses to hide her waistline bulge.

When medications were administered, Karen watched the tiny cups arranged on a tray directly above patients' names written with a Magic Marker. There was Thorazine. Mellaril. Tofranil. Dilantin. Dexamyl. Elavil. Dalmane. Nortriptyline. Karen recognized that these pills and capsules were the same confectionery colors as the Hundreds and Thousands that Veronica sprinkled on the tops of cupcakes. The wolf girl and even the fashion-zombie debutantes lifted their plastic shot glasses and sipped their morning dose in unison. Karen wasn't put on medication. She asked for a dollop of Pepto-Bismol now and then, while others chugalugged their psychotropic nectars. Her stomach trouble had actually improved. She was beginning to keep everything down.

IN ADDITION TO her attending psychiatrist, Karen was assigned to a resident doctor named Dr. Sheridan. Dr. Sheridan took her off the floor to perform an intake interview and to give Karen a physical.

The doctor administered the Wechsler Intelligence Scale, a word association test, and he asked Karen to draw some pictures for him. He told her to sketch her house in Woodside Hills. She took a pencil and the big sheet of paper and made an outline of the ranch house. She drew the big picture windows and the hemlocks at either end. She put a cat in one window. She told the doctor that the cat liked to sit curled on the silver tea service that was warmed by the sunny window.

The doctor took the drawing. He handed it back.

"You aren't finished yet, are you?" he asked. "Go ahead and finish the drawing."

"It's done," she said.

"Something's missing."

"You mean the people? Isn't a cat enough?"

"It doesn't have a door," he said.

"I guess I forgot."

"You don't have any access to the house. There's no entry?"

"Want me to do it again?"

The doctor gave her another piece of paper. "This time, draw a map of the world," he told her. "You know. The planet Earth."

Karen drew a modest circle. She didn't fill the paper.

"Okay," he told her, "where are you? Make an X."

Karen marked an X on the circle she had drawn. The mark was not in the center of the circle but at the rim in the lower right-hand quadrant. The doctor said, "You're not in the center?"

"Who is?" she asked him. She dropped the pencil.

"You put your X right on the edge—"

"So what are you writing in that folder?" she said.

"Just some impressions."

"Like what?"

He read from his notes: "Patient has short fingernails. Cuticles raw. Puncture wound on bottom lip. Right eye twitches. Raccoon circles, probably sinus."

"Sinus? Do my hands look bad? I can't have a nail file in my room in case I stab myself. Who reads that?"

"It's confidential, don't worry."

"Does my mother read that report?"

"No. Now tell me, what's your very first memory of home?"

"I don't remember much. It's a blank."

"That's a common amnesia mechanism. It's self-protective. But now you're safe. You can start to remember."

"Is that the law around here? I have to remember? I work pretty hard trying not to."

DR. SHERIDAN WROTE in his notes: "A compellingly sweet, still not completely embittered girl. Nameless dread is not of a neurotic nature, but grounded in poor family history. Maternal parent is gravely narcissistic. Condition underscored by prolonged homelessness with history of physical abuse and prostitution. Diagnosis: Disassociative with depressive features. Hold off on medication. In future, Ambar or another combination amphetamine and barbiturate, if indicated."

Karen had yet to endure a physical examination. Dr. Sheridan took her into a small exam room in the infirmary.

She was banged up from her last days in Virginia, and he noted her bruises. She sat on a table, and he tapped her reflexes with a rubber-tipped hammer. He listened to her lungs. He swabbed her chin with Silvadene cream where her tooth had protruded like a leather punch and the hole was still inflamed. "This is sore," he told her, "but it's too late for a stitch. Keep it clean."

She got down from the table and stepped on the scale. He noted her weight and her height. She got back up on the table. She feared he might ask her to put her feet in the stirrups.

He was letting her off the hook. It was policy at the hospital to be very sensitive to a girl's "signals," and a pelvic exam was optional. Asking a girl to endure an internal exam might set her back and ruin her progress after weeks of therapy. It was often overlooked.

He might have discovered that Karen's uterus was slightly oversized and exhibited the telltale "zone of softening" at the site of inception. But she had slipped down off the table and collected her clothes from the chair.

THE BAPTIST HOME
FOR LITTLE WANDERERS

———

THE WEEKS AFTER my arrest with Tony DelRose, Veronica gave me the silent treatment. If she was forced to address me, it was always a rhetorical statement.

"If a person saw the car keys, where might she have seen them?"

"The student who was looking for the thesaurus should know where it is. She was the last person to use it."

Veronica couldn't bring herself to say the words "you" or "I" or "us." These intimate pronouns unnerved her.

I started finding the French ashtray—QUEL RIT VENDREDI, DI-MANCHE PLEURERA—in odd places, as if Veronica had placed the moralistic dish in my path just to chide me. I found it on the bathroom sink, on my bureau, on the arm of the sofa. I found it tipped against my dinner plate.

I told her, "Are you using this ashtray?"

She didn't answer.

"I guess you want me to have a smoke?" I took her pack of Kents and lit up.

Veronica plucked the cigarette from my lips and stubbed it out in the little dish.

I ASKED RAY if he would drive me up to Philadelphia to see Karen. Ray told me that the doctors didn't want Karen to have any family visitors.

"But I'm her sister."

"They don't want family members anywhere near the place. It's like a quarantine," he said.

"But I'm flesh and blood."

"Flesh and blood" was exactly what the patient should be shielded from. All kin were considered toxic to patients. I would have to wait until Dr. Benvenuto scheduled a "family meeting." Ray seemed disturbed by this rigid house rule, but Veronica was grateful for the reprieve.

It was up to me.

The following Thursday, I left the high school with Melvie. We took the train from Wilmington and got off at Thirtieth Street Station in Philadelphia. Passengers eyed me; the sutures at my hairline had started to look angry.

Melvie was protective and tried to shield me from gawkers. He put his arm around my shoulder as we walked to the Cheltenham Institute, but I shoved him off me.

At the hospital entrance, the fantastic facade looked like the palace where Cinderella careens down the steps and loses a slipper. But instead of the fairy-tale heroine, I pictured Veronica dressed in one of her gold cocktail dresses. I could just see her racing down those wide stairs, playing cat and mouse with the model.

Inside the lobby, we asked for directions to North Unit. An unsuspecting soul offered meticulous instructions. We walked up to the kiosk at the nursing station and I asked to see Karen. The nurse talked to me through the tiny speaker grid in the reinforced Plexiglas. She said, "Do we know you?"

"I'm here to see my sister, Karen Mitchell," I said.

"Honey, she's not here right now. She's at school. Now you must be her little sister? Who's the doctor?"

"Him? That's Melvin."

"No, honey, who is *Karen's* doctor? Dr. Benvenuto?"

I recognized the doctor's name. I thought wheels were turning. "Yes, that's him," I said.

The nurse told me, "Karen's not taking visitors yet."

"But we haven't seen each other in over two years," I said.

"That's a good reason to wait a little more time."

Just then an alarm jangled. I thought she might have punched a button under the desk, like a teller might use to alert Security. Just as suddenly, smoked billowed from deep in the hallway on North Unit.

Melvie and I watched the smoke curling forth as we stood outside the kiosk. Staff ran onto the floor with fire extinguishers. In an instant, an attendant wheeled a gurney through the door. A boy was wrapped head to toe in a soaking-wet sheet, shrieking from pain. The boy had rolled a matchbook into a tube and tucked it in his rectum to smuggle it onto the unit. He set his vinyl mattress on fire and his clothes had ignited.

Security personnel steered us back into the central lobby. I was leaving the hospital without seeing my sister. Melvie led me back to the train station. Everything looked surreal. Trees were in blossom and pollen-rich tassels writhed on the sidewalks. Melvie understood that I felt stung and he didn't try to fill it in with conversation. He had watched me suffer for two years, carrying the folded Christmas greeting until it was torn and tattered. When the card was disintegrating, he offered me a wax paper bag to protect the specimen the way an entomologist might preserve fragile butterfly wings.

At home, I wrote a letter to Karen on Veronica's Olivetti. The shift mechanism was jammed and the keys struck only the red part of the two-toned ribbon. The margins were erratic and the letter looked like a red river snaking across the onionskin paper, a wounded red block of words. I wrote Karen that I had tried to see her but had been turned away. It was easy to romanticize about our reunion, the fantastic tryst was postponed—

I wasn't sure Karen would have wanted to see me.

RAY AND VERONICA TOOK me to my family court hearing. We sat in the front row of the courtroom next to Colleen and her parents. Veronica had dressed up for the occasion in a Chanel suit. She sat in her chair and crossed her long legs. Beside her, Colleen's mother wept, a familiar low whirring like a sewing machine treadle.

Tony had a separate court date. He had not yet been identified as an apprentice to Orsi in Philadelphia and was mistaken for a teenager from a broken home who took a fateful joyride with "loose girls," as if we had tempted *him* into the racket and not vice versa.

Colleen and I were placed on probation for one year. We didn't flinch until the judge told us that we were limited to a ten o'clock curfew and couldn't stay out at night. Colleen blurted out, "The Concord

Mall is open till eleven—" She was teary-eyed and quite beautiful in her disarray, like Faye Dunaway in the first scenes of *Bonnie and Clyde*. Her blond hair shivered like a doll's.

The judge told her, "All right. Curfew at eleven o'clock."

My probation officer collected imitation Hummel figurines and displayed them in cute arrangements on her desk. Clusters of diminutive forest animals and Slavic peasants marched across the desk blotter in itsy-bitsy domestic routines. Tiny milkmaids, toadstools, trolls and a circle of china kittens lapping a pool of ceramic milk that spilled from a tiny silver pail. Perhaps she imagined she could arrange her JD charges with the same ease with which she organized her figurines.

I went to Walter's shop after my afternoon appointments with my probation officer. On Friday and Saturday nights, Walter picked me up at the house for "dates." I was taking birth control pills without a prescription, pills that Walter's mother, a nurse, had stockpiled from hospital inventories over the years. I hid the contraceptives in the *Encyclopedia Britannica*, which lined the bottom rows of my bookshelves in my bedroom. Every night I rotated volumes, changing the location of my secret stash of hormones.

It was the same year as the "Summer of Love" and Ray didn't exactly like me dating a "longhair," but he didn't stop me. Ray had suspected Walter when he left his sickbed months ago and went down to investigate the "Underground" dressed only in his hospital johnny. He could see that the Underground wasn't a legitimate retail operation. There wasn't enough stock on the shelves. Walter's shop had only *one* of everything displayed. Ray knew how grifters set up salons like this. If a corner market has only one can of beans, one roll of paper towels, one jar of mayo, something else was happening. But Ray was relieved I wasn't driving around with Tony DelRose, who might be closer to my age but who had risked my life in a high-speed crash-up. Ray had seen the wrecked Continental impounded behind a chain-link fence across from the station house where he had picked me up. He told me that the luxury sedan looked like "a huge accordion. A squeeze box for Paul Bunyan." He couldn't believe I had survived.

Veronica liked Walter.

Walter arrived at the house prepared to barter for me with a Persian cat tucked inside his overcoat lapel. A tiny white kitten, like a fluffy sock on a darning egg. Veronica said, "Is this for *me*?" She was impressed by the pedigreed feline, a fancy few ounces of fur that Walter had picked up as a bread and butter gift. She was overly demonstrative in her thanks. She leaned against Walter, kissing him on the lips. An uncomfortable interval for me. The tiny kitten was pinched between them and mewled its distress. Veronica named the kitten Mini Bianco, and treated it as a fashion accessory, draping the kitten around her neck like an ermine collar.

The cat appeared at the same time that Veronica came home from Neiman Marcus with a pair of white leather go-go boots with tassels. She wore the white boots with her Blackglama mink. She picked up the white kitten and studied the whole ensemble in her full-length mirror.

She had seen dancers wear these tasseled boots on *Shindig* and *Hullabaloo*. Snubbing her middle age, Veronica impressed local fashion doyennes with her mix-and-match of hipster gear and legitimate New York fashions. When her estrogen pills caused mood swings or spotting, she went back to her doctor for increased doses. She refused to retreat into her "third age" and twirled in front of her mirror in her mink coat and white boots with the same far-off look in her eyes that she had had when she danced on the pedestal beside the marble nymph and in the private salon at Galeries Lafayette.

Veronica looked to Walter for a racy joke and basked in his tossed-off comments. I wasn't blind; anyone could see she was actually flirting with him. She told him, "You know, you look like that actor on *The Man from U.N.C.L.E.*, you know who I mean?"

Veronica understood that Walter sold candles and cigars and dabbled in gatorized guitars. Of course, I didn't tell her that Walter made most of his money selling drugs. He often enlisted my aid when he made connections. We drove to the Holiday Inn on Route 202, or to the Tally Ho Motor Inn right next to the Brandywine Raceway. Walter wasn't welcomed at these motels and was often intercepted by Security. Walter had that mongrel look, like a man who's got something happening, like a con in a critical phase of an operation. He needed me to soften his profile.

We walked down the row of motel doors until we found the right number.

If the connection knew us, we could make the payout and turn right around, but sometimes they wanted us to come inside the room and sit down for an info session.

One time, Walter left the motel room to have a private discussion in someone's service truck. He left me in the room with all of his money and the drugs he was buying, albeit under the supervision of the connection's bird dog. When we were alone, the man asked me, "Does Walter make you happy?"

"Sure, I guess so."

I saw how much money Walter was handling, sixty one-hundred-dollar bills and multiple twenties clipped in even stacks. I felt a remote tingling start at the small of my back and flood up to the roots of my hair. I looked into the stranger's eyes, which were the unnameable color of the spillway at the sewage treatment plant.

Another doper was in the motel shower. I could hear him singing the hit by Scott McKenzie, "If you're going to San Francisco . . ." This guy was into it.

The low-life before me was counting the investment from Stackhouse. He tapped the bills on the TV until it was an even green chunk. He tells me, "I bet you want some of this. You want some?"

"Maybe I do." I thought I might as well get a little of that cash since I was doing the public relations.

The man lifted two fifties off the pile of cash and set them aside. "One hundred if I spray your tonsils?" he asked me.

I thought about it.

A blow job for a hundred dollars seemed like easy cash. That would be a two-way chizz on Walter. I declined. Yet, his invitation haunted me. Was it a threat, or a missed opportunity? Maybe the next time I would try it.

Walter came back for me and together we walked out to his car. I sat down next to him and unwrapped the newspaper to show him the heroin he had just purchased. Two tubes of tarry mush twisted up in a dry-cleaning bag that said CORONA CLEANERS AND WASHERETTE. QUEENS, NEW YORK.

◆ ◆ ◆

As Veronica teetered at her midlife threshold, Ray had his hands full trying to bolster her up. Like a carney making huge wefts of cotton candy, Ray stirred up her ego, building its hive of pink sugar. He couldn't watch me.

Helplessly, Ray let me get into Walter's car on any given Friday night. I sat down in the front seat. Walter handed me a cherry Life-Saver, its hole smeared with a gooey knob of dung-black opium. I placed it on my tongue and sucked its bitter center. I looked back at my father and waved. Ray and I were in it together. He watched me drive away with Walter Stackhouse. Whatever might happen to me was sanctioned by Ray against his good conscience.

———

Dear Karen,

When are you going to write back? They must be holding your letters in a file. The "Family Meeting" has been postponed. It sounds fishy to me. You won't recognize me. I'm blond now, but Colleen didn't warn me how the roots grow faster than the ends.

Remember that abandoned house on the corner? The one where we stole the doilies from the backs of the chairs? The wife went to jail? Well, they tore that house down. A dozer leveled it smooth.

The Christmas card you sent me went through the washer. It's in a million pieces.

Last night I heard a steam train. It's been years since those steam engines came through regular. Now it's all diesels. Remember how they used to sound? Two short and then the long. We listened to those strings take the bend. Did I tell you about the woman who jumped onto the tracks? She was cut in half. Sometimes you don't know what people will do.

Didn't Veronica send you some stationery? Those blue sheets with the windmill? Did you write to me yet?

Your sister,
Maria

Dear Valerie,

I'm sending this letter to the Seventh Wonder. You'll never guess where I'm writing from. Thank Horace for telling Piers to look inside the Alum-a-room. If you see Piers, just ask him, "How's your symptom?" Tell him that's from me.

You like the windmills on here?

I guess I got a bun in the oven. Ruth calls it "an egg in the electric skillet." No one knows but me.

If you see James, don't say a word about it.

Tell Horace I'm writing to him at the Firestone Tire Center. Peaches won't find out. But if someone wants to tell her, that's Horace's duty, don't you think?

Who's been doing my lunches? Mr. McTinkle? Mr. Free Associate? Mr. Kilowatt? He brings his own electric toothbrush. I'm never going back to work. I can't have a tot and see clients. It's kicking right now like Joe Namath.

You going home to Trenton soon? When you go back, don't be surprised if your folks aren't glad to see you.

I'll write to Rose and Sharon next time, c/o the Seventh Wonder. You're my friend forever. Like a sister—

—Karen

A FTER SIX MONTHS Karen was earning seniority on North Unit. The average length of stay in North Unit was three or four months, a "fifth season," but Karen wasn't released.

Dr. Benvenuto saw Karen for twenty minutes once a week.

DR. BENVENUTO: "Karen, take a minute to imagine this. There's a body on the sidewalk. Another person is running away. Who are you? The *murder victim* or the *murderer*?"

KAREN: "Those are the two choices?"

DR. BENVENUTO: "The killer or the victim?"

KAREN: "What is this test? What does it prove?"

DR. BENVENUTO: "Just choose one. We'll go on to the next question."

KAREN: "Is this a trick?"

DR. BENVENUTO: "No trick. Sometimes it's harder to forgive the victim than it is to forgive the perpetrator. Sometimes we *hate* the victim. Sometimes the victim isn't even innocent."

The wolf girl still trotted the halls and Sharly wasn't going home anytime soon. Karen and Sharly had similar profiles: their bonds with their matriarchs had snapped. But Karen's "secret" was getting too difficult to conceal. She could no longer wear her blue sweater that Tommie had repaired. Sharly gave Karen a gaudy dashiki that belled out at the waist; it might hide her stomach. But Karen didn't like the African smock. "Shit, this will call attention to the problem."

Sharly placed the palm of her hand against Karen's stomach. "It kicked," she said.

Karen smiled. "Tell me about it." Karen liked the way it felt. She sat in Occupational Therapy, gluing popsicle sticks in a tower as the baby tipped or rolled. She felt the baby's antics and looked off in the distance, trying to hide her pleasure. The staff might have thought that these sudden spells were a new lunatic trait.

Many girls gain ten pounds or more when they first come to Cheltenham, and the staff wasn't alarmed to see Karen blow up. Then Tommie walked into Karen's room unannounced and found Karen standing before the plastic safety mirror. Karen's tight bulge was the size of a western honeydew. Karen dropped the hem of her shirt slowly and turned to look at Tommie sheepishly. "Guess what—" She grinned at the nurse.

Tommie took Karen off the floor for a full examination. Dr. Sheridan estimated that she was six-and-a-half-months pregnant. He was relieved that Karen had not conceived during her confinement at Cheltenham. That was welcome news.

He told her, "He's got a strong heartbeat." He didn't invite Karen to borrow his stethoscope to hear it for herself. She didn't know it was within her rights to ask for this privilege. The baby started kicking during the examination and the sheet pulsed across Karen's belly.

"That little stranger is busy," Tommie said.

It pleased Karen to hear Tommie talk about the baby. It was the first time anyone acknowledged that she was courier to a separate life, a sole individual, with its own reasons to be.

NORTH FIELD WAS A LUSH, wide-open lawn just off the North Unit residence wing. The garden was fully enclosed by a high stone fence crowned by broken glass. Patients got their "fresh air" for a half hour each day, if they had earned clearance. Karen strolled the lawn with Sharly. She told her friend, "The cat's out of the bag. They know."

Sharly said, "Are you allowed to keep it?"

"I don't know." Karen burst into tears. Just as quickly she stopped her tears.

"Look," Sharly said, "you better get away from here if you want to keep your baby." She pulled Karen behind a stand of hemlock that obscured a tight opening in the wall. Karen stared at the tiny gap between the wrought-iron gate and a fieldstone column. Sharly held her breath and wriggled through. She stood on the other side. "Come on—"

Karen tried to wedge herself in, but it was a ridiculous plan. Her belly was too big.

Sharly squeezed back through the fence. "Maybe I can pitch you over the top." She knit her fingers together and made a stirrup for Karen. Karen put the toe of her shoe in Sharly's cupped palms and Sharly tried to boost her up. Karen's awkward conformation prevented such an athletic feat. The two girls collapsed on the path. Their laughter carried across the grass, where two aides monitored North Field from Adirondack chairs. When the girls kept at it, the men stood up and strolled across the tufts of clover.

After their antics, the girls were not permitted onto North Field together.

Dr. Benvenuto telephoned Ray and asked him and Veronica to attend a roundtable with the psychiatric staff, the director of the PR office who was there to initiate damage control and two of the hospital's lawyers. Veronica was seething and she had buttoned her Chanel jacket out of sync. Seated at the mahogany table, before the circle of men, she discovered her error and had to turn in her seat to rebutton. When she again faced the group, her temper was hitched up a notch.

Ray couldn't understand how Karen's pregnancy had gone undiscovered for all these months. "She's right under your nose. You're doctors, aren't you?" he said.

Dr. Benvenuto said, "At Karen's intake examination, her blood was drawn, but the only tests ordered were for drug toxicology analysis and routine hemoglobin to see if she was anemic or had contracted hepatitis. We don't ask new patients for urine samples. These girls are highstrung and can't relax the urinary sphincter. She'll shut down just seeing the specimen container."

Karen was entering her third trimester. If an abortion was to be scheduled, it would be a complicated procedure perhaps resulting in a live birth. The only available methods for terminating the pregnancy at this late stage would be injection of saline or induction of labor with prostaglandins. Dr. Benvenuto said, "We can't wait much longer for either procedure. It should be done immediately."

"Now hold on a minute," Ray said.

The lawyers described to Ray his legal right to choose an appropriate "medical option" for Karen. "It's your decision. You're in control, Mr. Mitchell."

No one seemed interested in asking for Karen's feedback.

Dr. Benvenuto assured Ray and Veronica that it wasn't too late for Karen to have a medically sanctioned abortion. A full-term delivery posed innate risks and a higher mortality rate for teen mothers. The fact that Karen had a history of herpes complicated it further. Herpes might necessitate a cesarean delivery.

Veronica said, "Why wait and put her through major surgery?"

Ray tried to imagine Karen's ordeal on the operating table. He saw a shiver of light as a physician brandished a scalpel. He said, "No. I wouldn't want her to go through that. That's out of the question."

There was no further discussion. Karen would not be permitted to deliver a full-term, live baby.

Only Dr. Sheridan raised points of dissent; he had never considered Karen to be mentally ill, but merely "disassociative." There were private institutions where Karen could be admitted to carry her baby to full term and get the assistance she needed. "She could have a normal delivery," he said.

Veronica said, "She'll never be *back to normal* if we permit her to become a mother."

Ray winced at the medical diction passed back and forth. In a harrowing narrative, the obstetrician explained how the baby would be aborted. Amniotic fluid would be extracted with a needle and replaced with saline solution. The saline solution would instantly kill the fetus and cause premature labor in a matter of hours.

When Ray signed the papers, Veronica took out a cigarette. One of the lawyers showed off his exquisite new fountain pen. The doctors pushed the writing instrument back and forth across the conference table. Everyone had a chance to admire it and scribble on a notepad.

I WAS IN THE KITCHEN after school, teasing the cat with a spoke of raw spaghetti, when the wall phone jangled. I lifted the receiver. A man's voice said, "Karen?"

"You want Karen? She's not here. Sorry."

"And *you* are?" His voice was commanding but not without a ripple of mirth.

With alarming freedom I told him my name.

"Well, hey there, Maria. How are you doing? Tell me, Maria, when does Karen come in?"

"Actually, she's away for a while."

"That's what I heard. Is she at the Baptist Home for Little Wanderers?"

"Where?"

"The Baptist Home for Little Wanderers. For girls in the family way? You wouldn't know the address of that farm? I'll jot it down. Go ahead, I've got a pen."

I said, "The Baptist Home? No, I don't know where that is." Could Ray have been lying about where he put Karen? She had never answered my letters addressed to Cheltenham. Was she at the Baptist Home for Little Wanderers? "*Who* is this?" I asked the caller. I knew he was someone important, someone who had had a sinister connection to Karen, and now he was connecting with me.

He waited to tell me his name. When he started up again, his tone had altered. His voice was keenly modulated, expertly honeyed when he told me, "Sweetheart, this is James."

"James?"

"That's right. Excuse me. I should have told you right off. Now Maria, you're sitting right there in Woodside Hills? In that big house by yourself?"

The hair on the nape of my neck prickled.

"You home alone this afternoon?" he said.

I mumbled something to the affirmative, a helpless confirmation of his eerie presumption. "I'm here," I told him. I felt like a worm wriggling at the claws of a robin.

"You still on probation, honey?"

"Excuse me? You know about that wreck?"

"You should smooth it over with the law before you step all the way out of your diapers. You might end up just like Karen. Another Miss MINS—"

This man had known Karen. He seemed to know me. How had he learned his information? An elliptical circle of secrets and betrayals was forming in my imagination. This man was trying to talk through me to Karen. He was using me as a conduit. I feared his intrusion even as I felt its pull. I felt it working on me.

"You tell Karen—" the voice continued. Even as I was dying to hear what message he wanted conveyed to my sister, I *knew* the message, its every possible meaning. Its implication was the same for me. I hooked the receiver back in its cradle.

SINCE I HAD MET Walter, I ignored my equestrian life and never showed up at Highland Stables. Veronica told me, "I guess that saddle is getting cobwebs. Why are we paying for oats if you don't ride anymore?"

"Are you saying you'll stop buying his oats?"

"You decide. What's it going to be, Walter or Dreamboy?"

Alex helped me place an ad and we sold Dreamboy to a farmer from Chadds Ford, Pennsylvania. I watched the farmer load the horse into the trailer. Dreamboy rolled his eyes and snorted, high-stepping as horses will do when they aren't sure of the truck bed. His club foot looked all the more poignant as he pawed the air with it. My tears came and went in uncontrollable spells. Then I was over it, long before I had expected to stop mourning.

Walter had moved out of his shop and was living in a garden apartment complex where he peddled narcotics. Walter taught me how to weigh out, measure and bag up his drugs for retail sale. I learned to separate clumps of tar and sift loose piles of marijuana like miniature haystacks onto the shiny trays of a brass scale Walter had purchased from a Merck catalogue.

I liked the feel of the metric weights in my hand, icy brass discs of varying sizes, like refrigerator magnets. I stacked the weights on one tray to balance the load of dope on the other tray. I learned the math. When I bagged hits of meth, I had to measure it in "grains," which confused me, and it was difficult to separate the crystallized powder that looked like chunks of Moth-B-Gon.

Walter's old high school friend Ampy Nelson hung around the apartment all the time. I never had Walter to myself. Ampy was a car dealer who weighed almost five hundred pounds. He drove a big customized sedan with extra-strength suspension coils and special shocks. The car had a made-to-order front seat with wire reinforcement in the cushions. Ampy came over every night and sat with us at the table. He perched on Walter's metal footlocker since Walter didn't have a kitchen chair strong enough to hold him.

Ampy was a partner in Walter's dope trade and had also fronted money for Walter's gatorized guitar business. The fat man had once saved Walter's neck by hiding seven plastic bags of heroin under his dripping breast fat and stomach flaps when the police searched Walter's vehicle.

The only time Walter and I could be alone was when Ampy had to go home to use his own bathroom. Ampy was so obese that he needed a reinforced toilet. He had broken several toilets and refused to accept Walter's hospitality when Walter told him, "Go ahead. Try it out."

When Ampy went home, Walter and I had our private interlude. Walter pushed me down on the bed. As he fucked me, I couldn't help wondering if my sexual life might always be tinted by the image of a fat man sitting on the toilet.

ONE AFTERNOON, Walter came over to the house. He said, "Here, baby," and he handed me a little key.

"What's this for?"

"You'll see."

I looked at the tiny key, which looked like it might belong to a suitcase or a file cabinet.

Veronica was standing there grinning. She was in on it. She said, "He hid it in your bedroom."

"You took him into my room?"

I went into my room to search for the surprise. I rummaged in my closets and combed my dresser top but couldn't find anything. I looked under the four-poster bed. There it was, a glistening black leather guitar case. I tugged it from under the bed and inserted the little key. It fit. I opened the lid. The guitar was gleaming in its felt-lined bed. I recognized it immediately. A costly Martin Dreadnought acoustic guitar worth a few thousand dollars. I lifted it out of the case and propped it across my knee. Its hourglass front was polished Appalachian spruce, a golden wheat color. Its body was deep Brazilian rosewood. The fret board and tuning pegs were all handcrafted, and its trademark teardrop pick guard was genuine silk-white ivory.

I knew Walter had paid hard cash for the instrument, cash he'd earned from his dope trade, but that's not what upset me.

He was making a production, manipulating me somehow, and I felt vulnerable to his extravagance. "It's beautiful. It just *looks* expensive, doesn't it?" Veronica said, hooking Walter's elbow and leaning against him to watch me. I didn't like it that Veronica was in cahoots with him.

A CLASSMATE AT the high school told me she had seen Walter in Philadelphia. Walter was easy to pick out in a crowd because Ampy accompanied him everywhere. Ampy was a sizable landmark, indeed. My classmate had seen Walter dancing under the strobe lights at the Electric Factory with a nymphette dressed in a fringe jacket.

"This jacket?" I asked my friend. I opened the door of my locker and showed her my new "frontier" jacket, a suede coat with a thousand leather tassels.

I realized that Walter must have a rack of these fringe jackets. He didn't care who wore the jacket from one night to the next. He was seeing other girls in the same twenty-four hours that he was sticking me.

Jealousy was a strange accelerant. I had felt *envy* many times before. I had *wanted* things. I had coveted Karen's items, and once I had wanted a friend's lavish bicycle streamers, long plastic strips that snapped in the wind. In an avaricious frenzy, I sneaked onto her carport and snipped them off with a scissors. But without the rubber plugs, I couldn't insert them in my handlebars. They were worthless booty.

But jealousy was different from envy. When I heard about the fringe jackets, I lost all my confidence. I lost it the instant when I recognized I had indulged in *too much* confidence to begin with. Identifying my naïveté was a bitter pill to swallow.

When I confronted Walter, he told me, "You don't make up rules. You don't give me ultimatums, girl—"

He forced me to look at him, eye-to-eye, until I softened. He squeezed my fingers to give me hope. "That's right, baby. Live and let live—or get left alone," he said.

I came back to the house to sit with Veronica in front of the TV. It was *The Name of the Game* with Tony Franciosa. I *loved* Tony Franciosa, but he couldn't distract me.

Veronica too was in an agitated mood. She chained-smoked Kents and sipped her third or fourth scotch. Karen's procedure was coming up. Veronica got up, crossed the room and flipped the channel.

"Look, it's *A Place in the Sun*," she told me, and she tried to fill me in. Veronica berated the two actresses in the film. Both were vying for Montgomery Clift. Shelley Winters wanted sanctuary. Elizabeth Taylor wanted a cheap fling.

I was pleased to hear Veronica talk about a movie and compare the plights of these heroines. I told Veronica, "I feel sorry for Shelley Winters."

"You do?" she asked me, showing her disappointment. Veronica sided with the debutante.

I told her, "Walter is dating other girls, can you believe it?"

Veronica straightened her back. She put down her drink. "Walter's seeing someone else?" The look on her face was authentic alarm. Her eyes both hot and steely, she might have been picturing the Arrow Collar model.

I told her, "Walter's a pig—" Then I burst into tears.

Veronica said, "Just chalk it up to experience." She looked into the distant night outside the window, mouthing the words again, as if she had often said these phrases to herself. "Just chalk it up—"

Her animate instructions, after she had frozen me out for months, seemed heartfelt. "There are many fish in the sea," Veronica went on.

I looked at my mother.

"Nothing ventured, nothing gained," she said. She relied on these clichés as indisputable evidence.

She was giving me the spine to dust him off.

"I can't exactly rub the slate clean—"

"Because he bought you that guitar? Give it back. Sacrifice it."

"The guitar. Well, I can return *that*—"

Veronica registered my admission, and the expression on her face shifted as visibly as a curtain pulled across a stage.

Quite dramatically, she popped up from her seat. She called to Ray. "My nitroglycerin—"

"Are you all right?" I stood in front of my mother, my mouth frozen open.

"Deceiver. Trickster. Slut right under my nose," she said without pause.

Ray came into the room looking like he just woke up. His hair was pushed high over his temples in humorous tufts like an owl's false ears.

"My nitro," she whispered to Ray, holding her wrist to her forehead, as if she might die before he could find her medicine.

Ray returned with the bottle and shook out a pill. He waited until Veronica had placed the tab under her tongue. He asked Veronica what had upset her.

Veronica said, "Your daughter's been sleeping with Walter Stackhouse."

Ray turned to me, "Stackhouse?"

I nodded.

"You're pregnant? How many periods have you missed?"

"I'm not pregnant."

His relief was visible in his shoulders, which hitched and then relaxed to their normal slope.

"Walter's cheating on me, that's all."

Veronica said, "She's bedding down with that cowboy. She finds out he's got a harem."

"Is that it?" Ray said.

"In a nutshell," I said. I was regaining my footing, feeling some cheek. I picked up my mother's pack of cigarettes. I lit a Kent and tugged the smoke into my lungs.

Ray took my shoulders and whipped me around to face him. "Listen. You're a woman now—"

I was fourteen.

"You're a woman now. What are you going to do about it?"

Ray was trying to tell me that the burdens of my gender were not simple and not to be overcome overnight. I thought of my sister in her present predicament. "You're a woman now. *What are you going to do about it?*" Would he ask Karen this?

AGAIN, THE ASHTRAY emerged in the same awkward places as before. QUEL RIT VENDREDI, DIMANCHE PLEURERA. She left it on my nightstand, beside my dinner plate. She had the nerve to shove it in my purse so I might find it miles away from home, perhaps at Walter's apartment.

I wanted to dash it against the wall, but for some reason I was careful not to chip, crack or shatter the tiny ceramic dish.

I WAITED FOR WALTER to pick me up at the high school. He never showed. I had missed my bus, so I started walking. A car rolled up to the curb and crawled along beside me, an old sedan with butterfly fins. As I walked down the sidewalk, the driver was trying to talk to me. He tapped his horn. I stopped walking and bent down to look in the driver's window. He was sitting there with a grin on his face just like Dick Clark, but his hair was shoulder-length and wavy. "Honey, you miss your bus?"

"It's okay. I'm walking."

"You need a lift?"

"Are you asking me if I need a ride?"

"You saying you want to?" He watched my face. He was trying to confuse me with my own ideas. His smile was disturbing, half sinister, half infantile smirk. I wondered if he was the man who knew my sister. Ever since I had answered that telephone call, every strange man could be him.

He patted the seat beside him. There was a terry-cloth towel tucked over the cracked upholstery. "Climb in," he said.

I turned around and walked back down the sidewalk in the other direction.

Without missing a beat, the driver tugged the chrome bar on the steering column and pushed the car in reverse. He drove *backward* to keep up with me, until he met a parked car. I trotted into the high school gymnasium, walked over the basketball parquet and went out the field house door. I walked across the baseball diamond and trudged along the cinder lanes of the track field. I picked up the sidewalk two blocks down from where the stranger was waiting in his car.

BED OF ICE

W E WERE RIDING in Christine's VW Microbus. Walter was in the copilot chair beside my stepsister. I stretched out behind them on the bench seat. Ampy sat in the wayback, and was careful to center his weight over the rear axle. Christine was recently divorced and had left her suburban home in East Lansing, Michigan, to join the Peace Pilgrims and to work with the death and dying doyenne, Elisabeth Kübler-Ross.

But when Christine learned about Karen's third-trimester abortion, she contacted Cheltenham and had somehow convinced Dr. Benvenuto to allow her to sit at Karen's bedside during the procedure. Walter and I didn't have clearance. We were "crashing" the abortion.

Ampy planned to go shopping in Center City at the Big Man Store while we visited Karen.

Ray was golfing at the Du Pont Country Club to seal a business contract with Atlas Chemical. But I knew he was beside himself. For the past few days, he had been sitting in his recliner in the wee hours of the morning. I saw the lamp on at 4 A.M. when I got up to use the bathroom. Perhaps he hadn't slept at all.

On the morning of the procedure, he was dressed in his yellow Ban-Lon golf shirt with the fleur-de-lis on the breast pocket. He stood at the kitchen sink cleaning his golf shoes, using a steak knife to loosen the matted grass from the cleats. Veronica had a card game at Kiwanis Wives, and she had to go to St. Helena's Church to drop off a pressure cooker that was needed for the annual "New England Boiled Dinner" fund-raising supper. The church had fifty pounds of corned beef to prepare.

Veronica knew what we were doing, but she didn't interfere. Christine had left the Peace Pilgrims commune and was driving us to the hospital. "We're doing her dirty work," Christine said. "Veronica should be with Karen."

"Karen wouldn't want her there," I said.

Christine said, "Veronica's a bad mother, like a ewe that abandons her own lambs."

Walter said, "When that happens, they skin a dead lamb and put the hide on the rejected lamb so a foster mother will nurse it."

"Where do they get the dead lamb in the first place?" I said. For some reason, I envisioned Linda Morgan and her sister who had perished on the ocean liner. One sibling was spared, the other was swallowed up. Who decides who gets what?

Walter said, "There's dead lambs each season. Born dead. Or maybe a coyote comes along. Coyotes will tear a fetus from its mother even before the ewe delivers. The dog nips the baby's snout and helps it along, then it runs off with the newborn."

"Oh, please—" I said. I knew about these orphaned lambs from my Quaker neighbors who adopted lambs each spring, feeding them from bottles with crude latex teats. But Walter's description of lambing practices and coyote attacks, as we headed toward Karen's abortion event, was making me sick. In fact, I was having terrible cramps in my side and abdomen. Horrible pinching spasms. I groaned periodically from my perch in the middle seat.

"Those are sympathy pains," Christine said.

"Sympathy pains? God, can that really happen?" I asked her, hunched over. "It feels real to me."

"Sympathy pains can be stronger than real pain."

Christine was getting carried away. Ray said Christine was too theatrical. He joked that she was never the same since she auditioned at the Wilmington Playhouse, where she tried to sit down on the rope barricade in the lobby. The velvet rope toppled and she cracked her head on the floor. Ray linked the accident in the theater to Christine's melodramatic performances. But I thought maybe Christine knew what she was talking about because she had attended seminars with Elisabeth Kübler-Ross.

"Am I running a fever?" I asked. A fine mist erupted across my forehead. The Microbus was a sauna. I said to Christine, "Are you sure Karen wants us coming? She doesn't even know Walter."

Walter said, "I've been there. I've been there."

"Oh, right."

"I saw worse in Nam."

"You never left the boat," Ampy called out from the back seat.

"They brought the wounded *to* the boat. The worse cases. I'm not queasy."

I felt a pain slice through my groin and wrap around my back.

"You need some liquid cork. Kaopectate might help those cramps," Walter said.

"It's not those kind of cramps," I said.

When we arrived at the hospital, I was doubled over. Christine took me inside the Emergency Clinic and told the receptionist I needed a doctor. Christine left me under the supervision of the clinic staff and walked away with Walter to find Karen on the maternity floor. I saw Walter slip his arm around my stepsister's waist. He inserted his fingertips in the back pocket of her tight jeans; he squeezed her ass.

Ampy stood beside me for a while, but I told him I'd be all right. I sat down in the rows of chairs. It was my first time in a clinic. Different from the pine-paneled waiting room at Dr. Kerrigan's that was decorated with Audubon prints and Norman Rockwells, the clinic had a row of VD posters. Junkies, oldsters with walkers, single mothers with runny-nosed toddlers filled every available seat.

I pictured the huge needle that the doctors would use to perform the abortion—like the spiked nozzle of a bicycle pump. I would have preferred the naked information rather than have to endure the irrepressible mural of my imagination.

Finally, I was pulled into a stall to be examined. I told the nurse, "I have to get upstairs to Maternity as soon as possible. My sister's having a baby."

"Oh, really? How exciting."

"Well, she's sort of having a baby. It's really a procedure of some kind." I chattered and the nurse tried to acknowledge my rush of details. My whirl of anxiety alerted the nurse and she patted my shoulder. A doctor came into the stall. He was North African and reminded me of Imran. He spoke with a foreign accent, in a gentle, lyrical voice. He pressed his fingertips into my washboard stomach muscles, finding the landmark organs that were indistinguishable to me beneath the drumskin of my abdomen.

The doctor explained he wanted to perform a pelvic exam. I had not yet submitted to such an intrusion and wondered how I could allow a stranger to peer at me. My moments with Walter were poorly lit, blurred even, in the rush of our greedy impulses. But here the doctor switched on a high-intensity gooseneck lamp just like the one Veronica kept beside the pedestal stand with the O.E.D.

I put my feet in the stirrups. During the examination, a nurse stood beside the table like a charwoman or a guardian angel. The speculum was icy and the doctor apologized. His apology was a bridge. I relaxed when I heard him say he was *sorry*. As he had me opened up like a little pink wallet, I asked him if everything looked all right. "Is this normal?" I said.

"What do you mean?" he said.

"I thought a girl is just supposed to have the hole. You know, *just* the hole?"

The nurse lifted her hand to her mouth to hide her amusement. My misinformation had disarmed them both.

"Perfectly normal," the doctor said. "Pristine, except for these pains you're having."

I sat up and pulled the sheet around me. I was relieved to hear I was normal. I thought I was cursed by the tiny pink embellishments, the androgynous details that Walter prized and manipulated with my assent, but which were still a source of confusion.

The doctor left the room and came back with a medical textbook. He showed me full-color photographs, meat shots like you'd see in *Screw* magazine.

I looked at the pictures, although I didn't feel I had any license to see them.

"Another thing I'm worried about," I said. "Last week I went to the Strait Shows with my friend Melvie to see the Elephant Woman. Heard of her?"

The doctor nodded.

Every year, the carnival set up their tents on an airfield at Wilmington General Aviation. I told the doctor, "They have freaks working with the circus? We went inside the tent to see them lined up. Well, I saw the woman with elephantiasis. Her legs were swollen like tree trunks. Shit, just like an elephant's. That's how she gets her name. On my way out of the tent, I fell in a dirty puddle.

"I heard that's how people *get* that disease, from falling into stagnant water. It's been driving me crazy—"

The doctor rocked back on his heels, his arms folded across his chest. His personal attention to me had opened up a Pandora's box. He patted my knee, bemused, and told me I wasn't likely to ever come in contact with that rare nematode worm.

Why was I thinking only of myself? Why didn't I ask the doctor what was happening to my sister? A pain sliced across my back and I grabbed my side. The doctor said it was probably my kidneys. He asked me to leave a urine sample and he went on to his next patient. The nurse gave me a container and showed me to a bathroom stall. With a great deal of difficulty, I started a timid stream. I handed the cup to the nurse and was escorted back to the waiting room.

In a few moments, a woman in a lab coat walked out to get me. She gave me an injection of antibiotic and handed me a bottle of Gantrisin tablets to take home with me. Cash and carry.

After I signed a form and paid ten dollars, I was ready to find Karen. But I wasn't sure I wanted see what was happening up there in Maternity.

I loved Karen. The fact that I couldn't stop her from leaving home almost three years before and I couldn't effect any change upon her situation right then made me feel helpless. My kidney infection was the excuse I needed to avoid sitting beside Karen.

I sank down in a scoop chair in the waiting room and picked up a *National Geographic* magazine. I turned to a photographic essay about an arctic expedition. I was happy to stare at the ice floes; their cool expanse was soothing. I turned the page and found a surprising picture. A tiny mummy had been discovered embedded in a glacier. It seems that an Eskimo baby had been abandoned in an ice sheet in a ritual of sacrifice; or perhaps the child had been ill and was left to perish in a snowbank outside its village compound. One hundred years had passed, but its body was intact, without any trace of decomposition. In its bed of ice, it was perfectly preserved. Its fur hood was supple and unmatted; its red lips were hydrated and had sharp definition; its eyes were wide open and bright as if full-sighted; even its eyelashes were spiky and distinct. It was a very pretty baby in its petrified suspension.

The frozen infant in the magazine pages jarred me into tears. I could no longer ignore the events unfolding on the floor above me. The whole hospital seemed to crush me. A nurse walked over and handed me a tiny yellow box of Kleenex the size of a personal Whitman's Sampler.

Ampy found me in the Emergency lounge. He couldn't sit down in the tight chairs. He opened his shopping bags to show me what he had selected at the Big Man Store. Ballooning shirts and trousers. A pair of authentic, giant-sized Landlubber jeans. He offered me my choice from a set of colorful bandannas, one size fits all. I chose the purple one and tied it to my belt loop in the Haight-Ashbury fashion of those days.

KAREN AWAKENED FROM her woozy semiconscious state and was glad to see Christine until she understood that the strange man whose voice she had been hearing was somehow sanctioned by her stepsister.

"Who is that? Is he an orderly?" she asked Christine.

He wasn't the person who had come in to collect the rented television set from the foot of the bed. Walter wasn't a legitimate member of the hospital triage and she couldn't place him. Walter told her, "I'm here with your sisters. I'm family. I'm watching these dials—"

His patter was distressing, and he reeked of weed, a sweet and musty scent mingled with lemony British Sterling, just like James used to smell.

Karen tried to shake off the heavy cowl of the sedative, but she slipped in and out of awareness. She dreamed about the white footprints again. She woke up. She saw the nurses in their white oxfords.

Dr. Benvenuto arrived with the resident gynecologist who initiated the procedure. Walter was asked to leave the room, but Christine watched as the gynecologist aspirated amniotic fluid from Karen's abdomen. The gynecologist started the immediate intra-amniotic admin-istration of hypertonic saline solution. After a few harsh kicks, there were no more telling movements from the baby. Within the hour Karen could expect her first contractions.

"All right, then," Dr. Benvenuto told her. "We're doing great—" He left the room, giving his thanks to the other staff.

A nurse explained to Christine, "She's just under the wire for this method, another week she could've delivered a live baby."

The nurse checked Karen's blood pressure, but the nurse would no longer have to monitor the baby. "We're all set," the nurse told Karen.

Her first cervical spasm hit Karen by surprise. A tight, then yawing pain. Her lucidity increased in direct relation to the severity of her con-tractions, which crested and returned without pause for two hours.

Because it wasn't a birth but an abortion, the little courtesies a doc-tor might show a new mother were forfeited for the sake of expedience. Without preparatory comment, the doctor snipped a small episiotomy to ease the delivery. With the next contraction, the baby slipped from Karen.

Karen sat bolt upright to look at the tiny infant.

It was perfect. Fully formed. Motionless.

Its fingers were distinct and ridged at each knuckle. Its new eye-lashes were translucent like tiny white spiders. The doctor pushed Karen back on the table so she wouldn't eye the disaster any longer.

A nurse lifted the tiny body and clamped the cord. The baby was dead. They knew the baby would be dead, but no one expected that the baby would be dark-skinned. Its face was a deep, sunny color like pulled taffy, quite startling juxtaposed to Karen's fair coloring.

It was Horace's.

Her loss instantly crystallized and seemed like a tragic accident. Karen was still in love with Horace.

A nurse quickly toweled the little body. The doctor whispered with the attending nurse about whether the infant would be written up as "deceased" or described as "products of conception of unknown ges-tational age." If they wrote "deceased" on the chart pack, the baby couldn't be discarded with other medical wastes and would have to be put in the morgue.

"I need confirmation on the terms for the documents," the gyne-cologist snapped at the nurse.

They weighed and measured the corpse, writing down the figures. Two pounds, six ounces. The nurse inked the baby's foot and made a print for the records. She expertly swaddled the baby in a flannelette towel, securing its thin arms at its sides and folding the blanket across its breast, tucking in the flaps. When Karen wasn't looking, she lifted the swaddled baby from the warmer bed and switched off the heat lamp. She scrawled the code "Demise" across the chart pack. She carried the tiny body to the morgue and placed it in a drawer with its incomplete paperwork.

I RETURNED TO Wilmington never having seen my sister. I was stirring a vapor of remorse and self-pity when I entered the house and saw Ray. He was sitting on the edge of a dining room chair. His left arm was bandaged and elevated on a wand hooked to a thick leather belt. It was some sort of portable traction. "How is she?" Ray said immediately, without dispensing a greeting.

"My God, what happened to you?" I said.

"Dislocated," he said.

"You dislocated your shoulder?" I said.

"On the golf course," he said.

Ray had been driving a golf cart too fast. He couldn't stop thinking about Karen and had frightened his client, who had warned him several times to slow down. Crossing a slope on the course, the front axle dipped at an incline and the cart toppled. His client was thrown clear and landed on his feet, but the steel canopy that suspended the surrey roof pinned Ray's shoulder, compressing the ball joint until it popped from its socket.

"Who would think a golf cart was so dangerous," Christine said.

"How did it go up there?" Ray asked me expressly. He was squinting in pain, a furious wince that he couldn't shake.

I told Ray, "I didn't go upstairs with Christine and Walter."

"Stackhouse was up there?"

"I was chicken," I told him.

"Stackhouse was there during the procedure? Where were you?" he asked me in disbelief. Then he patted my arm with his free hand. He seemed to remember I was the *little* one—why should I be subjected to these harsh chapters?

Christine said, "Karen was out of it. I don't think she'll remember much."

"She must have been drugged," Ray said.

I burst into tears. My sister's enforced stupor during her ordeal seemed worse than the abortion itself. I tried to fall into Ray's arms. One arm reached for me already, but it was merely his splint, a stiff appendage that blocked my approach.

Veronica arrived carrying a fishbowl of decapitated roses and other floral beheadings, an elaborate potpourri she had won at her bridge game. She centered the fishbowl on the dining room table. The intense perfume was concentrated and immediately nauseating to everyone in our distressed circle.

I noticed all the bowls of flowers in the house. Guillotined lilies and slashed hydrangeas floating in vessels of clear water. Veronica cut flowers at their peak and launched them in tureens and urns. These blooms were disembodied, without roots, stalks, vines. Without any clue that they had been harvested from a mother plant.

Veronica's makeup had drifted and blotched as if she had been crying. I noticed how tiny she looked in her silk suit, its creased fabric hanging askew on her hips. She might have lost weight. Perhaps the weeks had been harder on her than I had acknowledged. Indeed, some tragic detail was visible in her face. It surfaced as she stood there, like an authentic drawing rising through a false picture, like Jesus' profile recurring on the infamous veil she was named for.

She surveyed the three of us. I felt a sudden twinge of pity for her. My voice snagged on a possible word of support; but what could I say to console her? Perhaps Veronica never deserved these troubles. Didn't other families fare much better? Some children might even prove to be a balm or gratification to a mother. Why couldn't Veronica have had those same rewards? I saw how Veronica needed *me* to love her. She needed my allegiance—how could I withhold it?

Veronica placed a bottle of codeine at Ray's elbow. She had had his prescription filled at Happy Harry's Pharmacy. He couldn't unscrew its cap with one arm immobilized. I lifted the little jar, snapped the lid open and gave my father the painkiller.

"Did you see the baby?" Veronica asked me.

The image I had been turning over in my mind all afternoon was that of the lovely Eskimo mummy, a glorious infant, its bronze skin gleaming like petrified wood.

Christine said, "I saw it. It was a black child."

Ray looked down at the glossy dining table where our faces were all reflected. He didn't seem to drink in what he saw.

Veronica said, "It's a relief, isn't it? Karen will be grateful one day. Imagine the heartache a Negro baby would have brought her—"

I stirred the rose petals in the fishbowl. Everyone responded to the piercing scent of the desiccated blossoms, a spicy breath like a withheld confession.

"Get rid of that," Ray said.

I took the bowl outside to one of the sunken garbage pails and toed the pedal to open the lid. I pitched the fishbowl into the empty can. It shattered.

Ray met me in the backyard. Together, we walked around the house, his arm hooked awkwardly in midair. We were both rebounding, and we took some comfort in one another.

His dislocated shoulder was causing him to sweat. I untied my new bandanna from my belt loop and offered it to him. He wiped his face. His golf injury would be the genesis of many years of relentless bursitis, aches and pains that radiated from the insulted humerus and scapula. The pain webbed through his clavicle and outward, all the way to the tips of his fingers—and reminded him of Karen.

WOODSTOCK

———————

Karen's "recuperation" in Cheltenham dragged out for another year. The date of her discharge from Cheltenham wasn't projected on any calendar, but Ray told the doctors that he hoped Karen would be released before the "moon shot" in July. Ray liked to think that Karen had been safe in the hospital during these volatile months of political assassinations and riots. He told me, "You'd be better off in Cheltenham instead of marching on Washington and going to those SDS meetings. I should lock *you* up." It was the first time he had slipped and had admitted that Karen's hospitalization was in fact an incarceration. He shrugged his shoulders in an exaggerated series until I smiled and let him off the hook.

Men walked on the moon, and Karen was still in Cheltenham. In August, Walter took Christine to Woodstock instead of taking me. I was working as a counselor at a People's Settlement day camp in downtown Wilmington, and Walter didn't wait for me to get home from work. WOR had reported that the traffic in upstate New York was already a bottleneck.

Walter had five huge barrels of Dutch pretzels he wanted to peddle at the music festival. He was going to make a killing. Christine let Walter drive her Microbus. Its VW shield had been soldered into a peace sign. Walter hoped to sell contracts for some gatorized guitars—maybe he'd sell one to Hendrix.

I came home from the day camp and discovered that Walter had fled with my sister. I asked Veronica, "How could you let Walter go to Woodstock without me?"

"You want to work as a pretzel vendor? That's slave labor."

I took my Martin guitar and drove over to his building. I let myself in the apartment. I took the guitar from its case and strummed a few harsh chords in a final farewell to the remarkable instrument.

I pulled back the sheet on Walter's double bed and placed the guitar in the little furrow that might have been my own imprint or someone else's. I tugged the hem of the blanket to cover the guitar's gleaming hourglass figure, leaving its golden neck exposed on the pillow. I took the tiny key to the guitar case and Walter's apartment key and placed them both on the metric scale, choosing the corresponding weights to offset them. It was a game I enjoyed immensely. When the little trays were level, I let myself out of the apartment.

In all the rain that fell that fateful weekend, the pretzels got soggy and Walter couldn't *give* them away. I was grateful to be spared the misery of that mud bath. If Woodstock was the pinnacle event of the Peace Generation, did we all have to be there in person? Karen didn't attend Woodstock, either. We both missed it—so what?

THE FOLLOWING WEEKEND, Karen was discharged from Cheltenham. Veronica didn't want her to return home, and she was released to live "off campus" in Philadelphia. She was still expected to attend group therapy meetings, but she never showed up. The wolf girl's father, Bennett Dixon, took Karen to Atlantic City to celebrate her freedom.

Karen took an apartment with Sharly, who had been discharged from Cheltenham a few months earlier. Sharly had already fallen on hard times and was glad to have a place to live.

"Are you going to call James now that you're out?" Sharly said.

"I thought about it."

"I guess now it's *the moment of truth*."

Karen looked at her friend. "I think that moment has passed."

Sharly giggled, a warm, infectious trill like a roomful of parakeets. Karen couldn't get enough of it.

First things first—Karen went to the animal pound and picked out a tom kitten. The next day, she went back for its little twin.

Without a real high school diploma, Karen applied for a few different jobs that didn't pan out. She worked one day as a receptionist at a travel agency. Her supervisor said she would need a new wardrobe. She didn't like people telling her what to wear. Ruth and Hendrick had supplied her with a limited uniform, a ratty selection of Barbizon nighties crammed into a Lane hope chest in Ruth's office.

She trained as a taxicab dispatcher, but she couldn't understand the street guide and had trouble operating the radio transmitter. She pushed the wrong buttons and squelched the exchanges. She broadcast the wrong instructions to drivers, directing cabs to vacant lots, or she transposed street numbers. Sharly told her, "How can they expect you to know the city when you've been locked up?"

Even without a job, Karen had some money coming in. Ray sent her a monthly allowance, and she was "dating" Bennett Dixon. Bennett owned a string of rug emporiums in New Jersey, and he sent her a Karastan carpet for the apartment.

Bennett took her on weekend trips to the Jersey shore. He gave her money. But he was careful to never put the cash into her hand. She never felt like she was hustling, and he would never unfold his money clip in front of her. He didn't sort stacks of bills on the bedspread as some men had done to try to convince her to do extra. Bennett never offered her direct payment for her company. He loaned her his BankAmericard and mailed her bank checks with the amounts embossed in little blue dots. Karen liked to rub her fingertip over the tight bumps in the paper. Sharly saw these embossed checks and called Karen's boyfriend "Mr. Braille."

"Thank God for Mr. Braille," Sharly said when Karen cashed a check.

Bennett's daughter was a hopeless case, committed to Cheltenham till doomsday or until his insurance company balked. His daughter was irretrievable to him, just as Karen was estranged from her own parents. Yes, they had met one another inside a loony bin. But their reconnoitering outside the hospital walls seemed sunny—a benign serendipity. They often laughed about their bond. Karen didn't worry that Bennett was married and kept a big house for his wife. She didn't want the complete burden of a middle-aged man.

Sharly was back to her old ways, hustling, shooting up and doing speedballs with the junkie population in Rittenhouse Square and every needle park. Karen saw the self-destructive neighbors in her building and moved into a row-house flat on Nineteenth Street in Center City, taking Sharly with her. They shared the flat with a gorgeous "high yellow" black model named Betsy Beeman, just like the pepsin chewing gum. Karen met Betsy in the camera shop where she had started a new job as a clerk.

Betsy Beeman ran the portrait studio in the camera shop. Families brought children into the studio to pose for baby pictures. Betsy arranged the infants and toddlers in front of a blue velvet drop cloth. Sometimes, watching people's babies, Karen thought of Horace's infant boy. How would it have looked on that blue velvet cloth?

Karen sold film and took orders for film processing and reprints. A local porn king came in to the store and walked all the way through to the back. Betsy's boss accepted requests for under-the-counter processing, and Karen saw the contact sheets. The client specialized in "snuff shots." Naked women were made up with daubs of cherry pie filling to look like they had been stabbed or shot. Karen remembered Dr. Benvenuto's words: "Do you want to be the *murderer* or the *murder victim*?" She watched her boss and his client push a magnifying loupe over the exposures, deciding which photographs should be enlarged for their mail-order business.

WALTER WAS IN JAIL. In September he was arrested for drug trafficking and with blistering speed the courts processed him, making his case a public example. He was sent to the penitentiary in Smyrna. It was a long drive to Smyrna in Ampy's customized sedan with its floating shocks like a rolling living room sofa, and I only went once.

The following week, I attended an SDS meeting in a condemned building on Ninth Street and was arrested with ten others for trespassing and "consorting." The police couldn't prove that our group was linked to any contraband substance, but our gathering itself was against the law. Again, I appeared in family court and was sentenced to another year of probation. Assigned to the same probation officer, I was surprised to see that the German figurines that had once lined her desk had been replaced by a perpetual motion machine, a distressing contraption with moving gears and levers that accelerated, paused and cocked up and down.

Ampy kept vigil for Walter and wrote in Day-Glo paint across his picture window in full view of I-95 rush-hour traffic: WALTER STACK-HOUSE STILL IN JAIL. DAY 45. Every day, Ampy erased the count and wrote in the new figure.

But I didn't think of Walter. I dreamed only of my reunion with Karen. For four years, I had not seen my sister. Yet, her secret life had created the very formula of my existence as a girl, sister, woman. Her disappearance had molded my own self-awareness; her disappearance had *filled* me, and perhaps it had even defined my physical conformation. Our sole connection was manifested in our broken bond; it was our one spark.

To see Karen again might jar me from whatever slim perch I had built for myself. I didn't think that Karen wanted the abrupt juxtaposition any more than I did. Wasn't it better to keep our distance?

Then one morning in late autumn, Veronica answered the telephone. I watched Veronica's face washed blank and her features assume their telltale glacial effects. I knew it was Karen on the other end. She handed me the receiver.

Karen told me it was her day off from work and she was taking a train into Claymont Station. Could I meet her?

I pictured her when she was still living at home, younger than she would be in true life, and never having caught up, still younger than me. Anything I knew about my sister was reconstituted from secondary sources. Most of all, from the blackboards of my imagination, like an endless quiz game of hangman, I pictured my sister: runaway, fugitive, whore.

"I'll meet you," I told her.

I had not stood beside my sister since the day we inked our footprints on a paper bag. As I dressed for our reunion, I realized I was still a string bean and decided to wear the one sweater I owned that made me look fat. Searching for the right clothes to wear, I realized that if I wore my "fat sweater" I was putting on a mask.

I WANTED MELVIE to come with me to meet my sister and I drove Veronica's Citroën to get him. I had my new driver's license but the French sedan had a gearshift mechanism mounted on the dash just like the arm of a slot machine, and I couldn't get the hang of it. I wrenched the knob across its *H* pattern and felt the mechanism vibrate down my spinal column. Melvie couldn't come with me. He had just had surgery on two ingrown toenails. The doctor had extracted the curved roof of each big toe, leaving the raw tips pink as melon balls. He would be useless to me.

I stopped to buy a box of Hearn's cakes for Karen. I watched the clerk tie the satin cardboard box with a tartan ribbon. The procedure was exactly the same as it was years ago before all of this snowballed.

Standing beside the open railroad trench made me queasy. Pure vertigo, I told myself. In fact, like Veronica, I had started to feel uncomfortable riding escalators and elevators or navigating busy streets. It was the dawn of a pattern of fears that would take decades for me to shake.

I was meeting my sister whom I had not seen in four years. I might have been meeting an icon, Bob Dylan or Joan of Arc, someone to whom I had no earthly connection. A string of cars emerged around the bend and rolled up to the platform. Its wheels locked in a painful stop motion and immediately Karen stepped down. She had brought her friend Sharly. They stood out from the afternoon stragglers, housewives and college students who took the midday trains. They were wearing too much makeup and resembled the girls I had seen in the Baltimore jail. Girls who had worn their baby-doll pajamas underneath Scotchgarded trench coats.

Karen's face was different from the last time I saw it. Her bleached hair and extra eye makeup gave her a startling resemblance to the trampy English singer Lulu, who had released the big hit "To Sir with Love" and whose hauteur was half whore, half schoolgirl.

As Karen walked in my direction, my throat contracted like the syrinx of a tiny wren or finch. I was going to be speechless, no matter how hard I tried to formulate a greeting.

I threw my arms around her. She looked into my face. I saw a few tears nestled like rhinestones in her eyelashes until she blinked. Yes, she was beautiful. I studied a tattooed snowflake on her chin until I realized it was the ragged edges of a scar.

"Nice," Karen told me, plucking the leather tassels on my fringe jacket. "Daniel Boone."

"Dan*ielle* Boone," Sharly said. "Oh, I've seen those jackets in *Vogue*. They're really glam. It's not just the western look anymore."

The fashion chat was an icebreaker. I told Sharly she resembled the British model Jean Shrimpton. Of course, she didn't look like that model very much at all. Sharly was too skinny and weatherbeaten. Sharly was one of these walking-stick working girls you can't imagine could attract clients.

Sharly admitted to me that she had actually done some runway modeling at Wanamaker's, long ago.

Karen was dressed in a full-length cornflower leather coat and blue platform boots, a zone of aqua hues matching her eye makeup. Sharly was wearing a maxicoat that brushed the concrete platform. Her miniskirt was so short that when she crossed her legs in the back seat of the Citroën, it looked like a tiny leather hymnbook thrown across her lap.

"With *that* skirt, you need a substantial coat," I told her. I was surprised to hear the fuddy-duddy tone of my voice. I was thinking Veronica wouldn't care to see Karen's new kidskin coat. It might not compare with our mother's Blackglama, yet how did Karen come across such an expensive item without the debt of marriage?

Already the car smelled like menthol cigarettes. Karen's Salem kings. Sharly's Newports.

"Just where in the hell did you get a coat like that?" I said.

"From the old man. Bennett Dixon."

"Who's that?"

Sharly said, "He's the father of that wolf girl in the bin. He starts chasing your sister."

"I didn't run very fast," Karen said.

"He buy you that coat?" I asked Karen.

"I bought it. He gave me his BankAmericard."

WHEN WE ARRIVED at the house, Veronica was out playing bridge, keeping her distance. We sat in the den and drank ginger ale, waiting for her to come home. "Ray's down at the warehouse?" Karen asked.

"Until about six," I said.

"We get the train at five," she said.

"You'll miss him, then."

"That's right."

To sit on the sofa together, we needed to move a card table where Veronica had left her needlework. Veronica was always doing a knitting project or hooking rugs. If she pulled little threads of yarn tight on an embroidery hoop or cinched fibers on a blueprint grid, she might control every loose end. Her wayward fears and unnameable regrets couldn't run wild and plague her.

Sharly helped collect the flecks of yarn, then she introduced herself to the liquor cabinet. She said "Hel*lo*" when she saw the rows of bottles. She tipped some scotch into her glass.

I presented the Hearn's cakes to Karen.

"Are these for me?"

"Yeah. I bought six."

"You know, I never liked these. The icing sticks to the roof of my mouth. Sharly, you want one?"

"What do you mean you don't like these cakes?" I asked my sister. "Since when?"

"Since the beginning of time."

I sat down on the love seat beside Sharly and stuffed a sweet in my mouth. I felt the choking sensation Karen was talking about.

As children we had shared our sweets. I often bit into jelly beans and handed her the severed nub, my teeth marks slashed across the gummy center. Why I had always licked the salt from pretzels, ate the first bites of apples, handing my sister little more than the core, why I halved the candy, choosing the bigger piece, was reason for my accrued guilt. But was it my fault if Karen was too pliant and never stood up to me?

Many times at daybreak, Karen and I had sat together on that same love seat. We watched the only television program broadcast at that hour, a live show called *Farm Report*. A craggy man in overalls stood in a pen with piglets and chickens to recite the weather forecast and give specific instructions about which crops should be rotated and which seeds should be sown in the coming week. We watched the dawn lift behind the farmer just as it was rising outside the window. The continuity of the sun rising on the television screen and rising over our house before our own eyes had a deep, almost religious effect. The world seemed ordered and made common sense; if the world had a beneficent monitor, if not a real God, then it was the host of *Farm Report* in his denim coveralls and dirty Wellingtons.

The dizzying pull of memory was making me queasy. It wasn't memory but all the menthol smoke in the room. Karen's cigarette fell from her fingers and singed the tassel binding on a silk throw pillow. She brushed the ash from the piping.

"Shit, what's Veronica doing at that bridge game? Do they play for quarters, or what?" Karen said.

I told Karen, "I think the winner gets the centerpiece from the lunch table."

"She gets the flower bouquet?" Sharly said.

"Well, that's something anyway," Karen said.

I saw a mark on Karen's inner wrist. "What's that?"

"That's my TB test."

I looked at the little wheal on her arm. "Is that positive or negative?"

"I have to call back if it's bigger than a dime."

Sharly leaned over Karen, her long hair falling in a straight auburn sheet. Sharly said, "Mine didn't look like that. Shit, yours is bigger than a dime right now."

"Let's measure it," I said. "Who's got a dime?"

"I used to keep a dime in my loafer," Karen said.

"I have one," Sharly said. She pulled a tiny beaded change purse from her handbag. She plucked a coin from it and placed it against Karen's arm.

"See," Karen said.

Holding Karen's forearm across my lap, I was filled with emotion.

"It's been a long time," I said.

"Life can be long if you're lucky," she said.

I said, "Did you really work in a whorehouse?"

"Is that what Veronica said?"

Sharly looked at Karen.

"Was it a real whorehouse?" I asked Karen.

"That's the long and short of it."

Sharly burst into laughter. Karen seemed surprised by her accidental pun, but Sharly wouldn't let it escape.

Karen removed a narrow strip of photos from her wallet, a row of four shots like you might buy at a booth in an airport or bus station. "Val sent me these. We took these at the boardwalk in Ocean City."

I looked at the column of shots showing Karen and James cheek-to-cheek. He was handsome, indeed, but his face had a disturbing resemblance to the familiar sly fox. Could this be the man outside the high school?

"That was him?"

"I guess it *still is* him," she said.

We laughed in a luxurious wave.

For one instant, every loose thread seemed to be gathered up, our collective tatters braided into our triple-pitched laughter. In our lives, together or apart, we had endured absurd conditions, hadn't we? "We were almost lost at sea," I reminded her.

"That's right," Karen said. "Now we're lost at land."

"Put that on my tombstone," Sharly said. " 'Lost at land.' "

We heard Veronica's footsteps in the foyer. She came out to the porch and set down an explosive arrangement of flowers, yellow carnations and asters bobbing, wild and frightening as a clown's wig. "Hello, girls," she said, her head bowed to the task.

"Did you win?" Karen asked Veronica.

"My Tuesday group is pathetic. Those ladies are weak players. I don't even try to win." She came across the room and pecked Karen's cheek. She looked at Sharly.

Sharly introduced herself in much the same manner she had greeted the booze. "He*ll*o, Mrs. Mitchell."

Veronica noticed the blue leather coat draped over a chair in the sunroom. She lifted it by its heavy shoulders. She stared at it. She set it down and walked out of the room. She came back with a figurine in the palm of her hand. It was a white ceramic cat for Karen. The cat's head unscrewed at its bow-tie collar. It was a bottle of perfume you might give to a child, an old Avon fragrance, probably long ago discontinued.

She handed it to Karen. Karen unscrewed its head and sniffed the cheap scent. The room filled up with it, a sharp smell like embalmed gardenias. But Karen seemed to value the little cat. The damage that came from these offerings manifested in our momentary confusion; each time we wondered, Is this love at work?

Poor Veronica, she might have been trying to re-create a time when Karen's desires were simple and easily satisfied by just these small trinkets from the Avon Lady.

"What's that smell?" I said.

There was an unmistakable scent of scorched polyester. The love seat was on fire.

"Did you girls drop a cigarette?" Veronica said.

Karen and I lifted the heavy cushions from the couch and saw the smoke billowing from the deep upholstery. Veronica picked up the telephone. She was dialing the fire department.

"We don't need them," Karen said, always shying from authorities.

I said, "Look, we can take the whole thing outside and hose it."

Karen and I tried to lift the heavy sofa and dropped it again. Sharly was useless in her miniskirt and platforms.

Veronica returned. "Where are you going with that?"

"Well, we're not going to steal it, are we?" Karen said.

Smoke was swelling over the room. Finally, Veronica held the back door for us and we carried the sofa out to the driveway. Veronica followed us onto the asphalt. "That's a nine-hundred-dollar upholstery job. That's Waverly fabric. Not cheap."

I went around to the spigot and tugged the hose, but the spool froze up. By the time I untangled it, the sofa had burst into flames, fully involved. Flames licked the wide seat like candles on a sheet cake, then climbed over the arms and up the upholstered back until the fire achieved the immediate perfection of a cartoon disaster.

The fire department arrived and the men unhooked portable extinguishers from the truck.

"These girls were smoking," my mother told the fire officer.

"What about you?" Karen said. "Your butts were everywhere. You smoke as much as anyone, don't you?"

"When I left the house this morning, there wasn't a fire."

The fireman said, "Well, if you get a cigarette down in the cushions, it can smolder for hours."

"That's what happened," Karen said.

Veronica looked at my sister as if every kind of trouble had Karen's form and outline.

Sharly said, "You're lucky we were sitting on it."

Suddenly, I saw Sharly as the Fire Department workers saw her. She was almost naked in her tiny leather skirt, shivering in the cold November air. Karen didn't look much better, in her tight jersey dress, the color of Italian ice.

The men squirted the sofa with chemical foam. They left it in the driveway, a charred wedge with dabs of suds.

Veronica thanked the fire officers. "Can you take that with you? It doesn't look very nice. That's something you might see in Philadelphia where they leave everything on the sidewalks."

"We can't take it on this truck. We'll call a waste contractor to pick it up. That's your cost, though."

"That will be fine. I don't want it here for long."

I couldn't help thinking that the sofa was becoming a symbol of Karen's presence. Veronica might have said, "I don't want *her* here for long."

The firefighters had left a circle of foam on the drive, and Karen and I tracked white footprints across the blacktop and back into the house.

I could see Karen had had enough of Veronica; she had had enough of me. She declined to stay for dinner when Veronica announced blankly, "I'm thawing the beef."

Karen wanted a lift back to the train.

When she was in the bathroom, Veronica tried on her coat. "Is this your sister's coat?" she asked me.

"I don't know."

"Did she come here in this coat or in that maxi?"

"Ask her yourself."

"You don't get a coat like this for nothing. You have to earn some money to buy this. You think your sister can earn this kind of money?"

She stroked its cuff, smoothing the supple leather under her hand. She adjusted the coat on her shoulders and fastened the two clasps which closed the beautifully tailored hides at the collar and waist. She walked over to the hall mirror. "What color is this? Is it delphinium?"

Sharly saw Veronica in Karen's coat and turned on her heel.

Veronica said, "I'd be ashamed to wear this coat. It says 'mistress.'"

"You wear your mink."

"Your father gave me that mink. It's different. You know what I'm saying. Tell me how your sister gets a Bonwit?"

"It's her business," I told her, alarmed at the noun I had chosen.

Veronica nodded. She didn't want to know about Karen's secret world.

When I drove Karen to the station, I said, "Maybe I'll go into Philadelphia with you and Sharly. We can have dinner—"

Karen was holding the ceramic cat, which wouldn't fit in her tiny purse. She said, "I guess Veronica thawed that beef for you. You better have dinner at home."

"She takes a hunk of something out of the freezer. So what?"

"That's more than I can do for you."

"What do you mean?" I said.

"I don't have a pot roast at my house, that's what I mean. Shit. You always find symbolism in what people are saying. That's going to be a pain in the ass if you don't learn to stop doing that."

Sharly saw the train coming in and said, "See you, honey."

I watched my sister follow Sharly into a compartment. I searched the windows for the two women as the train started to roll away. I spied Karen's cornflower coat in one window, but she stared over my head and didn't make eye contact. Her weary half smile suggested that her retreat was benign and in our best interests.

I trotted to the end of the platform and teetered on its brass lip when I was hit by a wall of vertigo much worse than my typical squeamishness. The sensation that I was falling off the edge lasted long after the train turned the bend and disappeared.

NEW YORK CITY

M Y REUNION WITH Karen had not engendered a new vision of us, but an after-flash. Despite the dramatic moment when the sofa had caught fire, I clung to each homely detail—her menthol cigarettes, her pastel eye shadow that matched her leather coat, the tiny wheal on her forearm from her TB test. I was haunted by it.

I was still riding out the bumpy wake of my unhappy liaison with a convicted criminal. Walter Stackhouse was in jail. I sorely missed his predictable schemes and routine diversions.

On our last outing together, we had attended a faculty party at the University of Delaware where antiwar radicals and intellectuals were assembled in several nose-to-nose clusters, arguing about music, politics, art. I liked hearing snippets of their conversation and I tried to keep up. A professor embraced my ideas about a threatened estuary, and I was introduced around to discuss the tidewater ecosystem. Walter had been invited to supply "extracts of the poppy." He was a big cheese, until everyone had skin-popped. When the crowd of geniuses seemed to forget about Walter, he led me across the cramped parlor to an overstuffed chair. He pulled me down onto his lap and reached under my ruffled gypsy skirt. He tugged the elastic of my underpants aside and entered me right there, in the room full of professors and English majors. He rocked me almost imperceptibly, my full skirt extended over the arms of the chair. He was angry at my immediate integration into the university milieu and he was thumbing his nose at the academics.

A student in wire rims came over to us, but Walter didn't stop bouncing me. Walter was disappointed that the fellow didn't have an egghead question and he just wanted to know about gatorized guitars. I felt Walter's wounded self-concept manifested in his giant hard-on. These college types were too good for him—well, he'd show them by banging me at their own soiree. Later that week, Walter was arrested.

AFTER DARK ONE NIGHT, Alex showed up at the house fully drunk. He had been having a bad spell with his ex-wife, who refused to let him see his son. She ignored his desperate feelings. The week before, still wearing his nail apron, he sat down on his sofa, held a loaded pistol to his temple and released the safety. He begged his ex-wife to show up and gave her one hour to decide.

He gave her another hour. And *one more* hour.

Alex sat outside in his car with the headlights off. He waited until Ray and Veronica drove away to a duplicate-bridge game. When he saw my bedroom light switch on and my silhouette on the curtains, he left his car and came into the house. In his stupor, his shoulder brushed the wall as he walked down the hallway, sweeping the picture frames off. Alex came into my room. He peeled back my blanket and got into my bed next to me. I didn't stop him.

I once read an article about a remote lake in western Africa that bubbled up, releasing a poison vapor. The mist drifted over a coastal village, killing everyone. Entire families, every infant, child and elderly patriarch were obliterated. Why didn't these mysterious mists stall across American families?

Alex took me into his arms, and I let him understand I would never accuse him of acting solely of his own accord.

In hushed remorse, he told me, "I'm trapped in a genetic pattern."

"You're what?"

"The weed he plucks from his garden, grows in his son's."

Alex was still brooding about the Arrow Collar model whom he had never laid eyes on. Perhaps Veronica had showed him her recent postcard from Curtis Pettibone.

RAY AND VERONICA never bothered to send away for college catalogues. My *D* average was rankly deficient. On my own initiative, I went to see the guidance counselor at the high school to talk about my academic options. The counselor shook his head slowly and said, "Have you thought about an equestrian college? Maybe in Virginia—"

"Are you talking about one of those horse schools for stupid Miss Debs? No thanks." I thought of Dreamboy. Where was he? I was sure he had long since been rendered and tinned.

Nights without Walter, I sat in front of the TV and watched *Laugh-In* until I got a phone call from Ampy. He was giving me glassine envelopes of cocaine, which I used judiciously, but it had become a daily habit. I tapped the powder onto a little Woolworth's pocket mirror and cut the clumps with a single-edge razor. It was an exacting ritual, and I spent several minutes scraping the white line left and right, careful not to spill any dust off the mirror's edge. I watched my face reflected beneath the white scrim. I sliced the razor blade up and down, jabbing my eyes, my lips.

On Fridays, when I could "lay out" for the weekend, Ampy gave me spoons of heroin, or it was morphine "bladder mix" in tall amber bottles straight from the closets of Wilmington General Hospital where Mrs. Stackhouse worked the third shift. The "bladder mix" had to be consumed by mouth; its route was through the stomach, and it made me deathly sick. I told Ampy I preferred to get fixed, despite its junkie stigma. At all costs, I wanted to bypass the digestive track.

I understood that Ampy might want to have sex. But how would we manage the physical aspect? Sex was the only way I knew how to barter for drugs, or love, or money. But Ampy told me, "Who said anything about sex?"

"What then?"

"Friendship, for one thing. Shit, you're a good listener, honey, that's just about priceless," he told me.

I calculated my substantial debt and figured how many hours I'd have to be lending my ear. I tried to change his mind and told him I could square everything if he'd let me get on top of him.

I FOUND SOLACE IN the antiwar movement the way someone might join a twelve-step program. It was easy to file in line behind local hipsters and hate Nixon. I cleaved to like souls and mingled with exotic loners, loners who were alone by choice or alone from unremitting circumstance.

Ray said my "social conscience" was only a Band-Aid for my generation's lack of productivity. He told me I should put my nose to the grindstone at school, but instead I went to organized marches. With Melvie, I attended lunchtime rallies in Rodney Square, where courthouse secretaries rolled pennies between the feet of hippies making speeches; each spinning coin made a little spectacle of its own.

I went to bed with activists who rehearsed antiestablishment doctrine ad nauseam in lieu of pillow talk. These boys were always stumping; if it wasn't about the war, they were campaigning to legalize marijuana. They were reciting environmental impact statements to protest a landfill or an interstate extension somewhere. I was against the landfill. I was against the war. I dated local Abbie Hoffmans, fucked them, Frenched them.

But I didn't feel loved. I didn't love them.

VERONICA FOUND my Woolworth's mirror, crosshatched with razor blade scratches. She discovered my stash of cocaine and the tightly rolled dollar bill. She stretched the dollar open and let it snap shut in a dusty scroll. "Explain this," she told me.

She telephoned Ray at work as I paced around my bedroom throwing clothes in a knapsack just like a Hollywood movie when gangsters lose their cover and have to pick up and flee their flop. I packed jeans and scarves, my Days of the Week panties. Only tattered Tuesday and Saturday were left.

Veronica said, "Where are you going?"

"Destination Anywhere," I told her.

My delivery was perfect, flat and icy like my Lenny Bruce record. Each punch line was so exquisitely refined and deadly bleak it was like an act of murder-suicide.

"You can't leave until you talk to your father."

"I'm not talking to Ray. I'm leaving," I told her.

"Talk to your father. Tell *him* you're a *dope fiend.*"

I brushed past her.

"Your daughter won't pick up the phone. She's going to the door.

She's walking out—" Veronica narrated my departure. She could have begged me to stay.

I STOOD ON THE SIDE of the road and waved down a classmate who was on her way to her modern-dance lesson. She was wearing a plum-colored leotard and tights. Her blond ponytail, enhanced with lemon juice highlights, was cinched in a chiffon scarf. I eyed her and said, "Shit. Life is *beautiful for you.*" The radio was screaming and she didn't hear my jab.

She turned down the volume, but was careful not to squelch Number 9 of the Top 40 countdown. I said, "Can you give me a lift to the Twin Bridges? I'm hitching to New York."

"Are you going to that abortion clinic up there?"

"Yeah. That's right." It was easier accepting her version of my exodus.

I climbed into another car at the Delaware Memorial Bridge and two hours later got out of the car far uptown in Manhattan. Right then, an off-duty cabdriver saw me and shoved his door open. Again, I climbed in.

I was like a house cat fluffed up three sizes and the off-duty driver was enticed by my huge wide-open eyes. He told me he was bringing me back to his garage to put me in Lost or Stolen. He pinched my knee and slid his palm up the inside seam of my blue jeans. I jumped out at an intersection. It was a shabby black neighborhood where I stuck out like a sore thumb. Some kids approached me and lifted my backpack off my shoulders the way a gentleman removes a lady's wrap at a coat check. With elegant reserve and little fanfare they snatched my possessions and trotted away.

In my pocket, I had the address and apartment number of an SDS connection of some renown to our local University of Delaware chapter. He was an NYU student ready to help anyone who needed a place to crash.

As I entered the white neighborhoods, refined people looked at me as if I was a stray mental patient. Without a book bag or briefcase, my arms loose at my sides, I tore across the sidewalks like a junior Miss Frankenstein. I wasn't used to stopping at DON'T WALK signs, and I climbed up the heels of businessmen and other startled pedestrians coming and going.

My square-toed boots were a size too large, and I was getting blisters. I searched for the right address until I discovered that there were *two* Eighty-first Streets, one east and one west on either side of Central Park. By dusk I had found the right building and was buzzed through the foyer. I took the stairs to the fourth floor, avoiding the scary elevator with its small black porthole.

When my SDS compatriot answered his door, four orange and white kittens scrambled to get out. He stooped to collect the cats as they circled our feet and gently tossed them back in the flat.

"Drew Johnston?" I asked the man.

He nodded and grinned. He wasn't displeased to find me standing on his doormat, a textured square in the design of a commemorative postage stamp. The postage stamp doormat gave me a queasy sensation. It branded me somehow, as if I myself might be some sort of special-delivery item. I knew nothing about my host except that he attended New York University and was an SDS captain. He seemed much older than the typical college student. His hair was thinning and his eyes looked sunken. He looked generally malnourished and had the wildly variating pupils of a typical junkie. Yet, strewn on the floor was a catnip mouse and a jingle bell tied to a string. I thought, Why worry about a man who adopts a house full of kittens?

My host showed me to a chair beneath the famous giant-sized FUCK THE DRAFT poster. He offered me a glass of "sun tea" which he had brewed on his fire escape. He poured the rest in a bowl for my blistered foot. "Tea is good for open sores," he said.

I wondered, What open sores has he doctored? He teased the kittens and explained that he worked part-time on a fireboat moored at a pier on the East River. "I'm not on shift tonight, but do you want to see her?" he asked me.

"Sure," I said, although I had walked too much already and I didn't want to wear my boots again.

He lent me a pair of huge socks with leather soles. In these medieval slippers, I could walk several blocks from the apartment to the dock where the fireboats were tied up in a line.

I padded along silently beside my new friend. "How often do ships catch fire?" I asked him.

"We respond to all kinds of fires along the river. Usually, it's sheds, warehouses or trash on the piers." He waved his arm across the expansive waterfront and looked genuinely intrigued by the endless possibilities of different conflagrations. "We might get a call from the harbormaster about a ship's fire out in the channel. A captain will radio if he needs a tow. Then it's the garbage scows, they always smolder. Did you ever hear about the *Normandy* disaster in 'thirty-nine?"

"The *Normandy*?"

"A French liner burned up in port. They thought it was sabotage, the Mafia working for the Nazis. The fire started deep under her decks. Every unit in New York was pumping streams. She took on so much water from fireboats she started to list. Then she rolled over. She sank in her own berth!"

"Is this where all the ocean liners tie up?" I couldn't stop myself from asking about the *Stockholm* and the girl in its crumpled prow.

"Liners sail out of the New York City Passenger Ship Terminal. That's on the Hudson."

There was a crew on shift at the fireboat. Men were looping hoses until they were in waist-high coils on deck. The collapsed hose was of an ominous flesh-tone latex. Other men stood on deck playing bagpipes. The musicians looked out at us as they played a mournful dirge, but they didn't seem to recognize my companion. I thought it was strange that they ignored one of their official brethren.

But after hitching 125 miles after fleeing my home, I didn't want to identify odd pieces that wouldn't fit the puzzle. I refused to acknowledge my needling suspicions. My joints were sore, as if the marrow had been extracted. Even my hair ached at the roots where the wind was blowing it against its typical drape. The soulful notes of the bagpipes sealed my fate. I started to nuzzle against the man whose apartment would be my safe haven.

As we walked back to his building, he asked me to shut my eyes. He said, "I want you to trust me."

"Sure," I said.

"No, I mean it. Shut your eyes. Pretend you're a blind girl."

"Pretend I'm blind?" Without protest, I shut my eyes. He took my elbow and steered me along the sidewalks. He told me when there was a curb, or when I needed to speed up at a crossing, or when I should halt for traffic.

"Trust me," he said.

For some wild reason, I was pleased to keep my eyes pinned shut. I took step after step in my soft-soled socks, as if following my sister's ghost footprints left here just for this purpose. Was this how Karen had disappeared? Was it as easy as this? I just had to shut my eyes?

Later that night, after soaking my blistered foot in a second bowl of tea, Drew led me across the kitchen to a foam pallet on the floor. "The guest room," he joked. The kittens scrambled after us. Without any formal announcement of his plans, he tied one of my wrists to the radiator ribs with a leather boot string.

"What are you doing?" I said, my voice still wry, as he cinched the knot.

"It's okay, honey," he said. I started to fight him when he threaded the other shoelace through the pipes and looped it around my other hand.

He tugged my jeans off. He raped me.

I tried to kick him, but he held my hips. He had set the radio to WCBS, "the All News Station." He twisted the volume dial until the announcer was screaming. As he fucked me methodically, with the efficiency of a criminal act, without unnecessary words, neither a consoling nor a lewd remark, I heard the traffic reports for the Hutchinson River Parkway and Brooklyn-Queens Expressway. Then it was the "Weekend Weather." Then again, the update for the "Hutch" and the "BQE." An accident in the high-speed lane. At his first penetration, I was dead silent in disbelief. My disbelief was like a constriction in my throat. Suddenly, my muteness was dislodged by the repetitive rhythm of the sexual act and I chirped with each thrust. I hollered my dissenting viewpoint, but he reached up to the kitchen counter and stuffed my mouth with an oven mitt on which I could taste a sour glaze of stale tomato paste and tuna fish from several open tins of cat food.

I couldn't breathe with my mouth gagged; my sinuses were stuffed. I thought I was suffocating and had a panic reaction. I drummed my heels against the bare wood floor until he pulled the rancid mitten from my mouth. He promised not to hurt me.

The kittens pounced and galloped back and forth.

I thought to myself, "I deserve this." I had left my suburban life and walked into this lurid sanctuary; the escape into sex had its price. I had delivered myself to the rapist's postage stamp doormat—wasn't I a hypocrite to struggle? Does every rape victim launch into self-examination even before the event is finished? I recognized my role in the sex crime. Had I not traveled of my own volition to that tiny soiled pallet, to the highly specific, isolated, yet universal zone of the victim?

I wondered about the little girl in stateroom 52. If she had lived, would *she* have been right here now, getting raped, instead of me?

At last, he froze. I recognized the familiar shudder across his shoulders as his hips locked at the trigger of climax. His eyes flashed open and refocused as if he had awakened and was surprised to see my face. He deftly unknotted the shoe strings and rubbed my reddened wrists as if erasing these pink bracelets might erase his wrongdoing.

Right then, the *real* SDS hero came home and alarmed the impostor. I was pulling my clothes back on when I learned that the man who had led me through the streets "like a blind girl" was himself a vagabond using the apartment as his crash pad and impromptu torture den. Despite the authentic Drew Johnston's reassurances that I would come to no further harm, I trotted down the stairs still tugging my boots on. I had five dollars on me, enough to take a Trailways home to Wilmington if I went on foot all the way to Port Authority. The next bus wasn't for two hours. I sat in the rows of plastic chairs and watched the arrivals and departures churn through the doors. Hundreds of people streamed in two directions as if following the pathways in a huge organic mechanism or veinal system. I too would enter that collective propulsion, but I wondered why in the world had I purchased a ticket back to Wilmington? Why did I choose to go home?

At the Wilmington bus terminal I dialed Veronica from a phone booth. Despite my disappearance for one whole night, she sounded remarkably chipper.

She said she would telephone Ray at his office. Ray left his desk and met me at the Trailways terminal. I sighted his unhappy face as he steered the car along the curb searching the crowded sidewalk.

I knew what was happening even before our eyes met. I saw a suit-case on the back seat of the car. The suitcase.

Ray was taking me to Cheltenham. And next to my suitcase—my portable typewriter. Veronica had thought of everything.

CHELTENHAM

———

R AY STOPPED at the White Horse Tavern. I hadn't seen the place in years. Its shabby disrepair made me see how easily my father took refuge in the tumbledown roadhouse next door to the Brandywine Raceway. Ray found anonymity and could relax with these weather-beaten grooms and sulky drivers getting tight. Here he could talk about working the open hearth whenever he wanted. He took his suit jacket off and blended in with truckers, racetrack personnel and farmers who smelled like they still did a modicum of work. The stinging manure scent on their boots softened their unmistakable wastrel traits and Ray liked being with them.

"Stackhouse is in jail. The fat one is next, and then they'll come after you," Ray said.

"Cheltenham or jail. What's the difference?"

He polished off his first tumbler. "You're not going in for as long as Karen. The doctor said it's just to review our options." Ray sipped his drink and winced. He wasn't supposed to drink scotch because of his ulcer. He was warned not to sprinkle pepper on his melon, but he *always* peppered his melon.

I didn't tell Ray about the man who assaulted me. How would I describe to Ray how I had shut my eyes and walked through the city like a blind girl? Marching like a blind girl was even worse than being raped.

Ray watched me with his begging face. He urged me to smile. After every transgression, his motto never changed. A smile was the cure-all. I pinched my shirt cuffs so my rope burns wouldn't show. My ribs felt sore from my little struggle; maybe I was bruised. Even my ankles were stinging where the kittens had scratched me in their explosive antics. I hadn't had any sleep on the bus ride to Wilmington. I didn't care where Ray was taking me. I just wanted bed and bath. I knew that I wasn't coming back home. Veronica wouldn't stand for it. I had snipped the cord. It was my privilege.

As we left the tavern, Ray walked behind the bar and lifted a bottle from the shelf. He took a tiny trinket from the neck of the White Horse scotch, a little plastic horse on a loop of thread. He handed it to me.

I wound the string around my wedding finger and closed the tiny horse in my fist.

AT CHELTENHAM, I tied the little plastic horse around the dummy doorknob of my hospital room.

North Unit was claustrophobic. Being locked in the same hall where my sister had been sequestered for years, I didn't feel any connection. Karen and I had been kept apart, and at that moment we were borne apart again.

DR. BENVENUTO: Maria, do you think you can draw a picture of your house?

Sure. I can draw a house with my hands tied behind my back.

DR. BENVENUTO: That would be a good trick. I guess you never heard of Ann Adams?

DR. BENVENUTO: Ann Adams? Who is she?

She's that artist who draws with a pencil in her teeth. Karen sent me a Christmas card.

DR. BENVENUTO: Just draw the house for me. A simple sketch will be fine.

Well, here it is. The house you asked for.

DR. BENVENUTO: I thought you lived in a ranch. This is a two-story house.

This house was abandoned. The police came after the husband and wife. I thought maybe Karen went to live there. But the city has bulldozed this house since then.

DR. BENVENUTO: You have sketched an abandoned house? Fascinating.

You think I'm *trying* to be fascinating?

DR. BENVENUTO: Well, aren't you? Now draw a circle to represent the world. Place an *X* somewhere in the circle, wherever you feel you are located.

I made a mark in the center.

DR. BENVENUTO: This *X* is in the center, but it's in the lower hemisphere of the circle. The world is *on* your shoulders. It looks like you're holding it up.

I guess so.

DR. BENVENUTO: This is a defensive mannerism. Some patients have started to call you "Mother Maria," because you try to solve everyone's problems. You're a "people pleaser" to avoid your own issues.

I looked at the doctor's tanned face. He had recently returned from a trip to the Andes, where he had purchased an alpaca rug for his office. There was new evidence of his comfortable life each time we met. His voice was cheerful and well rested. His gold rings were thick and smeared in the sunshine each time he gestured.

Just as he had grilled Karen, he asked me to choose one: murderer or victim?

ONE NIGHT I HELD a glass sliver. I wormed two fingertips between my windpipe and the cords of muscle in my neck, finding my jugular. Its pumping rope pulled and went lax, pulled and rested, like a snake climbing from the heart into the brain.

MY ENGLISH TEACHER, Miss Wurth, dropped off a copy of the *Living Bible*. The text had been combed and diluted until all its strong figures were tamed to the level of a Shel Silverstein picture book. Miss Wurth had also brought the high school literary magazine, *Collage*, in which I had published two poems.

I used the *Living Bible* to prop up my transistor radio on my bedside table so its speaker was at pillow level.

My window faced east.

The rising moon gained the pink tinge of a Canada Mint or a baby aspirin. I wrote down these observations on my Olivetti portable with its blood-red ribbon.

Veronica found an advertisement in the *New York Times* calling for manuscripts. Random House was publishing an anthology of poems by jaded teenagers, matriculants of the difficult sixties. I sent off a packet of pages typed on corrigible bond; the fragile tissue sheets made the poems seem twice as poignant, as if they might dissolve en route like saltine crackers. Seven of these efforts were accepted for the volume.

AMPY VISITED ME in Cheltenham, but he wasn't permitted on the floor. His obesity might cause patients with eating disorders to alter their successful routines. A five-hundred-pound man entering their environment could set them back weeks. Tommie brought me off the floor to an anteroom where Ampy waited. The leather sofa was grossly skewed by his weight; its clawed feet were lifted inches off the floor at the opposite end from where my friend was seated. The tight room was overwhelmed by the scent of Ampy's talc. Ampy went though bottles of Ammens powder in order to soothe his chafing folds of flesh.

An attendant remained in the room to ensure that Ampy didn't give me any contraband substance. Ampy told me, "Walter's doing great. They made him a trustee."

"A 'trustee'?"

"He wears whites and can work his way into minimum security." I nodded, imagining the brown-nosing Walter must be undertaking to earn his higher station at the penitentiary.

Ampy said, "Walter has to be a snitch to save his own ass. Who can blame him?" Ampy didn't seem happy about his friend becoming a snitch.

"Are you saying Walter could get out soon?"

"You know Walter. He lays on the charm, anything can happen."

After discussing Walter, Ampy and I had little else to say.

"THIS PLACE DOESN'T CHANGE," Karen said with a touch of awe in her voice. She seemed truly stunned that her inexplicable confinement in North Unit had not spared me the same sentence. For the first time, I felt that she was admitting to me that we had a connection, we were linked. Yes, the same maternal poison fell over us in equal doses.

It was here she had carried Horace's baby for almost seven months. "The happiest time in my life were those months I had the baby," she told me.

The wolf girl paced toward us and stopped. She eyed Karen with skittish recognition, the way a spooked horse throws its head back and shows the whites of its eyes. Then she loped off in another direction.

"She's growing hair on her back," I said.

"Really?" Karen said. "That can't be true."

"Her medication has side effects. She's so weird."

"It's a mystery."

"You still see her father?" I asked.

"He brought me here. He went to the bank, but he comes back in thirty minutes to get me." Karen stretched open my arm to look at cuts I had made on my wrist. Some were healed, but new lines were garnet red.

"When in Rome—" I said, looking at the situation with earned pessimism. How many times would I follow the wrong path because I was forced onto it and couldn't get off. "I've stopped doing it, really. Look. I promise I'll never do it again."

"Shit. I never cut myself," Karen said.

"Right. You never called attention to yourself. You just disappeared for *two years*—"

"You're still mad about that?" Karen said.

"You just walked out."

"Not because of you."

SETON HALL

I WAS RELEASED from Cheltenham in July 1970 in time for Christine's wedding that month. I had one more year of high school and would reside at Seton Hall Convent, a Catholic settlement in Wilmington that took in homeless girls. Veronica had made the arrangements with her diocese to have me admitted even though I wasn't a legitimate ward and didn't qualify as a child who suffered financial need. Veronica agreed to pay my expenses there.

I told Dr. Benvenuto, "I really can't imagine living in a convent."

"Just as a boarder."

"But I know some of these girls. They're on my school bus. They're hard up—"

"Then you'll be way ahead. You'll be the leader."

I tried to picture riding the school bus, getting off at the convent instead of at my old stop.

Christine had started a volunteer drug hot line in an abandoned merchant marine barracks on the waterfront in Providence, Rhode Island. Christine wanted me to come to her wedding and maybe stay for the rest of the summer to answer telephones. She described her wedding plans: She will walk down an aisle of Harleys lined up in two rows, a blinding runway of chrome. At a cedar stump altar, she will exchange blue denim wedding bands with her groom. She's going to distribute packets of bird seed so people won't throw uncooked rice; rice can kill wild chickadees and titmice.

Veronica told Christine, "Denim rings—I can't imagine symbols of everlasting matrimony made from someone's blue jeans!"

Christine said, "At least blue jeans don't rust."

Christine knew a Brown University student, a volunteer at the drug hot line, who could give me a ride to Providence when he returned from a visit to his parents' home in Delaware. The student's name was "Trey," a nickname he had earned because he was named after his father who himself was named after the father before him. Christine told me that Trey had the Roman numeral III on all of his stationery, handkerchiefs, Izod shirts and even on his tennis racket hood. She said, "If you want to see what Trey looks like, his picture is in *Newsweek*'s issue about Woodstock."

Before leaving Cheltenham I went into the hospital's library and found the issue of *Newsweek* with the famous centerfold photograph from the year before, a giant panorama of Yasgur's field. Thousands of hippies and tripped-out peaceniks are facing a remote stage at the bottom of a sweeping pasture. One reveler in the very *last* row has turned around in his seat to reach for a pack of Camel cigarettes in his jacket.

His face is the only full cameo in the wide-angle snapshot that documents our age. Yes, Trey had turned face front at the instant when our whole generation had their backs to the camera.

"Can you survive an afternoon at home before your ride comes for you?" Dr. Benvenuto had asked me as I left the hospital. "That's 1400 hours to about 1900 hours, military time." Dr. Benvenuto looked at his wristwatch.

"At home with Veronica? Sure, I can survive a few hours," I told him.

THERE WERE NEW ribbon streamers on the registers and an overwhelming scent of Endust circulating through the air-conditioning vents as I walked through the house. It was as if everything had been polished to remove telltale fingerprints. My bedroom had been completely remodeled, the walls paneled over, the furniture different. My bedroom had been transformed into a new guest room.

Veronica had sent all my clothes, books and records over to Seton Hall. She had given the convent everything, even the mock trousseau I had played with as a child. Veronica told me, "Sister Caroline says you can go through all that stuff as soon as you want, but the heat is too oppressive to spend time in the attic. You better sort through it in the fall."

Ray flinched. He was embarrassed and seemed as anxious as I was for the Brown University student to arrive, whoever he was. My stepsister's innocent acquaintance would be my unsuspecting getaway driver, my door-to-door conduit to a new life. Ray knew me. He knew I would look for any route to escape Seton Hall Convent. He too didn't want me to sleep beside Maryknoll orphans and refugettes with their tropical infections and scabies sores.

When Trey arrived, Veronica pulled him into the living room to grill him about Christine's fiancé. Instantly drafted to be the mediator or judge, Trey seemed a little puffed up by the honor. He told Veronica, "Well, he rides a motorcycle. The kind with black leather saddlebags and those silver medallions." I thought the student was a bit prissy in his description, but I was hungry to find any connection I could. I decided I liked his looks. He had a dirty blond ponytail and a golden mustache. He had a shy habit of wiping his index finger across his upper lip to smooth its wayward tufts. Again, he used the tip of his pointer to reposition his wire-rim glasses higher on the bridge of his nose.

I told Veronica, "Stop pestering him. We have to split or we'll never make the wedding."

Veronica ignored me and spoke directly to the young man: "You went to an Ivy League school? What's your educated appraisal of this union?"

I blushed. To what "union" was Veronica referring? I sensed a wholly different coupling foreshadowed the very instant that Trey had plopped himself on my front doorstep.

"Let's get going," I told him. I wanted him to understand I didn't revere that household. I was as rootless and perishable in that environment as one of Veronica's decapitated flowers.

Ray walked me out to the car. What I had believed was a wedding present for Christine was in fact a surprise for me. Ray had bought me a new Smith Corona electric typewriter. He looked sheepish as he placed the typewriter in the back seat of Trey's car. He seemed aware that such a gift was accompanied by an unmeasurable burden.

Ray had removed his French cuff links, and his loose white cuffs billowed in the wind as he waved good-bye. His wild sleeves exaggerated his last gestures until they appeared almost heartbreaking to me. Was he giving me the checkered flag or was it his final surrender? The effort triggered his trick shoulder and he dropped his arm.

I turned completely around in my seat and waved madly in return, until the car rolled over a hillock and I could no longer see my father.

DRIVING NORTH ON I-95, I told the Brown student, "I liked your picture in *Newsweek*. I never got to Woodstock—"

"It rained like hell," Trey said.

IN PROVIDENCE, I SPENT the day after Christine's wedding wallpapering the office at the drug hot line with hundreds of Hershey bar wrappers. "Who ate all these sweets?" I asked Trey, trying to win his complete attention. He told me that the chocolate bars had been donated to the volunteer organization. The wrappers were soaking in a bucket of wallpaper paste. I took off my halter top and smoothed the wet chocolate bar sheets over both my breasts.

Spontaneity is genius.

I had fallen in love with Providence. The fastest route to establishing residence there was to lie down in the arms of a settled constituent. That night I slept with the Brown student. When Trey saw my crosshatched arms, he lost his hard-on, but only for a moment. I was different from the debutantes he took on ski trips financed by his family, but he wasn't above a relationship with someone like me. He himself was working in a menial job that summer, pumping gas at a dock in Providence harbor, although he still received a monthly check from his father. He smoked dope on the job between the arrivals of pleasure boats that motored in to tank up. Nights, he worked at the drug hot line with my stepsister, and soon I was working there too. He was a certified preppy, from a wealthy Delaware family with the same wastrel characteristics common to the du Ponts and the Kennedys. He still wore a solid gold signet ring, a memento from his private school education.

Trey's one claim to fame in college was the time he forgot to turn off a hot plate and he burned down his frat house, a structure that was on the National Register of Historic Places. When Trey telephoned the house to tell someone to turn off the appliance, the fire marshal himself picked up the receiver. Another time, high on acid, Trey leaned against a balcony railing until the rotted fence toppled, spilling him three stories. He survived his sensational plummet and suffered only minor injuries, most noticeably a notch in his chin, a prominent cleft, but he lacked the corresponding aura of a Gable or a Mitchum. His plunge from the third floor was yet another event that brought him transient glory.

This was the profile I decided to marry, on the spot, to put an end to my childhood once and for all.

I WAS RESCUED FROM Seton Hall and I owed my freedom to Trey. I have heard of women in car crashes who fall for the paramedics who operate the jaws-of-life machine. The victim has a lot of time to think when she's trapped in a compacted hunk of steel; she listens to her rescuer's encouragement above the sawing metal. She falls in love with the stranger who cuts her out of death's hands. This phenomenon mirrors what happened to me when the Brown student extracted me from the wreckage of my household.

Trey rented an attic apartment in College Hill near the university. Greedily, he assumed his parental role. I soon saw how he needed me to fill out his self-portrait. He was raised under the duress of a patriarchal system and was forever trying to impress his father with his loyalty to the customs of the landed gentry. Firstborn son in the privileged class wasn't an easy role. Once, when he was small, he had sketched an army tank for his father. His father told him that his pencil drawing was deficient. "A tank doesn't have *wheels*, it moves on caterpillar treads."

His father took out his ink pens and rulers and went to work drawing a perfect replica of a regulation armored combat transport. This little scene from Trey's childhood was a microcosm for all that would befall my husband, and it guided him into his relationship with me, into the timeless juxtaposition of ruler and serf.

As surrogate patriarch, he gave me sanctuary in his house, but he wanted creature comforts in return. He needed someone to iron his shirts, sort his socks, cook his meat until it wasn't pink. This was our agreement, why not?

In good faith, he enrolled me in Roger Williams College. The small college was "progressive" and would accept strays without high school diplomas if the prospective student could prove her interest was sincere. I explained that I owned a new electric typewriter.

I was admitted to the college program merely on the *volume* of my poetry manuscript, which weighed in at four pounds of onionskin.

DICTIONARY

OF THE SOUL

———

1970–76

RITTENHOUSE SQUARE

⸻

S HARLY CUT HER finger with her Tandy rhinestone puncher. Karen gave her the Kleenex box. Sharly had a row of shiny stones going up one sleeve and she was working on the collar.

In one week, Karen will be "maid of honor" at the wedding. She once put on a wedding dress to strip for the peep window. Ruth passed that gown around to all the girls, but Karen had never been a maid of honor. She went shopping at Lord & Taylor and bought some floor-length crepe de chine culottes to walk down the aisle.

"Those are lounge pajamas," Sharly told her. "Shit. You going to wear pajamas to that wedding?"

"The clerk called these 'cocktail culottes.' "

"You taking Julian to the wedding?"

"He's not coming. Shit, he just got back from Nam."

"Betsy says Julian was in the stockade for fragging his superior officer. He's a bad character."

"Betsy doesn't know her cousin like I do."

"I hope she doesn't know him like that."

Betsy Beeman's cousin Julian Richwine came over to the house looking for a flop. It was like a memory crawled out of Karen's mind and stood up on its two legs. Julian looked just like Horace. Big shoulders, skinny hips, dark golden eyes the color of root beer LifeSavers.

Sharly told her, "You're always seeing someone who looks like Horace. You got a fixation on Horace."

"You never saw the original."

"If you ask me, they all look the same."

Betsy let Julian stay for a few days after his grandmother had thrown him out. He was supposed to get enrolled at the junior college, but he started to operate instead. Mrs. Richwine recognized his type even if it was her own grandson. She was a city tax collector and she wasn't somebody to play with. She had the posture of a prison guard. Betsy said, "Mother Richwine practiced walking with a hymnbook on her head."

Sharly said, "You mean with a *basket* on her head." Sharly started a mini–race riot with Betsy.

Betsy told her, "You have no respect for black pride or for Dr. King's memory."

When Julian left the war, he went right back to his partner who had a racket. Julian said he's the number-two man and has his own crew under him, but Karen heard his boys saying that they are number two, which means Julian is telling them that *he* is number one.

Mother Richwine saw all the shaggy commerce in her kitchen at all hours and she had the locks changed.

Julian received food stamps. The first night they walked over to the A&P, Julian bought a whole beef tenderloin. Julian said, "This is for my dog. It's against the law to buy Alpo with food stamps."

Betsy said, "Are you crazy? This is prime beef. You can't feed this to a dog."

"I ain't going against the law," he told her.

It turns out he *did* have a dog. One of those skinny Doberman pinschers. Every pimp and operator in Philadelphia had to have at least one. He called his dog Mr. No Shoulders. Julian told Karen that means "snake" back in the jungle. Julian didn't see what's wrong with giving prime beef to a dog. Since he came back from the war, he thought everything was equal, man or beast.

He said, "Don't worry, beautiful, Mr. No Shoulders is outside watching over this house."

She told him, "We have cats in here. That dog can't come in."

It was an instant thing, like that magic bottle that says "Drink me." Soon the dog was sitting on the sofa, and Julian was in Karen's bed. The cats hid behind the clothes hamper.

JULIAN TOLD KAREN she didn't need to work at the camera shop.

Sharly asked her, "You really quit your job? That's a nice arrangement. What's Mr. Braille going to think when he hears about Julian shacking up here?"

"Bennett doesn't own one freckle on me."

"He *rents* those freckles," Sharly said. "When he sees you have a live-in boyfriend, he's going to put a block on his BankAmericard."

"Sharly, you're just jealous Julian looked at me first."

"You love any dinge that walks in here. You can't get hot for white guys unless they're old-timers? Ever since that gorilla pimp in Norfolk, you run from your own kind."

"He's waiting in that Alum-a-room for someone just like *you*. What's taking you so long?"

Sharly said, "Julian is conducting business right in this house. Selling dimes. First fix is free. Taster's choice. He's back here three weeks and he's rounding up dopers."

"I guess you were first in line."

"First fix is free," she tells me again. "Yellow jackets two for a dollar."

"How you going to finance that? Julian can't fuck a popsicle stick without getting splinters."

She stuck out her tongue. It was coated with scum. Karen wondered if Sharly had caught trich again from a ten-dollar blow job. She'll have to pay that much at the clinic just to get a script to clear that up. But Sharly was laughing.

They both felt lucky.

Karen had *Love Story* happening, and if there was a panic in Rittenhouse Square or Franklin Park, it didn't bother Sharly. Sharly didn't even have to put her shoes on to get fixed. But she wasn't bringing clients back. Julian told her, "This place isn't your trick pad."

"It's not your candy store, neither," she told him.

He told her she'd have to use that junked Oldsmobile behind the A&P if she wants to work.

SHARLY HAD HER rhinestone jacket almost finished. Little glass swirls on its shoulders and down both sleeves.

Julian walked in. He heard Karen talking about her sister. "I'm not going to that wedding in Dupontville," he tells her.

"Who asked you?" Sharly said.

Julian fingered her jacket. "This ain't too fly. You don't see *me* wear these Elvis doodads."

"Elvis says, 'Thank you, God.' "

"I'm needing this table," Julian said. He wanted the dinette to cut his dope. He plugs in his new electric coffee grinder. He doesn't wait for Sharly to clean up her supplies and sweeps her Tandy kit right onto the floor. Loose rhinestones bounce like a thousand raindrops on the linoleum. Sharly screams. Julian grinds his boot heels on the little gems. These diamonds are instant dust. They're not even made of real glass.

JULIAN WAS TOKING weed in bed. Karen told him she might as well smoke it herself. He said, "You think this is strong? You want to taste *real* dew. The jungle was a greenhouse of premium dew."

She never liked inhaling dope with James and didn't like breathing it secondhand.

"When did you go to Nam?" she asked Julian.

"I went over right after Christmas, December 'sixty-seven."

"I was in Cheltenham then."

"You were safe and sound when they set me down in that Jiffy Pop. It was the last days of Rolling Thunder. These bombs aren't winning us the war. We drop half a million tons right in their lap. We're just making them mad, like when you tease a hornet's nest. You see that movie *Jason and the Argonauts*? Jason fights these scrawny skeletons. They pick up their own broken bones to fight? They fall down but they just get back up? That was Charlie.

"Then Tet happens in January. Tet is the fat lady singing. Fourth week in-country, and we take fire. That's when I get hit. My ass is fragged. Not a high-class casualty." He showed her one cheek of his buttocks. A row of pebble-sized scars in a line like the valves on a trumpet.

She told him, "That's a terrible reminder—"

He said, "But it's not good enough to ride out on the dust-offs. I'm still in. I got ringworm, crotch rot, toenail fungus. Fungus on my eyelashes. I'm walking around with crud on me that can't survive in a toilet bowl stateside until I get short. I'm notching my stick, what happens? I'm with the Hundred and Worst for suicide practice—where's that hemostat? I had it a minute ago—"

Karen gave him the hospital tweezers so he could pinch his joint. She wished he'd crush that roach. The room was beginning to stink. He told her, "Third Battalion goes into A Shau Valley to take Hill 937. Operation Apache Snow. It's a termite mound of VC loonies. We get Osterized. GI puree. I guess you heard about Hamburger Hill on Cronkite?"

"On Cronkite? I think so."

"We load up medevacs with fifty-six Glad bags. WIA are all in small parts. We didn't even hold that peak."

Half of him talks, his other half listens.

It was like Ray when he described how the steel industry had become a "dinosaur." She can't ask these men to stop telling their stories without hurting their feelings.

Julian said, "I'm near my Date Eligible. I see brothers everywhere doing U-turns, you know? It's a black power mutiny. These mutinies are happening all over the jungle. We decide we're not jamming with this rat fuck operation—"

James Robinson watched the TV war on the network news every night in Ruth's trailer. James would lean forward, tap the screen with his fingertip and point out the weapons. "See that? That's an M-16. That's a 50-cal. That's an M-60. That's a four-deuce—" He touched the TV screen like a kid pointing out his favorite Tonka toys. There was always a parade of heroes walking past the camera with greenery stuck in their helmets. A single file of jungle Marlboro Men marching through scorched clearings. James told Karen, "The White House tells the networks to give lots of air time showing troops and ammo, so it looks like we can pull it off. The VC watch tapes of Cronkite and the *Today* show."

But James didn't have his own story to tell Karen, not like Julian, the real McCoy, wounded in action.

JULIAN WASHED HER HAIR and combed it out. He said he loves her gold hair. Sharly said dope kings need to have a blond on their arm, just like they have to have a Doberman with a spike collar. Sharly was just jealous Karen had her arms full when hers were empty. Julian kissed her. He smelled like her Camay soap and his sickening dew. When they made love, she found his wounds—five hard bumps, like touching a stranger's fingertips. Whose fingertips? she wondered.

SOUTH
OF THE EQUATOR

—————

Veronica received a cable from Lima, Peru, where the model lived with his seventh bride. When Curtis Pettibone relocated south of the equator, Veronica boasted, "It drives him crazy to be in the same hemisphere with me."

Ray looked at her. Could she really believe that her spell had never broken? Veronica monitored the potency of her sexual allure by how many postcards she received from the model each year. But the cable message was confusing. It said, "Curtis has flown away, probably in your direction."

Alarmed that Curtis Pettibone might appear at her doorstep at any minute, Veronica dissolved a nitroglycerin pill under her tongue. Then she dialed her hairstylist to make an appointment. Nothing happened for a week. Veronica had her hair fixed and had it fixed again. Finally, she telephoned South America. Veronica couldn't speak Spanish, but the young bride spoke French. She told Veronica that Curtis Pettibone had passed away from liver disease. His widow was a little miffed. During his last days, the model had talked only of Veronica.

"Curtis is dead?" Veronica said.

She asked the widow for a copy of the death certificate. Veronica still held an insurance policy on her first husband and needed the death certificate to file her claim.

After two weeks, she opened an air-mail envelope and found the coroner's slip, a tiny ribbon of paper no wider than a ticker tape. The slip stated the time and date of the model's death. Veronica took sick for a week. She flagged at her tasks as if someone had opened a tiny door in a doll's back and removed its AA battery.

Veronica went to St. Helena's and requested a mass be said for the model. She kept a deck of mass cards on the front-hall table and used them for bookmarks or message slips. For weeks, these official mass cards appeared on the refrigerator under little cat magnets. At last, the remaining cards went into the end-table drawer with the yellowed *Doria* tickets.

It was just the two of them, Veronica and Ray.

Ray had again been feeling ill and he double-dosed on his prescription antacid. When his stomach spasms didn't improve, he self-medicated with Glenlivet scotch. The pricey brand seemed more consoling. But alcohol was a serious insult; it bathed his ulcerated epithelium and worsened his flare-up. He gulped a jigger and winced.

Why was Veronica's first romantic tryst her enduring taproot? I didn't think I would ever feel that way about my first tryst with Walter Stackhouse. His jail time might hold a soap opera fascination for some, but it didn't seem glamorous to me when I drove through the gates at the penitentiary and I saw the coiled razor wire like a nightmare Slinky stretched across the towering electric fence.

All my life, I watched the Arrow Collar Man's grasp on our family. Perhaps Karen interpreted Veronica's romance with the model as true love enacted in absence, loss, unanswerable flight. To earn Veronica's affection, Karen understood that she must disappear from the scene early on and retreat forever.

But what launches desire and perpetuates its fiery orbit?

Was I steering toward that "certain someone"? I would know when it happens. My nerves will unravel beneath his touch; my soul will whip open like a bedsheet torn into wild, sun-bleached streamers. Yes, that's what real love will do to me.

PROVIDENCE, R.I.

———

Trey and I were married in Wilmington during my midterm break from Roger Williams College. Ray walked me down the aisle. Veronica waited in the first pew wearing her new suit, an elegant watermarked green silk, like lithograph fabric used to print counterfeit money.

Veronica thought that I should at least *look* like a virgin bride. No denim wedding bands for me. No love beads. I wore a handmade dress that had never been claimed by its legitimate bride and was sold at cost right off the dress dummy. What, indeed, had happened to the first bride? The dress billowed with stiff taffeta ruffles stitched over a satin camisole. The slick fabric was the same material used for casket linings.

I stood on a footstool in my discount wedding gown as the seamstress tucked and pinned the bodice. I felt weighted and numbed like a bumblebee when its legs and abdomen are entombed in pollen. I remembered the wedding disaster when a bride and groom were siphoned into a cistern. Certainly, no bride could climb out draped in these heavy skirts. I thought of married life in incongruous images—bumblebees in their tedium and astronauts sealed up in fireproof suits—all of us programmed to endure relentless orbits, hive to flower, earth to moon, in an inscrutable passage to the unknown. I fingered the slippery satin and pictured myself standing beside Trey at the altar with the dazed countenance of zombie couples in *Night of the Living Dead*.

Veronica had booked the chapel at the Brandywine Battlefield

Church. Ray told me, "So you're getting married at the site of a famous bloodbath." He winked. The reception would be held at the posh Concord Country Club. Wedding gifts stacked up on the dining room sideboard. Revere silver, chafing dishes and fondue sets from the city fathers, bank trustees, the state governor and even from the du Pont family, the reigning monarchs of Delaware. Trey's guest list was daunting and Veronica worked furiously on wedding details. But Veronica's elaborate plans for a posh wedding were undermined when I insisted that we invite my friend Ampy who weighed five hundred pounds.

Veronica said, "You can't mean it—"

Veronica had already resigned herself to the fact that Melvie was escorting Colleen, who was seven months pregnant with Tony's baby while Tony was in Juvenile Detention Hall. Karen was dragging in her skinny collaborator, Sharly, who might arrive in mango hot pants. But it wasn't Colleen's huge belly, Karen's lounge pajamas, Sharly's leopard miniskirt a la "Francis Francine," nor my secondhand wedding dress like Cinderella's shroud that alarmed guests at my wedding reception. My wedding day reached its absurd climax when Ampy stood up in his custom tux with a crimson cummerbund. He interrupted the wedding toast to say, "Excuse me, folks. Can we have a moment of silence for Walter Stackhouse, still in jail. Day three hundred seventy-five."

On our way back to Providence, Trey stopped at an interstate motor inn for our wedding night ritual. I mentioned to the desk clerk that we were newlyweds. The clerk eyed me and grinned. He told me, "Is that right? I'll have to give you the Honeymoon Suite. That's got *your* sunken tub. *Your* heartshaped king. *Your* vibrator mattress. No extra charge for newlyweds. That's room 336." He handed me the key on its bright plastic medallion.

When Trey unlocked the door to room 336, I saw that the clerk had made fools of us. It was an ordinary motel room with a double bed and pay TV. The bathroom had a disposable bath mat, and when I stepped out of the shower, I left my notorious footprints on its cheap paper sheet.

I SAT ACROSS FROM Trey as he sorted our mail. I was still surprised to see my married name printed on the envelopes. He handed me a letter addressed to me. I tore it open to find a greeting card from Ray along with a crisp fifty-dollar bill.

My husband looked at the cash. "Who sent you fifty dollars?"

"Ray. Who else?"

Trey plucked the fifty from my fingers. "This gets deposited in the household account," he said, dropping his tone an octave.

"But it's my money," I said. "Ray sent it to *me*." I swiped the fifty from his hand.

Trey snatched it back.

I pinched a corner of the greenery and we sawed the money back and forth in a tug-o'-war battle. When Trey lost his grip, I held the fifty-dollar bill in front of his face and tore it in half. I ripped it into tiny pieces and tossed the ragged snips into the air. Confetti rained down on Trey's sandy locks. I cackled like a witch and stomped out of the room. When I returned moments later, Trey had glued every piece of currency to a loose-leaf sheet in a jigsaw rectangle. He was headed for the bank, where they would accept the pasted fifty and credit his account.

His ingenuity alarmed me. He had salvaged the money, but only to rob it from me. His actions had nothing to do with thrift. He was showing me the ropes of our union, in which oppression of my freedoms would be common practice. He was my husband, my new patriarch. I was only seventeen, after all. "Act like a child and be treated like one," Trey told me.

When I married, I thought my childhood was over. My teen years were behind me, uncoupled from the present moment the way a string of empty boxcars is disconnected from the engine of a train. I felt no nostalgia for those early years as they coasted to a dead stop. I was married. I was "someone else."

But domestic accidents in my first months of marriage suggested I was still a novice. One night, I filled the kitchen sink to soak the dinner dishes. I left the apartment to go to the washerette. There was a little action happening and I bought a hit of coke with my roll of quarters. I wouldn't have any change for the dryers. I carved a line on top of a washing machine after brushing away the spilled soap.

In my absence, the taps weren't shut off and the dishwater spilled over the lip of the kitchen sink. Water flooded the apartment below, soaking the chenille bedspread and mattress of a new divorcée. It was my good fortune that the victim was seasoned, and she rolled with the punches pretty well. She saw my Golden Girl eyes and recognized my high-speed chattering even if Trey didn't yet know. The woman understood that my union with Trey was a cracked egg and the chick would peck its way out. But events like these proved to my husband that I needed management. Every night, he made a production of twisting the taps to make sure they were tight.

In turn, when Trey wasn't looking, I spiked his glass of Miller High Life with Heinz vinegar and watched him take a swig.

Trey maintained the upper hand until I discovered his secret. I came across a tiny key in a china saucer on my husband's desk. The key was too small for the car or for his office at the University of Rhode Island, where he was a Ph.D. candidate. I brushed the key with the feather duster and left it in the dish. For days the key drove me to distraction. It recalled the key Walter Stackhouse had awarded to me that had opened the velveteen guitar case and unlocked his unwholesome attentions.

The key fit a suitcase on the floor of Trey's closet. When I tried to lift it, I was startled by its weight. The Samsonite was filled to the brim with hard-core pornography. Photographs, paperbacks and magazines, amassed over many seasons, spilled across the carpet. Hundreds of dog-eared tear sheets and stroke books cherished from many harvests of triple-X commerce. And worse—a curious collection of little Polaroid snapshots. Someone, perhaps Trey himself, had been out on the twilight streets snapping pictures of interior rooms from the bird's-eye view of a peeper. These instant pictures were shot from odd angles, the camera lens nosing through gaps in Venetian blinds and peeking under curtain hems.

I found a flesh rag called *Sore*. The violence of that one word *Sore* so distressed me, I thought I would be sick. Of course, the magazine's name was *Eros*; I had read the word backward standing over the heaps of issues fanned across the floor.

I had discovered a trunk of smut.

Ray once warned me "Snoops have to live with themselves" when I had tried to read a letter over his shoulder or if I picked up the telephone receiver to eavesdrop on my mother. I couldn't run to him now.

That winter, I attended college poetry readings. I stopped at a den behind the washerette to tie off before coming back to the apartment. No matter what hour it was, I'd see Trey had set up the Bell & Howell projector. He rented a post office box and ordered eight-minute stags from foreign catalogues and black-market mailing lists. The sex flicks had poor translations that ran along the bottom of each frame, with invalid idioms and awkward words. Trey asked me to read the English subtitles out loud in my furred junkie voice.

Trey sought the anonymity of mail-order sex. As a practicing voyeur, Trey was never forced to connect with his love object. In sex, he looked at me funny, as if from a great distance. I could be unconscious, as far away as I wanted, across a football stadium, across a dreamy prairie of my own making. He wanted my identity erased, just as black bars obscure eyes, or like TV crime reports scramble the victim's cameo in a cubist smear.

BLACK DOLLS

R AY LEARNED THAT Karen's boyfriend, Julian, had been in the
stockade after being arrested for trekking AWOL two miles behind his battalion. Alex assured him that there were hundreds of kids
in Nam walking backward, away from the hot spots; it wasn't that unusual.

Julian was one member of a trio of black soldiers accused of fragging a noncommissioned officer who had tried to foil their retreat.
They bunted a live pineapple at the NCO and the fellow was blown to
bits. After a hearing, the report concluded that the officer's death was
SIW. Self-inflicted wound.

Julian wasn't charged with murder.

He did short time in the stockade and was released with a general
discharge.

Ray said, "We'll give him the benefit of the doubt."

Veronica didn't want to see Karen or the suspect GI. Ray telephoned me in Providence to ask me to accompany him the first time
he met Julian. Ray wanted to take us to lunch, but he was a little
squeamish about sitting down to break bread with the black vet. When
Karen and I were small, Ray took us to the annual Kiwanis pancake
breakfast. Free tickets were circulated to urban families and the cafeteria was packed. An actress dressed like Aunt Jemima greeted families
at the door and showed us where to sit. Black families sat in one part
of the cafeteria. A desert of bare Formica separated them from the
whites. The huge room smelled of Virginia-smoked bacon and maple
syrup, a smell I associated with the black mammy dressed in a long
skirt and calico kerchief.

Ray always sat on the white side where his business links were set up and he could participate in the shoptalk. But once I went ahead of Ray and sat down beside a girl in the black section. The girl held a gorgeous *black* doll in her lap. The doll's formidable size and noisy crinoline smock made it seem far superior to my floppy Tiny Tears that cried saltwater if I filled her with an eyedropper. Ray saw me seated beside the black child and whispered, "I've got to talk business, honey. Over there—" He jerked my elbow. The black girl and I blinked in unison, our communion dissolved. Ray walked me and Karen over to the white side.

"You want one of those black dolls?" he asked me. "I'll buy you one."

Karen said, "That black dolly's going to feel pretty lonely at our house." Karen might have been speaking for herself.

Ray said, "Karen's right. She won't feel at home."

WE WALKED INTO Karen's apartment to see Sharly in her sleeveless nightgown. She brushed her works into a kitchen drawer. I realized that in Karen's household people got up late in the morning and had their coffee, toast and tar. Ray ignored the syringe and invited Sharly to come to lunch with us. I saw her bare arms; the ivory troughs at both elbows were inflamed like she had worried flea bites. I knew she must be using the same old spike until it's dull. I told her, "Shit, will you cover up?"

Julian walked into the room, picking his 'fro with a long-tined comb. He smelled of cannabis. He pushed the comb in his back pocket where the tines protruded like a tiny pitchfork.

Julian asked me, "Where's the heir?"

I ignored his remark. We were just getting started. Ray said he could drive us out to the Paddock Steak House or did we want to go to Trader Vic's or to Kon Tiki?

"Kon Tiki," Karen said. "They have drinks with those little umbrellas."

Karen was trying hard to make Ray feel more comfortable. Certainly, she didn't really want to get ahold of those little paper umbrellas with their toothpick spokes.

I was surprised when Karen slid into the front seat of the car between Ray and me. We sat three abreast. This left the whole back seat for Julian. He sat right in the middle of the bench, which must have obstructed Ray's rearview mirror.

Ray tried some small talk and asked Julian, "So, you've been discharged for a few months? Have you contacted the Veterans Administration?"

"What for?" Julian said.

"Just to register your name with the VA, you know, for making some contacts. They might have some programs—"

"I don't need those clerks 'n' jerks watching over me," Julian said.

Ray said, "Now, I hear you finished your tour in the stockade? Does that mean you lose your benefits? What's the ruling on that?"

Julian asked Karen, "You tell him about that?"

"I didn't tell him."

"Maybe your sister has a big mouth," Julian told Karen.

I pulled my biology text from my bag and started to tell Karen about my laboratory science class at college. I told my sister, "Last week we put a mouse into insulin shock."

Julian said, "Listen to her. Miss Coed."

Karen was pleased to talk about something besides Julian's time in the military jail.

I said, "We injected insulin solution into this mouse and it went into shock. Then the professor mainlined epinephrine into its heart. He stuck the needle straight into the ventricle to wake it up."

Karen encouraged me to continue. She wanted me to talk about this neutral mouse who wasn't a member of our tense outing.

Ray was impressed to see that live animals were sacrificed in the service of my higher education.

Karen said, "I guess the rat died?"

"You know how we could tell it was dead?"

"How?"

"There was one golden drop of urine. When an animal perishes, it *voids*. Everyone does."

Our group seemed to stop for a moment to visualize this common denominator. I let Karen take my biology book in her hands. She quickly gave it back.

Julian said, "I guess she reads lots of books." He referred to me in the third person once again.

I turned around and told him that I was currently reading three books by the same author. "F. Scott Fitzgerald, heard of him?"

Julian said, "How do you read three books? You only got *two* eyes."

Julian insulted my college experience for a good part of our journey. Karen laughed at his stingers, and I understood that he went after me just to please *her*.

Karen was wearing Sharly's jacket and Ray began to tell us how they manufacture rhinestones from "plastic resin." They're not even real glass anymore.

"Rhinestones," Ray said, "were originally authentic quartz pebbles collected from the Rhine River and sold as costume gems."

A police cruiser pulled up beside the car.

The cruiser's blue bubble twirled in ridiculous tight circles, much faster than seemed normal. It nosed us over to the shoulder.

Ray said to us, "What was the speed limit, anyway?" He reached across Karen's knees to open the glove compartment.

"You weren't speeding," I told him.

"We were *crawling*," Julian said.

The officer stepped up to Ray's window. He took Ray's registration. "Is everything okay here?" he asked Ray. The officer examined Ray's ID. "You have any trouble here, Mr. Mitchell?" The officer stooped to look into the back seat where Julian was sitting with his arms folded across his chest.

"You're making a conclusion," Ray told the officer.

"Who's your passenger back there?"

"That's Julian," I said. "He's a Vietnam vet."

"I can speak for myself," Julian said.

"You're telling me all's well?" the officer asked, and he put his hand on Ray's shoulder.

"Shit, are you deaf?" I said, bending down to glare at the officer.

"She's a bit snappy," the officer said. He stepped back from the car to wave us on. I could see he hadn't finished with his first line of thought.

Ray put his blinker on but hesitated before pulling away from the curb. In what direction had he been driving? Where was he taking his girls?

Julian began to talk, "I could be holding you all hostage."

Ray apologized.

"Yes, this happens all the time," Julian was saying, "when they see a black man in a late-model. That cop thinks I'm hijacking your car. Maybe I'm taking these white girls, Mr. Mitchell." He began to laugh, an ugly slurring sound. Karen said nothing. She had remained silent through the long minutes of it all.

Ray said, "You know, I guess I might have been going too fast."

"We were *inching* along," Julian said. He didn't want to confuse the issue.

"I'm sorry," Ray told Julian.

"Don't be sorry, Daddy," Karen said.

When Ray heard Karen call him "Daddy," it was as if he took a punch in the diaphragm.

We parked at the Kon Tiki. The same cruiser pulled up behind us; its blue light twirled over the restaurant's huge replica of a primitive god's head from the Easter Islands.

The cop walked up to the car.

Karen stared ahead at the giant god's head with its straight nose and protruding jaw. The officer leaned down level with Ray, who didn't look good at all. He told Ray, "It seems to me you might have some trouble here. I'm going to radio downtown and ID this passenger of yours."

Ray said, "Officer, you're harassing this man. This is my daughter's boyfriend—he's a member of our luncheon party."

The officer said, "He's with your party?"

"Yeah. We're having a *party*," Julian said.

INSURANCE

———

Veronica received an insurance check after submitting proof of the model's death. She decided to split the money between all of us. Karen and I were not the model's true offspring, but we were exposed to the runoff and concentrated toxins of that union. We had side effects to be recompensed.

My husband assumed management of all my assets just as he had deposited Ray's fifty-dollar bill after taping it back together. But Ray insisted that we spend the insurance money on something "crazy." After putting up with Curtis Pettibone for years, Ray might have liked to have had a big party.

Trey took the money and purchased matching five-speed Schwinn bicycles. I rode my bike in single file behind my husband, up and down the streets of Providence. Trey always took the lead. If I overtook him, he circled around me to reclaim his position in front.

I thought about the model and how he couldn't disappear gracefully from our family's changing blueprint. Even after his death, he had furthered my imprisonment by engendering these ritual bike outings with Trey. I pedaled behind my husband for miles and watched him make dramatic hand signals. Once I split off down a side street hoping to be on my own, but it was a cul-de-sac and Trey found me on my way out.

At twilight, a sheet of bats twisted across the sky like iron shavings pulled by a magnet. I envied their mysterious freedom as they pulsed and dispersed. What had Karen used her insurance money for? I tried to picture Julian seated on Trey's Schwinn. I almost wished it were him.

JULY 9

———

I N 1974, Karen and I had babies born less than one month apart.

Karen brought her baby home from the hospital and was immediately visited by a caseworker from the Department of Human Services. The city was routinely informed of any baby born to a disadvantaged mother who might need to be interviewed and evaluated for social services. When Karen was admitted to the maternity unit, the OB nurse noted in Karen's chart that the patient had a black eye. A fig-green crescent fanned across her cheek.

The staff noted that the patient wasn't accompanied by any family member when she showed up to deliver. Karen was the primary or even the sole parent responsible for the newborn and the young woman might not be equipped for motherhood.

Julian was in the street when Karen went into labor. She walked over to a shooting den across the vacant lot, but no one had seen Julian since that morning. Karen waited for him as long as she could. Finally, she took a cab to the hospital.

Her infant was six pounds, at least three times the size of Horace's baby, which she had never held in her arms. The newborn's hair was silky coils and his skin was warm bronze like unrefined honey. After two days in the hospital, at last Julian visited, bringing a huge stuffed rabbit, as tall as he was. The rabbit was too large to be put into practical service and Mrs. Richwine, who had come down from City Hall on her lunch hour, convinced Julian to return the toy to Strawbridge's and exchange it for a crib mobile for the bassinet.

When the social worker visited the apartment, she told Karen that Karen's neighbor had reported an incident that had happened the week before. In a sudden spat, Julian had shoved Karen against the wall and the concussion had knocked two landscape pictures off their hooks in the next apartment. The tenants had reported the fight. They were sending a bill from a frame shop where the items were being restored.

The social worker said, "You were full-term when he shoved you into that wall?"

"I guess I was," Karen said. "But I tell him, don't throw me against *that* wall with that nosy bitch on the other side. We got *other* walls—"

"Well, I've heard everything. You tell him which wall he should throw you at?"

The social worker looked around at the messy room where the baby was sleeping in his bassinet. She opened all the kitchen cupboards to see if there was food. She checked the bathroom to see if there was a diaper pail or somewhere to throw away the Pampers. She told Karen she could get these items free from the city—a diaper pail for cloth diapers or a garbage can for the Pampers. Which one would she need? She noted in her folder that the plaster was cracked. Paint was chipping off the door lintels and it should be tested for lead.

Karen tried to keep the cat box clean, but the apartment had an overwhelming odor of cat spray from her toms. Karen told the social worker, "Julian remembers to buy Alpo for Mr. No Shoulders, but he forgets to buy the cat litter."

"How many cats do you have here?"

"Just four."

"Four cats? One dog? That's a large number of pets to maintain."

"I'm just about a zookeeper," Karen said. "I guess I should get rid of some of these—"

Karen wondered if Veronica had sent the official to harass her. Veronica had once told her that she kept too many cats. Veronica had even suggested that Karen had had another black infant in premeditated retaliation for what had happened to her first baby. Veronica had asked her, "Wouldn't it be better if this baby grew up in a black family? With a black mother?"

Karen told Veronica, "End of conversation," and she hung up the telephone. When Veronica dialed again, Karen told her, "Since when do you know what real mothers are supposed to do?"

JULIAN HAD THROWN Sharly out of the house. Betsy Beeman had distanced herself from her cousin, and with the arrival of the baby, she too moved out. Bennett Dixon waited to see what Karen decided about Julian. In fact, the wolf girl's father had financed the baby's layette. When Julian saw the new baby clothes and tiny washcloths spread out across the bed, he asked Karen, "Did you get money out of my box?"

Using this as his premise, he collected the little nightgowns and booties. These colorful terry-cloth items from Wanamaker's were brand-new; he could trade them back for a cash refund. He saw the diminutive sterling silver cup from Shreve, Crump & Lowe that Veronica had sent in contrition after she had asked Karen to give up her baby.

"Shit, I can get a bill for this cup," Julian told her. "A baby don't have to drink from a *silver* cup."

Karen didn't care what happened to Veronica's trinket.

"Here," she told Julian, "take the cup. But he needs the other stuff."

Julian went over to Jersey twice a week and needed a white girl on his arm to push him up a notch in his curbside negotiations. If Karen could no longer come, he'd find someone else. She watched him dress up in his copping clothes, an acetate shirt with giant flesh-tone paisley designs like severed ears. He put on his fur-collared flight jacket, picked his 'fro and told her, "I'm serious with you." He said he would marry her and they'd grow old, but she knew he was handing out applications to all the white girls in the neighborhood. He never dated black girls. He sprayed himself with Brut and put the solid-chrome collar on Mr. No Shoulders until the dog's pointy snout dipped under its weight.

Mrs. Richwine used her connections at the Tax Department to find Julian a job in her offices. Julian told Karen, "I'm not hiring on with the city. I'm not a wage slave," and he didn't report to work. Instead, he sold spikes at local shooting dens, brand-new syringes packaged in long cellophane sleeves like a row of lollipops. He sold one of these spikes with a hit for ten dollars. When the needles ran out, he sold spoons and decks. Julian told Karen, "Junkies use the same spike until it breaks off in their arm."

RAY STOPPED AT the Scott paper plant to get Karen a big case of toilet-paper rolls. The foreman on shift helped Ray load the carton in Ray's Buick.

"Can't eat toilet paper," Julian told Karen after he helped Ray carry the heavy box upstairs. Julian took the Doberman outside because the dog made Veronica nervous. Julian said it was the other way around.

When Julian was gone, Veronica presented Karen with a handmade baby sweater she had knitted for Nathaniel. Karen folded back the leaves of white tissue paper and looked at the tiny yellow garment. She fingered its intricate rows of stitching and saw Veronica's skilled hand-iwork. Karen didn't know what to say.

Veronica sat down in a straight chair and Ray sat on the sofa; he ignored the dog's slobber marks on the armrests. The cats entered the room to sit with the strangers, their tails switching. Veronica stared down the scruffy felines.

"This is a nice imitation Turkish," Veronica told Karen when she noticed the Karastan that Bennett had long ago provided. It was a skewed compliment, but Karen expected as much. Veronica's Persian rugs were authentic antiques, with complex designs—labyrinths, pyramids and opposing columns like Parcheesi boards, each rug knotted by hand by craftsmen who went blind from their work.

Ray wanted a turn holding Karen's baby, and she was pleased to arrange Nathaniel in Ray's arms. Ray gently tugged the cuffs of the baby's nightgown and tried to smooth the baby's crinked hair with the heel of his big hand.

Veronica said, "May I hold him?"

"You want to hold the baby?" Karen said, her eyebrows frozen high.

Veronica waited, her arms extended until at last Karen offered up her baby.

"My goodness, he doesn't weigh anything. Isn't he gaining?" Veronica said, with checked criticism.

Karen said, "He's eight pounds now. That's almost two pounds already."

Veronica had not yet lowered her gaze to the baby's face, and for an absurd, prolonged interval she stared across the room and out the window. Veronica wasn't comfortable holding *any* baby. At last, Veronica dropped her face to examine the infant.

"He's not what we thought, is he Ray? *Il n'est pas chocolat, il est plutôt café au lait.*"

Karen remembered the breakfast trays left outside their hotel doors in Paris. Steaming pots of coffee and plates piled high with croissants. Veronica had taught Karen how to mix café au lait. The milk should never be *added* to the coffee; it should be *merged*. The tradition required a little finesse. Veronica lifted the coffeepot and pitcher of milk in either hand and poured simultaneous streams into a cup, mixing a tawny froth. With the cup brimming, she dipped her roll into the masterful concoction. Veronica had told Karen that this ritual was an important part of her French heritage, but Veronica's queer remark about the baby's skin color did not seem so warm and inclusive.

The baby squirmed and Karen took her son from Veronica, who didn't mind giving up her privilege. Julian had not returned with the fried chicken she had sent him to get for her parents. Karen said, "Do you want saltines? I have crackers and cheese until Julian comes back."

Veronica pulled her sweater on. She told Karen that Ray was taking her to lunch at the famous Bookbinder's restaurant. She wouldn't need any crackers. Veronica looked down at the infant in his bassinet. He was a pretty baby. "He's irresistible," she told Karen. It didn't kill Veronica to say so.

JUST THREE WEEKS after Karen had brought her baby home, I drove to Providence Lying-In Hospital with Trey. I counted my contractions and watched my mortarboard tassel shiver on the rearview mirror where I'd hooked it after my college graduation the month before. It was a heat wave and the interstate had buckled. Huge chunks of asphalt heaved and overlapped until the traffic was stopped. The cracking asphalt was mysteriously in sync with my first stage labor. Trey steered around the obstructions, seizing opportunities to climb over medians and weave around barriers to avoid the broken surface in the expressway, but he lacked the madcap bravura Tony DelRose had shown in the driver's seat. Driving in the breakdown lane to the birth of our child seemed an appropriate final aspect of our brief union.

It was July 9, my birthday. The coincidence made my labor and delivery seem like a spontaneous event; it had nothing to do with Trey. What biological oddity or red-letter day in numerology had made my daughter's birth fall upon mine that same hot day, with just two decades between us?

In a few hours, my baby daughter was born; her face was the glowing nimbus I had longed for. Not since I had seen the photograph of the frozen Eskimo baby, in its serene suspension, had any face seemed as fresh and promising. One infant was excavated from a glacier; the other surfaced from my own flesh but seemed equally immaculate.

The nurse penciled in the exact time of day, 4:08 P.M., checking the big clock on the wall of the delivery room. Until that moment, I had perceived the passage of time most often in increments of misfortune: the skewed minute hand on the kitchen clock the moment my sister disappeared; the *Doria* collision that claimed my impostor; and even farther back, the model who had deserted his station beside Veronica— these were linchpin events that formed my deepest ravines of feeling. But with the birth of my daughter, I was shedding my first self—my unhappy childhood was over.

Trey stood beside the delivery table dressed in a green smock and its corresponding mask and beanie, as was the tradition in the baby hospital. His features were hidden except for his teary eyes. His tears startled me.

I was thinking, Who is this man? The stale archetype of the Woodstock generation? Why was he standing there beside me at this private instant, intruding upon the first moments of my recovery.

My ejection seat marriage was a completed mission. The birth of my daughter Kate was my "Dilbert dunker." That's military slang for ditching aircraft, why not say the same for matrimony? I looked at Trey's bewildered squint. He was moved by the birth of his child, but his tears *didn't move me*.

◆ ◆ ◆

DURING THE TWO DAYS I recuperated in the baby hospital, Trey toured the peep shows on Washington Street with full liberty. When I was discharged, I stole baby clothes from the hospital nursery—tiny shirts with mitten-cuffs so a baby couldn't scratch its own eyes—and I packed these in my suitcase. I waited all afternoon for Trey to collect me and my swaddled newborn, and still he didn't come get me.

There was a famous Continental Productions triple bill at the Columbus Theater.

I knew it was over with him.

WHEN TREY AND I separated, I moved to a small cottage in Newport. Trey came to the house twice a week to see his toddler. On one of these evenings, after Kate was bathed and safe in bed, Trey and I took off our clothes in the dining room under the glare of the overhead fixture.

Trey had even thought to bring a flashlight.

There in the blinding room, we examined one another for lice. One of us, in our last days together, had infected the other. We didn't make accusations, since we really couldn't be sure who had proffered the first louse. Trey had been seeing coeds and business girls and he routinely visited peep shows where lice might crawl up his pants cuff. Or perhaps I might have ferried the plague home. I was tutored by local barflies, indiscriminately. I had my choice between the most seasoned slime and the greenest punk rockers. I never bothered to inspect anyone for parasites.

In our last act of kindness toward one another, Trey and I combed and picked the crabs and nits from ringlets of our pubic hair, concentrating on places we couldn't see for ourselves. We decided we would do better to shave one another and search again. We lathered and giggled at our own expense. Trey might have found the exercise erotic, but I didn't reciprocate. "Bend over," I told him. "There, I got it. Here's another one, good glory."

We took turns searching. In our final communion we mingled our vermin in a dish of alcohol.

DICTIONARY

OF THE SOUL

⬥

THE TENANT DOWNSTAIRS was starting his barbecue grill. It was against the rules to cook on the fire escape. It wasn't good for the baby to breathe charcoal smoke, and Karen went to shut the window. She saw Julian down in the alley with the checkout girl from the Royal Market. The girl was still dressed in her uniform from parochial school.

Julian had his hands on her hips. He was trying to fast-fuck that girl right in broad daylight while Karen watched him from the second floor. She asked herself, Does he think I'm so deep in his pocket he can put on a show for me?

If he looked her way, she'd have to do something. She hoped he wouldn't look. Then he saw her.

She put Nathaniel in his bassinet and walked over to Julian's stereo set. She lifted the turntable. It had wires coming and going. She dropped it back. Instead, she took his records from the window seat. His spool of 45s and his favorite LPs. The Maytals' "Pressure Drop," Otis Redding's *"Dictionary of Soul,"* Jimmy Cliff's "Many Rivers to Cross." Karen tried to choose one of these, but she took the whole stack. She leaned out over the alley where Julian kept banging the girl. She pulled the records from their sleeves and tossed them into the air. They hit the sidewalk, bounced off their edges and burst into smithereens. One record rolled right up to Julian's feet. Sam Cooke and the Soul Stirrers. Percy Sledge. Sly. The Temps. Jackie Wilson. The Chambers Brothers. She knew she was throwing out his whole lifelong collection, but why should she stop?

Julian tugged his pants up. He collected some records that didn't break in half. The rest were in slivers. The girl smoothed her skirt and slipped behind the building. She came back to get her satchel. Julian held two halves of a record. He tipped his head back and howled. It was his *Dictionary of Soul* in two pieces.

Nathaniel started to fuss and Karen picked him up. She sat down to nurse him, but she heard Julian running up the stairs, taking three at a time. She thought, I've done it now. Julian burst through the door.

He had the electric charcoal starter from the neighbor's hibachi. It was glowing.

He chased her with the red-hot fork. "Shit—I've got the baby," she screamed. He didn't care what was in her arms.

He brushed her sleeve with its blazing tip. The polyester melted against her skin like burned sugar. Karen couldn't lift her cuff off her wrist; it was stuck to her.

Julian twisted the electric fork in front of her face.

She threw an ashtray at his head. The butts flew in a swarm, but the ashtray missed Julian. The baby cried.

Karen remembered: I'm somebody's mother even when this is happening to me.

Julian tossed the electric fork out the window. He tore the baby's mobile off its hook. He walked over to Karen holding the string of yellow ducks. He wrapped it around her throat but the elastic snapped.

"Are you through?" she said.

He wanted her to forget that business with the girl.

She told him she had already forgot. She said, "I don't care about that cashier from the Royal Market. She's just a schoolgirl—"

He was ashamed of himself. Shame makes men angry; she'd seen it happen to James. Julian slammed her face against the window bench. Hot tar filled one side of her head. One ear was roaring, the other was dead.

HER EAR BECAME so painful she feared her milk would dry up. At the clinic, she showed them her wrist where her sleeve wouldn't peel off. A doctor looked at her ear. He said it was a ruptured eardrum. It was permanent.

They gave her some ointment to put on her arm. She was asked to sign a form. She signed it first, before she read the small print. Then a nurse pulled the form away. Karen asked her, "What does it say on that sheet? Is that about coming to arrest Julian? Is that about foster care?" She wished she had signed her fake name, Cindy Stevens. Why didn't she think of it?

"Your baby is underweight," the doctor told her.

He gave Karen samples of Enfamil. He told her that when she had used up the samples, she should fill out an application for public assistance.

"I'm not filling out more applications. These forms backfire on people."

JULIAN TOLD KAREN to mix the baby formula with water to stretch it.

"I don't think it should be diluted," she told him.

She called Bennett Dixon and told him, "My milk is gone because my eardrum exploded. I have a second-degree burn on my arm." She made it sound as bad as she wanted. The truth was, it was bad enough on its own.

Bennett told her he was leaving for Florida. He'd be back in three months. The next day, an S. S. Pierce truck pulled up in front of the building. The driver unloaded cartons of Similac. It was hundreds of dollars worth of formula and big silver restaurant-sized cans of corn and baked beans and sliced peaches. The driver stacked the silver cans of fruit on the floor until they were high as a drum kit.

The living room was crammed with cartons. Karen couldn't turn around. It was just like the old days with James and his towers of S&H stamps.

Julian looked at the free stuff. "That crumbly geezer wants to feed my child? That feels just fine to me." He chucked a heavy can of peaches at Karen's head for whatever reason. It hit the wall. The plaster was gashed. The neighbor on the other side began to scream. Her pictures kept falling off.

MRS. RICHWINE WAS on the telephone. She told Karen, "Think what's best for the baby."

"Which baby you talking about? *Your* grandbaby's selling needles in Franklin Park."

She told Karen, "You'll never be a black mother."

"That's a news flash."

"I've seen these mix-breeds grow up. They try to be *all white* or *all black*. It's pitiful."

She tried to pull Karen's heartstrings, but Karen's heartstrings were already plucked off.

Mother Richwine was trying to get the baby out of her hands, but Karen couldn't understand why. She was telling Karen, "Mrs. Whitney from the DHS is coming right over."

Karen slammed the telephone receiver.

Mrs. Whitney showed up ten minutes later. She saw the cartons of formula. "Where did these come from?"

"They're paid for," Karen told her.

"These cases suggest an impropriety somewhere along the line. Are these cartons stolen property?"

"They're not bootleg," Karen said.

"I'll have to report what I see with my own eyes."

Karen told her about Bennett Dixon and how his daughter thinks she's a wolf, so he adopted her instead.

Mrs. Whitney didn't lift her eyebrows. She said she hears all kinds of stories. She wanted Bennett's phone number to check it out.

"Truth is—he's gone off to Florida with his wife. His wife has to spend winters in a tropical climate."

This time, Bennett didn't give Karen a phone number for him. He had reached his limit.

Mrs. Whitney told Karen, "I can help you fill out these foster-care petitions now, or I can come back when you've had time to write them out."

"I'm not signing those."

"Right now, it's still voluntary. That's when decisions can be made for the baby's welfare. You know what's best for your baby, don't you, Karen? He'd do better in a drug-free house. With your signature, the baby can be placed out—"

"Placed out?"

"It's your choice now. But if push comes to shove, we don't need your signature at all. We decide when that happens."

"I'm not signing that form. I'll kill anyone who comes near my baby."

"If you make threatening statements, I have to record your remarks. Everything you say goes right here on your sheet."

VERONICA WAS EXPECTING Brandywine Cleaners. Ray's habit of drinking antacid straight from the bottle left aquamarine stains on his shirtfronts. She pinned a note to the laundry bag and answered the doorbell.

Two men in tight panty-hose hoods charged past her into the foyer. The masks smeared their features, but she recognized their domed Afro hairstyles glistening like anthills under the taupe nylon.

One man leveled a pistol at Veronica. The second man heard the TV in the bedroom and shot through the wall, right through the headboard of an antique four-poster. The first man tugged his hood off, seeing no need for it now that he was inside with his victim. He tapped her knuckles with the tiny nozzle of his gun. "Those diamonds. The gold rope."

"Did Karen tell you I have good jewelry? Is she the mastermind behind this?"

"Shut up." The man shoved her. Veronica peeled her rings off her fingers and unsnapped her heavy charm bracelet. He pushed them into his pocket. He steered Veronica down the hall and into her bedroom where he rifled through her dresser drawers until he found a quilted envelope tied with a satin ribbon. She didn't have to show him where to look for her jewelry. He found two ruby rings. Her diamond bracelet. Diamond clip earrings. Her Cartier brooch. Her jades and heavy Italian knots. The square emerald framed in diamond chips. An opal the size of a cocktail onion—that ring belonged to her daughter, what was it doing here? The man rolled up the pouch of gems and plunged it into his shirt.

"I see, she must have drawn a map?" Veronica eyed her bottle of nitroglycerin on her dresser and asked the man, "Can I have my pills?"

"Not now. Later, take all you want."

In Ray's cluttered desk, he found a stack of loose fifties, a mere two hundred dollars. "Shit," he said. He went to the closet and tore open her summer pocketbooks; he turned her beaded evening bags inside out. Each purse was empty except for random linen hankies, loose mints and souvenir ticket stubs.

The accomplice was trigger-happy and fired his pistol at the closet mirror, shattering the peculiar trio. Their reflections collapsed on the rug.

"Where's the rest of the cash?" the first man said.

"It's in the bank. We're civilized—" she said.

He found her wallet and plucked her credit cards from their plastic windows. He walked her back through the kitchen and tugged open the sideboard, grabbing handfuls of sterling—nested cake forks and teaspoons, spilling the silver on the floor in a loud clatter. Veronica was breathless. Her palpitations shifted and stalled in an odd arterial calypso. She thought she might be having a heart attack.

They grabbed a new carton of Kents from the kitchen counter and added it to their booty before going out the back door. They climbed into a car idling on the street across the lawn. Veronica tried to see the man behind the wheel. Was it Julian?

The police assured her that she wasn't singled out. There was a robbery profile happening in North Wilmington. A car gets off the interstate. It comes into the wealthy neighborhoods, does a job, gets right back on I-95 and cruises back to Philadelphia or to D.C.

Ray told her, "You're being hysterical. Crooks look for a lady's jewelry case in her dresser—where else would she keep it? Karen wouldn't tell them—"

Ray installed convex mirrors on the porch trellis so Veronica could look out the peephole to see possible intruders who had ducked out of view. Diamond State Telephone came out to add a second line to Veronica's bedroom. If anyone lifted the receiver in the kitchen, she could still dial out from the bedroom on her new emergency-red princess phone.

The thieves had not seen a diamond soaking in a dish of Lux liquid. It was Veronica's original engagement ring. She had never returned it to the Arrow Collar model. Where would she hide it now? Veronica put the ring in an ice cube tray in the freezer.

THE

SEVENTH WONDER

———

THE RAIN WAS coming down like needles.

If Karen took the baby to the clinic in this downpour, he was going to get worse. She had been putting mineral oil in Nathaniel's ear as the doctor told her. The baby had a Cheerio stuck in there, or it was some white bread he pushed in with his finger. It bothered him. Sharly came into the apartment without ringing the buzzer. She was soaked. Her voice was almost gone from her chronic sore throat. Since Julian kicked her out, she catches naps at Deverel's pimp post but she won't tell Karen where home is. Last week Deverel put a mirror to her lips to see if she was breathing. She was skulled and he couldn't wake her up. He called an ambulance, but first he dragged her up the street two blocks. He didn't want rescue personnel arriving where he organizes business.

Sharly invited Karen to come in with Deverel. Deverel would take care of her, Sharly said, but Karen saw what he had done to Sharly. He removed Sharly's moles with a Schick. He shaved one off her neck and nicked one right off her chin. She used carbolic Vaseline on these sores, but they didn't seem to be healing.

Karen looked in her Band-Aid box for little adhesive "spots," so Sharly could cover up her raw marks.

Karen looked at her friend and couldn't see getting back in the Life. But if Sharly didn't stop by, *who* was going to check on her? If Julian stepped over a line, who would know about it if Sharly didn't poke her head in?

Karen told Sharly, "My little sister split up with Trey. She has a little cottage with an extra room and wants me to come."

Sharly said, "You're not going up there with *her*, are you? She needs to find her own way. It wouldn't work out. Your sister has big ideas. 'Ideas' are a luxury."

"That's right. I look at things one day at a time, but Maria looks at all the different angles. She goes backwards and forwards in her mind."

"That must make her life miserable," Sharly said.

Karen agreed.

They got the baby ready to go to the doctor. When they walked out the door, they turned right around. Mr. No Shoulders galloped up the stairwell. Next came Julian and his partner Gerry. Gerry flopped on the sofa and started scratching all over. Karen saw he had his cough syrup hives again. She knew these boys weren't straight.

Julian said, "Where you taking Nathaniel?"

"Going to the doctor," she said.

A long teardrop of mineral oil rolled down the baby's cheek.

"What's wrong with his ear?" Julian said.

"That's baby oil."

Sharly took Nathaniel in her arms and pulled the diaper bag over her shoulder. She moved to the door.

Julian chased her in a circle around Karen. "You lettin' that whore hold my son? She's a pig, look at her. That's trick juice on her collar."

Karen didn't notice it when she put the Band-Aid spots on Sharly's sores. She asked her, "Sharly, is that cum on your collar?"

Sharly lifted her lapel and scraped it with her fingernail.

Then Gerry stands up. He waves his gun. It isn't like Ruth's tear gas revolver or Julian's pistol. This one has a long muzzle like a trick gun with a flag that drops down that says BANG. Gerry sees that Karen doesn't believe it's a *real* gun. He shoots right through the diaper bag and into the wall. Karen sees a bullet hole in the vinyl. Sharly lifts out a diaper. There's a hole right through the plastic Pampers.

Gerry shoots again and the bullet hits the hot-water riser. The pipe makes a loud gong. The whole house must hear it. Karen sees Gerry is going to have his shooting practice until someone tries to stop him. He shoots up the sofa. Dust rises off the cushions in smoky puffs. He shoots the end table, but it's just an old carton of baby formula covered with a scarf. It squirts a milky stream onto the Karastan.

"He's going to kill us!" Sharly yells.

Karen grabs the baby and climbs out the kitchen window right into a rainstorm. The fire escape is rusted and the ladder won't drop down. She hears the gun popping off in the apartment. I'm going to have to jump, she thinks. It's raining pricks and needles. She can't even see the ground.

Julian pokes his head out the window. "You can't get down from the second floor unless you can fly. I don't see you holding that little feather like Dumbo."

Sharly is shrieking, "Don't shoot me. Don't shoot me—"

Karen thought of Dr. Benvenuto's questionnaire. Murderer? Victim? That came into her mind once a day. Sharly pushed past Gerry and ran out the front door, but the Doberman bounced up the stairwell and galloped inside. He saw Karen on the fire escape and leapt out the open window, teeth first. Silver strings of dog saliva sail through air. She held the baby tight. She jumped.

Sharly ran around the house and pulled her up. Karen's spine was vibrating like when she hits the wind chime pipes and grabs them in her hand. She lifted Nathaniel's face up to hers. He was wide-eyed, but he seemed all right. Sharly tugged her sleeve and they ran down the street. The pistol cracks never stop. Mr. No Shoulders barks from the fire escape, too chicken to jump.

SHARLY LED KAREN onto a city bus and they rode nine stops. Karen's back was tingling like a school of fish shifting behind her ribs. She limped into the clinic and a nurse took Nathaniel from Sharly's arms. Nathaniel's temperature was too high. The nurse stripped the baby and put him in a sink of shaved ice. He reached for his mother.

"He wants me," Karen told the nurse.

The nurse told her, "He doesn't know *what* to want."

"Excuse me?" Karen said. She wasn't going to take any attitude from that nurse, but then the doctor came into the stall to look at Nathaniel's ear. He told Karen that the fever was from an infection. He said, "Everything is connected—the sinuses, the eustachian tubes. Ears

and sinuses have minute cul-de-sacs vulnerable to secondary bacteria."
The doctor gave Karen a bottle of antibiotic medicine as pink as Pepto-
Bismol and told her to give the baby three teaspoons a day.

"What about that bread in his ear?" Karen said. "Baby oil didn't get
it out."

The doctor came back to the stall with a Teledyne waterpick.

"Is that a waterpick you have there?" Sharly said.

"To flush the ear canal," the doctor said. He turned on the machine
and squirted water in the baby's ear. Nathaniel kicked his legs and
wailed.

Karen said, "He doesn't know why I'm letting you do this to him.
He must think I'm crazy." She recognized her passive role in the trans-
action. She really didn't like these doctors and how people have to have
them. She remembered Dr. Kerrigan and how he made her pick up
marbles with her toes. She recalled the time she peed stars and they
stretched her open with stainless pipes. They painted her blisters with
Gentian violet just to make a spectacle worse. Now this one aimed his
waterpick. Where did they get their nerve?

Bread came out of the baby's ear in soggy crumbs. The doctor said,
"Look here. These look like some insect parts. See this?"

She stared at the tip of the doctor's finger. In the wet bread crumbs
there were some shiny black flecks.

"That's a thorax," the doctor said.

"A thorax?"

"And this is a wing sheath. These insect parts were in your baby's
ear." He stared at Karen and Sharly.

"Insect parts? Something crawled in there? Maybe an ant?"

The nurse said in a flat voice, "That's a cockroach."

The nurse wouldn't let Karen take her baby off the ice.

"He's shivering," Karen said.

The nurse said, "His fever's come down. But he'll be admitted
tonight."

Karen said, "What are you writing in that chart? Please don't tell
DHS about these insect parts. I don't know how these insects got in his
ear—"

"If her building's infested, is that Karen's fault?" Sharly said.

"Does DHS have to hear about this?" Karen asked again. The doctor left the stall before he answered her question.

The nurse told her, "The clinic reports to DHS every time you come in. We have to write it up. Your bashed eardrum is in writing."

"My eardrum is in writing?"

"Domestic assaults go on the top line."

"You keep a sheet on me?"

"You look worse each time. Your baby's sick again—"

"Shit, that's why I come to the doctor. Because he's sick. Does that go against me?"

"It's a coin with two sides. If you come in for help—*help starts coming and you can't stop it*."

The doctor returned from the nursing desk. He told Karen, "Mrs. Whitney from DHS is coming in to assess your baby's situation."

"His situation?"

"I told her we'd want to keep him in the hospital one night. That's a little extra time for you to get things in order. Maybe you have a relative and can put something together? Why don't you girls go to the cafeteria and have a cup of coffee until Mrs. Whitney arrives."

"I've got coffee right here," a different nurse told Karen. She asked Sharly if she wanted some too. The nurse tugged the curtain wide open and left the stall. She walked over to the coffee station next to the nurses' desk. She was giving Karen a minute to absorb the news. With her back to Karen and Sharly, the nurse poured two coffees and spooned the Cremora into the cups.

Karen lifted Nathaniel from the melted ice. She couldn't find his playsuit and wrapped him in her coat. Sharly tugged a drawer open, she knew exactly which one she wanted. She hid a box of disposable spikes in Nathaniel's diaper bag. The nurse took her time. She tapped the plastic stick on the rim of each cup and finally turned around. Karen had walked out of the hospital. This nurse, whoever she was, had an instinct about people. She knew Karen must escape with her baby.

AT DEVEREL'S FLOP, Karen said, "I'm here to get dry, but I'm not settling in."

The floor was littered with White Castle wrappers and stale hamburger buns, empty paper cups and soda straws colored with silver lipstick marks. Karen hadn't seen that metallic shade since she did her Goldfinger routine for the peep window. Karen sat down on the bed next to two little chocolate almonds someone had pulled off an Almond Joy candy bar and left there on the mattress.

Karen collected the gooey nuts and put them on the table. There were bottles of Lavoris with the caps left off, giving the place that cinnamon stink Ruth's office had when the girls rinsed their mouths between clients. It was the same routine. Karen was startled when she saw her face and beside it, her face again. Two identical washed-out, exhausted familiars trapped in a line. She realized it was just *two mirrors*, side by side. Deverel's girls needed these mirrors to primp between tricks, but the repetitions were unnerving. Karen didn't wish to wait too long in the legitimate pimp post. She told Sharly, "I'm never going back to Julian, so where am I going to go?"

She thought of Bailey's. She couldn't believe she was homeless again. "Do you think Ruth would put me back in the ticket cage? If Horace comes around, we can get reacquainted. It could happen naturally."

"He would see it coming a mile away," Sharly said.

"I don't know. Maybe I'll go back to Virginia Beach," Karen told Sharly just to hear her voice say it.

"Shit. Don't go all the way down there to get back in. Deverel will bring you in, right here. If you stay, we'll have each other. We could get a place—"

Sharly's face looked pale and miserable, like turning a stone over and finding a bare worm. Karen told her, "I'd stay if it was only Julian, but it's the DHS. When they hear the apartment got shot up, they'll take Nathaniel. Can I use this phone?"

"Deverel won't pay your long-distance pimp-to-pimp phone calls. Karen, Deverel will work you into his book, why not? He's not a gorilla."

Karen picked up the telephone. Instead of calling the Paris, Karen called Information and asked for the Seventh Wonder Diner. She dialed the number. Her heart was slamming. She asked a waitress if Ruth was eating there. The waitress said it was just the work crews from the Bay

Bridge-Tunnel. There's always a crew painting that bridge. As soon as they're finished, they have to start over. Karen asked for Valerie, for Peaches, Rose Pearson or Sharon Martone. She almost asked for Sharly. Sharly was sitting right next to her.

The waitress told her, "It's a man's world right now, no girls sitting here." She clicked off.

Sharly said, "Happy now?"

Karen saw Nathaniel playing with a teddy bear, a trick gift someone brought to one of Deverel's girls. Karen didn't want him touching that filthy toy. She told Sharly, "Don't let him suck on its ear."

Sharly said, "It's all right. This little bear belongs to *me*."

Karen stayed the night in Deverel's punch house. Some of his girls worked from a book and the phone kept ringing. Girls came in and out from the rain, soaked to the bone and shivering, without one umbrella between them. They looked Karen over. She told them, "I'm not coming in, don't worry." One of these girls was a nervous wreck. She creeped a trick and thought he had followed her back.

Karen picked up someone's half-eaten burger from White Castle. "How old is this?" she asked.

"That's from this morning. It should be all right," Sharly told her.

Next thing, Sharly was pulling the plunger on a syringe, red-flagging the last of her bag of heroin. Her blood splashed into the bulb and she pumped it back in.

Sharly told Karen, "You could use some of this. Your back must be hurting, right? And you're so wired."

"No thank you."

She told Karen, "I saved a birdseye for you. This is just a painkiller, that's all."

Karen was thinking Sharly must really love her to share her dope. That's her last teaspoon. Sharly would have to grab a client tomorrow morning, and if it's still raining, it won't be easy to find one. How could Karen say no?

The next day, Deverel came back and started right in on Karen. "Shit, you could have all the white collar you want. I need girls like you for Happy Hour. Suits cruise between six and eight P.M. before they get the train to Cherry Hill—" Karen didn't listen. She collected her diaper bag and jacket and took Nathaniel in her arms. She was still a little furry from her small hit of dope. Sharly was fully wasted and Karen didn't wake her. Karen saw the toy bear tucked in with her friend. Nathaniel might need it. She pinched it from Sharly.

The baby should have breakfast. Karen lifted some quarters from a saucer next to Deverel's elbow as he talked on the phone. He didn't try to stop her. She went out to the street to find her own telephone. Ray might let her come home with the baby if she explained he was sick. But when she called, it kept ringing. She hung up and tried the number again in case she had misdialed it. She recognized the ringer, a short, warbly tone the same every time.

THE NIGHT KAREN LEFT Julian, Veronica and Ray were sailing on a Caribbean cruise. Ray had received a letter of invitation from Compagnie Transatlantique announcing the farewell cruise of the luxury liner SS *France* before it was to be retired from transatlantic service. Preferred customers would be offered a discount rate for five-star compartments reserved ahead for the final party cruise on the *France*, with ports of call at Martinique and Barbados in the Windward Islands. By the 1970s, passenger ship lines had been defeated by the aviation industry. These great ships would be relegated to clownish vacation cruises in the tropics and in the northern fjords. Ever since Veronica was robbed at gunpoint, she insisted that she needed a change of scene, and Ray bought tickets.

Ray had been losing weight because of his ulcer; in his loose-fitting cruise attire, he looked like an invalid on a supervised retreat. Terminal cases booked cabins on these tropical cruises. The doomed often seemed to lose any imagination for how they should spend their last precious days on earth.

Ray sat on deck with Veronica in a row of lounge chairs. She was annoyed by people's reactions to him. He looked ill. His face was white, with the flat pallor of a roll of blank newsprint. Veronica slathered herself with Bain de Soleil, an exotic pink oil that resembled transmission fluid. She dabbed some on Ray's nose and forehead so he wouldn't burn. Bain de Soleil was the most expensive brand, but Ray told her, "Where did you get this, did you drain a radiator?"

Karen dialed four times and didn't get an answer. She left the receiver swinging on its silver cord and walked up the city block.

Veronica unpacked her new resort fashions in the sunny stateroom on the SS *France* as the liner steamed into bright tropical waters the color of mint ice cream, past barrier islands like golden fingers of shortbread.

NEWPORT

K AREN TELEPHONED ME in Newport. I picked up the receiver
and slid it right back in the cradle.

Again, Karen dialed my number.

I lifted it off and slammed it on its hook.

In recent days, I'd been harassed by an ex-boyfriend, a wastrel I'd
met at a waterfront disco. Now he called at all hours and wouldn't announce his name. He held the line in dead silence. I didn't expect to
hear from my sister, and at its first chirrup I plucked the phone off the
hook and crashed it against the wall console.

After Trey moved out, I sometimes sent my daughter next door
where a teenage girl watched her until I came back late at night to retrieve her. I patronized the working-class lounges, where I met lobster-
men, jai alai jocks, America's Cup mates, whoever discovered me in
anonymous serendipity, night after night. Each union was a combus-
tion that burned off in an instant, until I got entangled with an unpredictable misfit.

He had just stolen a collection of vintage hubcaps from the annual
Boston Auto Show, an array of antique chrome badges worth a few
thousand dollars. He stored the stolen hubcaps in my basement, in
three blinding towers. When his possessive nature erupted in violent
instants, I quickly broke it off with him. But he started to stalk me. I
still had his booty.

I held a cold compress to my daughter's forehead. She had a huge
egg on her forehead after tripping on a cement riser on the back stoop.
The doctor instructed me to keep her awake. She must not be allowed
to fall asleep in case she had a concussion. Keeping my fussy daughter

awake all night coupled with my phone intruder was wearing on my nerves.

Again, the phone jangled and I picked it up. Karen said my name in rigid syllabic enunciation. I hardly recognized her voice. "Is it you? Karen? Have you been trying this line? Thank God it's you. I'm scared to death—"

"You're scared? You should see *me*," she said.

Of course, she must be in trouble to try a third time after I rang her off twice.

"Julian's friend shot up the house. He shot right through the baby's diaper."

"My God, is the baby all right?"

"I'm beginning to see anything could happen."

I was relieved to hear my sister's voice. I told her, "Karen—there's this nut after me."

"Shit. Are you trying to copycat? Are we in a race?" Karen asked.

Karen had called me in her distress and I had spilled events specific to *me*, but did she really think I was competing with her?

"I thought you were someone else," I told my sister. "You see—I dumped this guy. Now he follows me. He trails me through the Almacs supermarket, taking everything out of my cart as soon as I put it in. He looks awful, his clothes are crumpled. He works for Marcy Oil. He doesn't change his uniform. He sat down in my booth at Newport Creamery when I was on shift. He swiped my order pad from my apron pocket and tore it in half. It wasn't exactly a phone book, but it impressed the customers. I shower with the bathroom lights off so he can't see through the vinyl curtain—"

No matter how I criticized the scoundrel, I guess I was still impressed by him.

Karen said, "He's bad news. But you're not reading the police report, you're just reading the want ads."

Karen never thought any of my relationships could add up to the malevolence of one Julian or James Robinson. I wanted to say, "What about Walter Stackhouse? He's back in jail, and what about the SDS rapist? How did they stack up?"

"I can't shake this guy," I told her.

"I'm dealing with the DHS. That's worse."

Was she saying that she would never have left Julian if not for the authorities? Yes, life has to have a man in it, even if it's the Wrong Man. That was the one natural law we both cleaved to. We learned it from Veronica.

"We really can choose them," I joked.

"You could have had that sweet Jewish kid from Wycliffe, what was his name? He was decent."

"I guess I missed my opportunity," I said.

Melvie Hirschon was killed in Nam in 1972. Because Julian had walked away from the action, I wasn't going to mention it to Karen. Each time I thought of Melvie, I saw him on the sofa right after his surgery for ingrown toenails, the raw tips red as mango peelings.

I told Karen to come to Newport until things settled down.

Karen said, "I can get a Trailways to New York. From there, I take Bonanza Lines."

My daughter had fallen asleep in my arms. I shook her.

I MET KAREN at the bus station. Nathaniel's nose looked sore and crusted with a greenish discharge. "I've got this pink bottle," Karen said, explaining Nathaniel's ear infection.

I described Kate's wakeful night. Our maternal ordeals broke the ice. We drove to my house behind the Newport Airport. I tried to explain my irresponsible tryst. I told Karen, "I guess I've been doing a 'Venus thing.'"

"I'd say you're acting like someone from *Mars*," she said. Of course, she hadn't recognized the literary reference.

We walked up the garden path to my door, holding our toddlers on our hips. The sea breeze was sweet and despite my lurid confessions and Karen's shaky predicament, our reunion seemed promising. Karen was a world away from the Philadelphia row house where she'd leapt from the second-floor fire escape, holding her baby. And with my sister coming to live with me, I wouldn't feel so isolated or act so recklessly, would I?

Roses clutched the trellis in a centenary commitment to bloom and bloom and bloom, each season. The one unsteady aspect in that seaside vista was a huge drifting shadow cast by the Goodyear blimp, which was moored right behind the house at the Newport Airport. The blimp was used to film the Bicentennial Tall Ships and to monitor the America's Cup races. That year, Ted Turner's *Courageous* was the favorite, but Karen had never heard of it.

The airship drifting on its tether often obstructed the afternoon sunlight. In fact, the blimp had become a peculiar superego. I imagined looking down at myself from its high cage. How would my everyday routines and tawdry episodes look to a bird's-eye observer?

Karen took everything in. The drifting blimp, the little hillocks of beach roses shaking their clusters of golden hips. If she was glad to be there with me, she didn't seem glad.

Nathaniel was asleep and I showed Karen the crib I had borrowed for him. She put him down on the fresh flannelette sheet. My daughter had recovered from her fall, and I gave her a squeeze toy, hoping she wouldn't wake the other child with its piercing whistle. Kate's milk-white skin was a shocking contrast to her cousin's deep complexion, but it was Karen who remarked on it, not I.

Karen sat down in the living room, exhausted.

I asked her, "You want a drink?" I spilled Old Crow over one cube each. I crushed four Valium with the bowl of a spoon and sprinkled it into our tumblers. "Dust works faster than tabs."

"Is that Valium?"

"Welcome to the Lowland of the Dolls," I said.

I watched a smile creep up one side of her face. She embraced my humor sometimes; other times she stiffened.

Several college brochures from graduate English programs were scattered on the coffee table. I should have put these brochures away before her arrival.

I said, "I'm applying to graduate school—"

Karen said, "Shit. You lead a double life, you know that? Which part is bullshit?"

Her interpretation of my world was stinging. I lit a cigarette and handed it to her. I lit another for myself. "I've always wanted to be a writer, ever since I stood in the manure pile beneath the RIDE AT YOUR OWN RISK sign at Highland Stables right before that place was condemned by the Board of Health."

Karen said, "Writing everything down must be a pain in the ass."

I saw she was right. Karen's whole life had been a naked scheme for survival, but I couldn't withstand my human journey unless I halted at every crossroads to scribble in new maps and windows. At Highland Stables, hadn't I begged the inspectors for a turn with their ultraviolet lenses so I could see for myself the vivid rat trails that squirmed over the woodwork. I read about a new military invention called night vision goggles. These must be like the rat glasses, and wasn't the literary life like donning precision eyewear in which the darker terrain might surface? Like a military fanatic's obsession, I wanted the privilege despite the risk.

My electric typewriter was set up on the dining room table next to my college application forms.

Karen took it all in and shrugged. The contrast between us was substantial. I thought if I brought Karen down to the cellar to show her the three stacks of vintage hubcaps we might meet our common level. She peeled back the bubble wrap from different chrome specimens: domed moons and convex plates said CHRYSLER, CADILLAC, THUNDER-BIRD. One mirrory dish even said FIAT.

"You better get rid of these fast," she told me.

That night, Karen and I went to our rooms to sleep under one roof for the first time since 1964. Karen was restless. I heard her shift in bed and plump her pillows with angry punches. I heard her flick her cigarette lighter. Again I heard it. I wanted to tell her, "Think of a field of daisies. And count each one." I got up and took her my bottle of Seconal.

"Jesus, that's a big jar of reds," she said. "You're a pillhead, you know that?"

"Trey calls me a 'walking apothecary.' Fuck both of you."

We laughed, but I went back to my room and swallowed two capsules. Seconal always made me dream that I was *having a dream* but I couldn't wake up. I had even started sleepwalking, and once I had breezed outdoors with my car keys. I didn't wake up until I heard the fly wheel screech. I leaned back in the icy vinyl seat of my Chevy Vega and maybe that's what roused me.

Once or twice, I thought I heard Karen weeping, but in the morning, she was level. She never showed her tears to me.

◆ ◆ ◆

AFTER ONE WEEK, Karen was thinking of going back to Julian. I told her, "You'll feel better if you find your own apartment. You have to take the next step."

I divided up my pots and pans, my kitchen gizmos, my sheets and blankets. I took new bars of soap from the bath vanity, shampoo bottles, hand lotion. I stacked canned goods and household cleaners.

For some unnameable reason, I needed to give her *half* of everything in my house.

Karen tried to stop me. "Fuck this CARE shit. I'm not an underdeveloped country."

Ray and Veronica were still sailing with the farewell cruise on the SS *France*, but I knew Ray would send Karen some start-up money. "He'll be glad to hear you left Julian."

Karen looked down at her feet.

I saw that she hadn't decided to give up on Julian.

"Oh, Christ," I said.

Until she made her decision, I had child-support checks from my ex-husband and I imagined giving Karen *half* of the money.

I stood back from the towers of canned goods and took stock. I was trying to make up for everything—for Karen's Halloween candy that Veronica transferred to me, for the opal ring like a knuckle of soap suds and for each pat on the head I had vied for, bumping my sister out of arm's reach.

"Why did you buy two of everything in the first place?" Karen said.

"One in use, one in the pantry," I rationalized. I saw the luxury of having *more* than was necessary. Could I have always been hoarding things for Karen?

Our toddlers played together on the carpet. When the two children hugged one another, their contrasting limbs entwined, they looked like *one* calico doll of light and dark scraps.

But they weren't going to grow up together, were they?

As I filled out my graduate school applications and financial-aid forms, Karen looked over my shoulder. She told me that she was making it her policy to *never sign her name on the dotted line*.

She would keep this promise for decades to come.

❖ ❖ ❖

THE TELEPHONE CALLS started up again. My ex-boyfriend, Rick, broke his oath of silence. He asked me who was making a second silhouette on the vinyl shade? Who was there with me?

We saw him standing across the street in his rumpled Marcy Oil uniform. His shirtfront was streaked and he looked more disheveled than the last time. Karen depressed two slats of the window blinds to study his sinister figure. "He's fried," she said, "or does he always look like that?"

"Don't you think he's kind of attractive?" I said.

THAT NIGHT, I ANSWERED the telephone expecting Rick, but it was Julian. He told me, "I know Karen is there. Tell her I'm coming to get the baby."

I told Karen, "We should inform the police that he's making threats."

Karen said, "Look. Don't tell the police, they report to DHS. It's all one big machine. But how would *you* know, living here in this little cottage—"

I reminded her that I was a single mother too. I was being stalked—

"Having a lark with a scumball isn't front-page news to anyone but yourself. You go on a spree to *research* the underclass."

"It's a form of self-examination," I said.

"Self-examination is a hobby for the privileged class. *People like you* don't know that *people like me* never talk to police."

"I won't talk to them," I said.

THE CALLER WOULDN'T announce his name when I picked up the phone.

Karen said, "Can you hear the El in the background?" That would confirm if it was Julian trying to break down Karen's resistance. I held the receiver and listened for the elevated train.

Karen had more street savvy than I had. She had learned to think on her feet. Even when still a child, like the year before she disappeared, Karen had impressed me with her composure in an emergency.

Ray had met a tycoon in the chemical industry who raised cattle in West Chester, Pennsylvania. He sold Ray a side of black Angus beef for Veronica's new freezer.

Ray drove us out to West Chester one Sunday to close the deal on the meat. Ray could choose which steer he wanted from a corral of fattened Angus segregated for slaughter. The idea of looking eyeball-to-eyeball with our table meat didn't please Veronica. "That's a man's task," she told Ray. "I defer the privilege to you."

While Ray and Veronica shared a pitcher of martinis with the weekend rancher and his wife, Karen and I approached two Shetland ponies grazing in a field. Karen said, "We weren't invited to ride the horses—maybe we shouldn't."

"Ponies love us to ride them," I told her. She shrugged, quite used to my self-serving inventions.

I attached a nylon lead to the halter of one horse and boosted Karen up on its back. I grabbed the long mane of the other pony, thinking I might ride it without any bridle at all. Then I saw a piece of baling twine on the ground and tightened a slip knot behind the pony's ears. I jumped on its back.

We galloped bareback over the pastures while Ray and Veronica sat with their hosts on the farmhouse veranda, tipping the martini pitcher with full liberty. "They'll be there a while," Karen said.

We cantered over the steep hillsides until Karen told me to pull up. Something didn't seem right to her. "He's strangling," she said.

"He's what?" I leaned over to see the pony's frothy tongue fully extended through his toothless notch. He was fighting for air, his eyes rolling back in his head. I tried to loosen the twine noose, but its tight glossy skein wouldn't budge.

The pony fell to its knees as if performing a clumsy trick curtsy.

Karen had the presence of mind to jump down from her horse and approach the felled pony. She used her long fingernails to pluck apart the twisted baling twine strand by strand. With precision, she snapped each golden filament, which required brute force and concentration. At last, she freed the pony's airway. It snorted and stood up, shaking its thick mane.

◆ ◆ ◆

I CONGRATULATED HER again for her heroic feat, freeing that poor little horse, did she remember it? At that instant, all of our sweet childhood seemed imperiled in that chokehold.

"If it had died, Veronica would have had to freeze it."

Again the telephone clanged. We didn't pick it up. I watched Karen arrange her few possessions on the bed as if she planned to terminate her visit.

"Where are you going?" I said.

"Shit. I can't stay here forever. How can you stand it?"

WHEN OUR TODDLERS were asleep, Karen and I sat to watch *Police Woman* with Angie Dickinson.

"Don't you love her?" Karen said.

"This is Angie's greatest role. She looks good in that uniform. You just know she's still wearing Frederick's of Hollywood beneath the badge."

"She's hot."

Our nights had begun to take a familiar shape, as if we were still young girls in Wilmington choosing our TV fare in democratic negotiations.

Outside, garbage cans clanged as if they'd been drummed with a stick. "What's that?" I said.

On the backside of the house, a drainpipe pinged.

Karen sat still, eyeing her foot in concentration. She was tracking the sounds that encircled the house. Next, the gravel drive crunched under someone's boots.

"Julian?" I said.

"I don't know. Julian's just about a cat burglar. He wouldn't be making a racket."

I went to the window. In the darkness I made out a lean figure standing stone-still in the yard. I looked again. It was the maple sapling.

"I guess no one is out there," I said.

Karen said, "I don't like people looking in windows. In Virginia, those field preachers spied on me. I'll never forget the feeling."

Her description disturbed me. Again, I brushed the half curtain aside with the expectation that a mug might be squashed to the window. Instead, I saw the Goodyear blimp centered between 200-watt floods on the airfield, its silver skin luminous. The garbage cans were spilled. I let the curtain fall back. I said, "It must have been raccoons. Raccoons tear up the garbage like they're looking for one particular thing. They've got hands, you know. They're like monkeys."

When I went to take a shower, I felt especially vulnerable when I took my clothes off. Julian might be stalking Karen, and I showered with the overhead light off. With only a four-watt night-light, the bathroom was as dim as a vampire movie.

The showerhead made a high, pinging whine, a defect in the "pressure reducer valve" that the landlord had promised to fix if he ever got around to it. With the shower whining, I didn't notice when a little blade slit the window screen, top to bottom, making a vent in the netting.

I didn't hear the window sash shriek as it was jerked up in an instant.

A man reached through the vinyl curtain and into the shower spray. He grabbed my wrist. I dropped the shampoo bottle on the bony knob of my instep, a broken marble of pain. I must have cracked it.

The man levered my forearm at an unaccustomed angle, igniting a remarkable twinge. I screamed. Karen's trouble had finally caught up to her. Julian had discovered her hideout.

"Who's with you?" he said none too playfully, as he peeled back the vinyl curtain. I recognized the voice, its drunken pitch was a unique marker. It was Rick. My ex-boyfriend still wore his Marcy Oil jacket; its petroleum stains reeked. He hauled his whole torso across the sill and perched on his hip. With his feet off the ground, he twisted my wrist and held onto my slippery waist. He hissed through the shower spray. "I'll kill you—"

His jealousy was ludicrous, but I relished its cheap flattery and fell under its chintzy spell. Hadn't I encouraged him by hanging up the telephone each time he called, knowing it drove him crazy? It was a free-form seduction, when every no meant yes to him.

Rick burst into drunken laughter. It was a joke to him.

Karen came into the bathroom and flicked the light switch. She jerked the shower curtain across the rod and the metal hooks popped loose. She saw the embalmed invader balanced on the window ledge as he choked my soapy neck with mimelike embellishments, his elbows flapping. He wasn't serious about strangling me, but was too drunk to temper his performance.

Karen took a scissors from a bathroom caddy and jabbed his tight biceps. Tiny red globes of blood surfaced through his uniform and dripped onto the porcelain. Rick didn't even twitch as Karen stabbed him; he might have been a rhino pecked by a little bird. She grabbed a can of drain opener from under the sink. The tin of caustic crystals shook like a maraca as she hammered his head. She struck him square in the temple and again in the same gorgeous hollow above his high cheekbone. He collapsed forward into the bathtub like a heavy fish reeled into a rowboat, his jeans tugged off his hips.

He was out cold.

I stepped out of the shower and turned it off. "You might have killed him," I whispered. I was ashamed to show my allegiance to my attacker.

Karen handed me a towel. We stared down at the soaked disco star and petty racketeer.

"Shit," Karen said. "He's nuts."

I was stung by her observation. Karen could have at least acknowledged how *pretty* he was.

His face was a dreamy, seductive mask, albeit he was unconscious. His drenched black hair swirled like glistening licorice pipes. Symmetrical red stripes of blood like a tiny American flag scored his jacket sleeve. Certainly, Karen could understand how I had fallen for him?

"Now what?" Karen said. "Sooner or later Beauty's going to wake up."

I was limping on my bruised instep and feeling sheepish as we dragged Rick through the house and out the kitchen door.

I saw the blimp's silver hide, bloated like a fish that rises to the surface of polluted waters. I was suddenly embarrassed by my crude romance with the disco punk. Next, we had the embarrassing task of combining our brute strength to put my mistake in the car.

I told my sister, "Thanks for everything."

"Next time, he's your problem," she said.

Karen didn't like to leave the kids alone, but I assured her that it would take only five minutes to drive Rick to his sister's house. He was no longer a dangerous opponent when we propped him against his sister's front door and rang the bell. His pants had slipped down on his narrow hips, and in a beneficent gesture Karen hooked her fingers in his belt loops and tugged his trousers higher. The sea air would refresh him. I wondered if he had lost any brain cells in his bout with Karen; he wasn't someone who could afford to lose more.

We were back at the house in five minutes.

A figure was silhouetted on the kitchen curtains. His slender frame and exploding crown of loose frizz revealed it was Julian. He had sneaked into our haven at the instant we had abandoned our post to discharge our victim.

Karen walked into the kitchen. Julian gripped Karen's waist and kissed her hard on the lips. I watched to see if she froze or melted. He was an imposing presence in my disheveled pantry, and I felt his alarming pull myself. His arrival had shifted my bearings, turned me around, like a riptide catches a swimmer in two opposing slurries.

Julian released Karen and looked into her face. In wounded confusion, he said, "You left our son here alone. What kind of mother does that—"

The phone was ringing. I picked it up. It was a call patched in over VHF from the SS *France*, still underway in the Atlantic. I recognized Ray's voice, his inflection broken from the relayed connection.

He asked, "Is that you? Are you there?" Again, it was his familiar interrogatory greeting. "Honey, Veronica has had a mild heart attack. We're coming off the ship early—"

The ship-to-shore message, not Julian, jolted Karen out of my hands. Just when our lives had merged, again Veronica came between us, even there, in my cottage with its wraparound roses. Karen let Julian take his son from the crib beside my daughter's bed. He pulled a jacket on the little boy. It was my daughter's parka, but I didn't say so. I helped Karen collect her things in one vinyl bag.

They left on foot in the middle of the night.

STONEGATES

―――◆―――

Today, KAREN WORKS in a twenty-four-hour emporium of dollar slots at the Hollywood Riverboat Casino in Aurora, Illinois,
just outside Chicago on the Fox River. Karen reports at six-thirty with
the Early Birds, usually a busload of seniors, and she gets off before
three o'clock, when charters head back to the city.

When she explained her new position at the riverboat casino, the
word "slots" had amused me. It seemed like slang, a shorthand, a trick
word to incorporate everything—every loss and every possibility.

"You're working slots?" I said.

"It's just like Glitter Gulch. They're going to teach me the tables
down the line, you know, blackjack, craps, minibaccarat. Sometimes I
relieve the cashier in our retail store, the Golden Era Gift Shop, but I'm
usually watching the machines. Video slots. Video poker. All comput-
erized. Guess who's coming in this weekend?"

"I don't know, tell me."

"Helen Reddy. 'I Am Woman' "

"Christ. She's a Johnny-one-note. She must be ancient—"

" 'I Am Granny,' " Karen said.

She was silent for a moment, as if in respect for the passage of time.

Our lives are again in tandem motion, but at a safe distance. Our
first kids are in their twenties and we both have remarried and have
children in grade school. Her new husband works as a short-haul truck
driver for a soy products company, and he's home with Karen each
night. Yet when I connect with my sister, we are standing shoulder-to-
shoulder before Veronica, holding our broken heirlooms. I try to align

the porous edges of the blue Canton dish until the jagged seam meets and I can't see where it's cracked.

"Did you get my last letter?" I asked Karen.

"Don't think so."

Karen won't accept mail from me. She insists my letters never arrive. She denies receiving snapshots, birthday cards. For some reason she will not admit that she's received my correspondence, torn it open, tossed it away.

My intrusive courtesies unnerve her.

When I telephoned her at the riverboat casino, she was disturbed to hear from me. She still feels the desert of our youth between us. "We have to talk about Veronica," I tell her.

A bell clanged. Someone had made an instant jackpot. Karen said, "You should see this. Everyone has to come over and meet Mr. Lucky—"

I listened to the haunting chides and random congratulations from the video poker consoles. Voice simulators announced the lucky "Wild Cherry" in eerie celebratory tones.

She didn't want to discuss our mother.

"Karen, Veronica's not doing so well."

"Her hip replacement?"

"No, she's over that. But she's acting strange. You should see what she sent to Harry."

"She sent your boy something?"

"A newspaper clipping cut out from the *Wilmington Journal*. It says a family ran over their pet dog with their car. They buried the dog in the backyard. It wasn't even dead. It clawed its way out of the grave and ran to the doorstep, all bloodied, half-alive. Their little kid answers the door. He sees his pet—"

"Veronica sent that story to your seven-year-old?"

Veronica writes to our children from her apartment in a posh retirement center. She's invested her money in a life-care condo. From her retirement complex, she sends notes to my son and Karen's little girl scratched on daily menus from the opulent dining hall where she has checked off her selections for the week: filet mignon; lobster bisque; butterflied veal chop.

Her notes on these menus are bizarre non sequiturs: "Feet cold." "Barometer falling." "Meat tough." "Show canceled." "Potatoes raw."

My sister was quiet on the other end.

"A clipping about a dog buried alive," I said.

"Say no more."

"So, I telephoned her to ask her not to send these things to my son. She tells me that there's a black butterfly outside her window—"

"A butterfly? In February?"

"A *black* butterfly. She asks me if she should let this butterfly inside."

"What did you tell her?"

"I told her it must be an optical illusion."

"Everything is some kind of optical illusion. You should have just said there are no butterflies in winter."

Karen's perception that "everything is an optical illusion" had a weird common sense.

I said, "If you ask me, I think she saw the 'butterfly of death.'"

"Oh, shit. Veronica will live forever. She's had everything replaced. She's bionic."

VERONICA HAD BEEN GIVEN every refurbishment offered by modern medicine. After two heart attacks, she underwent a triple-bypass operation. She had a second bypass procedure in which doctors used her "mammary artery." It disturbed me that the mammary artery was used to nurture the matriarch herself.

At the time of her first surgery, Ray wrote to me about her impending medical ordeal. In his letter, he had made a mistake and had written "open hear*th*" surgery. His upsetting lexical slip seemed more tragic to me than Veronica's medical condition.

When I visited Veronica in the hospital, she insisted that I go home to get her one of her lacy nightgowns. "I refuse to wear this boring hospital johnny," she told me. In the ICU, she sat up in her bed and pestered the young interns. She worried that her breastbone, sawed in half and stapled together, had ruined her décolletage. But she knew her breasts were buoyant and symmetrical as ever, despite a line of steel sutures up the middle.

Ray died in 1991. After attending to Veronica through her major surgeries, Ray was stricken with lung cancer, the result of his fifty-year Chesterfield habit and his exposure to asbestos in the steelworks. Sometimes, I think of Ray's enforced retreat from his children; perhaps that's what killed him. He lived with a rime of guilt that finally ate through his system.

I visited Ray before he died and stood by his hospital bed. I propped his pillow and saw that its rubber case had caused a rash across his shoulders. I scolded the nurses for ignoring his erupted skin.

They didn't think it made too much difference at this stage of the game.

I tipped the tiny can of high-cal chocolate Ensure to his lips. The milkshake was tepid and unappealing to him.

"Can't you at least chill this shit?" I said to the staff.

Veronica rolled her eyes and said, "What are you whispering in Ray's ear? I've been trying all morning. You think he's going to wake up just for you?"

Veronica had crawled into the empty twin bed beside my father. She pulled the sheet to her chin just as she had done in Wilmington General Hospital when Ray was recuperating from his ulcer. She monopolized the nurses' attention. Could she try some of that milkshake they had offered Ray? What did it taste like? Nurses tried to indulge her, believing that her behavior was a once-in-a-lifetime lapse of good manners in direct response to her husband's decline. How could they know she had acted like this at each and every crisis?

I told Veronica, "Maybe you could hold him in your arms."

"He's peeing in his sheets," Veronica said.

As I stood beside Ray's bed, I had recognized the warm breath of ammonia and had tried to ignore it.

Ray's body was transported to a teaching hospital and there wasn't a burial. Soon after his death, I walked a secluded trail on the National Seashore near my home. In the middle of the forest, I saw the undergrowth pulse. Something invisible rustled the brush, making the low canopy twitch its green hide.

I found a common sparrow struggling to free itself; its tiny leg was cinched to a branch by a snip of monofilament. These strands of fishing line are often discarded on the back shore by surf-casters and scavenged by songbirds building seasonal nests. I tucked the bird in my hand to unwrap its talons. Its raw shin glistened like a wet toothpick. It wasn't serious and the sparrow swooped away.

I remembered my grandmother's remark about the afterlife: "A white pigeon will land on your head." I wanted to think that at the same instant I had freed the bird, I had released Ray's soul from its mortal tangle, its human trap.

I TOLD KAREN the story. She enjoyed the part where I rescued the bird, but she didn't see how it had anything to do with Ray.

I asked Karen, "Sharly's in Allentown, right?"

"Yeah, she runs a day-care center out of her house. She's got a state certificate. She's licensed. Doing great."

"Pimp den to playpen. That's an amazing story, isn't it?"

"One story fits all."

Karen didn't think Sharly should win highest honors. She didn't like the distinction I had made.

I said, "It's good she got straight before HIV."

"That goes for us too. I wonder about the other girls. Where are they now?"

"They must have got out long before the pandemic, right?"

"Pandemic? Is that what it's called when you have a degree?"

I ignored her snipe. I was used to it. "Look, you could spend one afternoon with me and Veronica and then go straight to see Sharly. I'll meet your plane and we'll drive to the retirement village together, okay? It's a strange place, kind of like—"

"Did anyone ever tell you it's better to shut up? Let people paint their own pictures."

THE STONEGATES LUXURY retirement complex is walled by stone fences, and to enter the compound, drivers must pass through a security kiosk, a tiny structure jeweled with mosaic tiles, like a Fabergé toll booth. We stopped at the gate as a uniformed security officer verified that Veronica expected us, and then he waved us on.

I understood how prisons, mental hospitals and now these lavish retirement communities must have police cabanas put in place to siphon away the unwanted. Karen was uncomfortable during the trans-action. She preferred to be invisible and slip past the authorities unidentified.

As I steered around the winding drive to find Veronica's wing, Karen read to me from a sales brochure the security guard had pushed on her at the booth. " 'Plan for your retirement. Reserve your *little pocket of posh.*' That's good alliteration, isn't it? You could have writ-ten this brochure," she said. It was clearly a ping, but Karen grinned at me.

Veronica's apartment was an elegant seven rooms nested in a cen-tral building. I noticed that her front door was propped open with a rub-ber wedge so she wouldn't feel locked in.

Veronica looked good. Her hair was cut at a crisp shoulder length and she had let it turn ashy silver. "Like Bacall," she said, "why not?" Her features seemed more refined and delicate in her retreat; her eyes looked even greener. But her figure had changed. She was too thin; her hourglass shape had narrowed down to a fragile pipette. Her gait was hesitant due to her recent hip replacement.

"I've lost my knitting bag," Veronica said. "Can you both help me look? It's that canvas *New Yorker* bag, remember?"

"Sure. Where did you have it last?" I said.

"If I knew that—"

Karen said, "You always find something in the last place you look."

It was unlike Karen to join in the verbal helixes that Veronica and I created, and we both stopped to peer at my sister.

Karen's face looked lined and haggard in the harsh sunlight stream-ing through the bay window. The room was brilliant, intensified by the white-on-white wallpaper. I noticed how even Karen's shoes looked scuffed against the thick ivory carpet.

Karen and I both showed our years. Karen had had neither the ad-vantage nor the encumbrance of an education. Her lined face was marked by her workaday world, her lost and stolen nights, her human dreams, the mars and crinkles of love and guts and Marlboros.

I peered at myself in Veronica's rococo mirror. Was it because of my schooling that my face always looks hungry?

Then there was Veronica, the sole survivor in our family's tentative grip on the privileged class. She made it perfectly clear that the reason she was spending her last dollars on these sublime digs was so she wouldn't have to live with any one of us. Ray was gone. We shouldn't begrudge her a bit of last-minute luxury. The opulent dining hall was set each night with gold-rimmed Lenox and Waterford goblets. The waiters sometimes brought finger bowls between courses. Veronica said, "The trout is deboned at tableside by expert sous chefs. That's what we pay for."

"God forbid you should find a bone," I said.

Karen and I searched the sitting room for Veronica's knitting supplies, her skeins of boutique yarns and her various-sized needles.

I noticed a little contraption on the dining room table, a tiny box with a built-in guillotine. I picked it up and saw that it was a "pill slicer." Veronica said, "I have trouble cutting my pills in half."

Karen eyed me as if I might swipe it. I took the pill slicer and the little French ashtray with the familiar warning—QUEL RIT VENDREDI, DIMANCHE PLEURERA—and slipped them in my pocket.

When I searched her bureau for her yarns, I discovered that Veronica had lined her drawers with the letterpress menus from the SS *France*. One menu sheet displayed the gory red circle of a wine goblet, as red as the day it was spilled. What more did Veronica need to document her life but memorabilia from a luxury voyage?

In the closet, Karen found several different sacks of Veronica's knitting projects. Each bag held different sweaters started and abandoned before the job was finished. Here was a gorgeous red sweater with a glamorous shawl collar, but the arms weren't yet attached. In another bag, a baby's wool cap with a pompon of delicate ribbons not yet snipped to an appropriate snowball. For whose baby?

I understood the peculiar nature of our search, and I tried to appear nonchalant when I asked Veronica, "Which sweater are you looking for?"

"I'm making a new one," Veronica said.

"For who?"

Veronica said, "I won't know *who* until we find my knitting bag. I don't have favorites, if that's what you mean."

I had once seen a movie in which a war widow knits a sweater for a soldier even after receiving a telegram informing her of his death; her beau will never return, but she sits in her parlor and knits a new sweater as if for his shivering ghost.

"You must know who you are knitting these for?" I said.

Veronica turned to me and spoke with sudden bile. "Whatever you think, I'm not responsible for what happened to any of you."

IT WAS A LATE spring day. In a month, the Delaware heat would be oppressive. I asked Veronica if she wanted to go outside and take a little walk with me and Karen. "Just to get the bugs out of your new hip," I said, hoping she would allow her circumstances a bit of humor.

"They're always trying to get us to walk. It's like boot camp," Veronica said.

"Walking might help those dizzy spells you're having," I said.

Karen said, "We'll take a walk. Then I have to hit the road, all right?" As she spoke, Karen was looking at Veronica's Mastercard receipts impaled on a spindle. Hundreds of dollars worth of fashion merchandise and upscale attire ordered from Neiman Marcus, Bloomingdale's, Marshall Field's and other pricey catalogues.

Veronica saw Karen eyeing the evidence of her pampered lifestyle. "I *have* to dress for dinner. It says so in the bylaws in the *Resident Handbook*. We voted on it. But believe me, it's a trial to look different every night."

"You have to look different every night?" Karen said.

"Coco Chanel once said that she can provide the visual palate—the textures, the color—but women have to *paint the picture*."

WE LEFT THE HUSHED LOBBY of the retirement center's main wing and walked out into the humid air. It had rained at night and apple blossoms spotted the sidewalk like snips of pink silk.

"Where do you want to walk?" I asked Veronica.

"There are only two walks we can take. The *White* Path and the *Blue* Path. The White goes a half mile. The Blue Path is a mile. I can't go a whole mile."

We started on the half-mile trail. I had seen these mapped trails at nature centers and zoos; even cemeteries direct visitors to their family plots by using colored markers. The exercise paths had been marked with stenciled dots, an ellipsis line like white tennis balls, one after

the other on the asphalt sidewalk. The spots advanced in a straight column until clear of the spilled blossoms, continued up a rise and grew
diminutive as they trekked on into the distance.

We followed the White Path, walking slowly so Veronica wouldn't
lose her breath. The white spots marched ahead of us and crested each
tiny hillock. *One-half mile.* One-half mile or eternity—which would
come first?

Veronica walked between Karen and me, her gait a bit tentative on
her new artificial hip. We took her elbows and she hardly assumed her
own weight. Veronica enjoyed our tender crunch, the forward propulsion that we provided even as we steadied her. Perhaps she deserved
our fawning, our protective clutch right then, and she might have deserved it all along. How had the three of us wronged one another, all
these years, by withholding our touch?

A man approached us on the sidewalk. A groundskeeper, I thought,
but then I saw his disheveled hair and clothes. I saw his eyes, a searing
twinkle as he acknowledged us in an artful, sidelong glance. He startled me. I looked down at my feet before I looked back at him. A typical indigent or homeless con, he was finding respite in the beautiful
landscaped acres of the retirement complex, defying the security officers who patrolled in balloon-tired quads.

The man wore a clear plastic parka although it didn't rain. He wore
all his clothes, at least five layers of shirts and sweaters underneath his
plastic raincoat. He was like a human hanger. And yet there was something about him—his features were sharp and his grin was immediate
and tantalizing, as if he well knew he still had his powers over women.
He acted as if he might have known one of us, long ago, in a better life
than this one. I watched his prominent Adam's apple hitch up and
down under his numerous shirt lapels. He tipped his ratty baseball cap,
pinching its long brim. He dropped his voice, finding a remarkable
emollient tone, and delivered the classic salutation, "Ladies—"

He carried a stained *New Yorker* tote bag, of all things, stuffed to its
burdened seams with his walk-around possessions. Veronica looked at
it as if weighing the chances that it could be *her* knitting he was carrying. Karen saw her mother's confusion and told her, "Those totes are
everywhere." Karen stared blankly at the homeless man, as if he were
a seedy landmark she had seen a hundred times. He might be any fa-

miliar throwaway or an intimate scoundrel from her own history, but whoever he was, she wasn't stirred up. It was Veronica who spoke first. She said, "I always thought Curtis Pettibone would end up like that if woman after woman didn't take him in." The man had heard her remark, and he skirted our trio and climbed back onto the sidewalk on the other side of the lane.

The stranger had upset all of us, each in our private way. I looked at my sister. She rubbed her lips with the back of her hand as if to withhold her more seasoned opinion.

We stopped for a moment on the queer roadway. In the middle of the path, Karen had found a tiny shrew, dead on its back. Although the creature was dead, its carcass twitched with life. Its miniature hide contracted and wriggled; its velvet haunches shivered and pulsed with regular hitches of movement. It even seemed to "breathe" with false aspirations. But the rodent, indeed, was stricken.

I turned its carcass over with the toe of my shoe.

We saw what jolted the impostor. Its hide was tight with a swarm of bright yellow beetles. The gaudy insects were coring its limbs and chewing through its interior, making the corpse come alive. Even its skull was infested with these bright yellow daubs in constant motion, until the rodent's snubbed face turned slowly to the right, then to the left, in expressive disbelief.

My son had described these marionette beetles to me after he attended Audubon Camp. The beetles invade a cadaver to polish off entrails and muscle until en masse they wear their victim's skin, moving its limbs in mockery of the living.

I enjoyed its scientific aspect, for it seemed to represent our universal fate in its horrible comic slapstick. We watched the infested creature, the industrious golden vermin puppeteering the perished form as if to return it to life. Veronica said, "It gets another chance this way. Like it or not."

Karen stooped to take a closer look. She straightened up, smiling.

We walked until the demarcations abruptly ended. We could turn around. "That's it," I said. "A half mile."

Veronica said. "We don't need the markers, do we? I have my second wind. Let's keep going."